by

EDWARD

HUNTER

NEW YORK: THE VANGUARD PRESS INC.

New and Enlarged Edition

BRAIN-WASHING

IN

RED

CHINA

the calculated destruction of men's minds

MANUFACTURED IN THE UNITED STATES OF AMERICA

DESIGNER: MARSHALL LEE

STANDARD BOOK NUMBER 8149-0121-2

THERE WAS A TIME WHEN I COULD IDENTIFY EVERYONE I interviewed by his true name. Nowadays if I were to do so I should leave a trail of death behind me. These persons, their relatives and friends, would die.

I look forward to the day when I shall once more be able to use true names in my interviews. That day, when I and my fellow correspondents can do so without endangering the lives of these people, the world will be free. This will be the test.

I have taken every possible precaution in this book to disguise the identity of my informants. I hereby inform the Chinese Communist authorities that if they discover a similarity of names, they will be those of the wrong men and of the wrong women. As for the men and women who might have given me the information, they are legion.

This material was gathered in the Far East and southeast Asia during 1950 and 1951. I have made generous use of excerpts from articles of mine which appeared in *The Miami Daily News* and *The New Leader* magazine, for which I thank them.

I would have been very happy indeed if, between the time I completed writing this book and its present, new, enlarged edition, events would have proven that I had exaggerated or had given undue importance to isolated instances. Unfortunately, events were to confirm every detail of the "brain-washing" pattern; and its imposition on American and other UN personnel captured in the Korea fighting was to put the word firmly into the English language and into newspaper headlines.

I say unfortunately, because the basic struggle in the world today that we call cold war, psychological war, ideological war, is in essence a life-and-death contest between concepts of brotherhood and of "brain-washing."

EDWARD HUNTER

May 1, 1953

To Tate (Tatiana Hunter), whose typing and typing and typing made my work possible, and to Tate Ann (eleven) and Bob (seventeen), whose patience in living alternately between the roles of waifs and the unwanted was just as important to ultimate achievement

FOREWORD

CHANGE THE WORD CHINA TO CUBA, AND THIS BOOK IS A description of communist warfare against the mind—brainwashing—in Cuba as well as in China. This is the world pattern the communists employ; what might, in military parlance, be called mind attack. It is the new dimension in warfare, added to artillery attack, naval attack, rear and frontal attack, air attack. Brainwashing's dual processes of softening-up and indoctrination have been added to the arsenal of warfare, girding the Trojan Horse in Twentieth Century accoutrements.

Change the word Cuba to China in the article from Camaguey, Cuba, in April of 1960, by William L. Ryan, Associated Press news analyst, and you have what happened on the Chinese mainland, the pattern for communism everywhere. Such details in Mr. Ryan's dispatch, for example, as the new Cuban textbooks that "make an undisguised attempt to focus youth hatred on the United States," beginning with "children just learning to read." The cartoon book with a cover showing the United States as an octopus, marked by a dollar sign. A geography teaching that Cuba won its freedom from Spain only to have it stolen by the U.S. The "extravagant glorification" of Castro in the schoolbooks, which teachers "are required to read daily."

This should have evoked no surprise, for *Brain-Washing in Red China* described not merely the phenomenon as imposed on the poor Chinese people but an international strategy, the model the communists take with them wherever they go.

They impose it on themselves as well. Its subterfuges, falsehoods, rewritten history and upside-down language are inseparable from communism. Knowledge of these techniques can save a nation, as well as lives. One of the rewards, the principal reward, that came from writing this book is the kind of statement made by persons like Ben Krasner, the marine captain captured in Hong Kong harbor and held a year in captivity in the Canton area. "I was able to keep a jump ahead of the Reds all the time," he told me. "I had read *Brain-Washing in Red China* and knew what to expect." The book probably saved his life. Knowledge of this fundamental communist strategy can save free peoples everywhere, including our own, as it very probably saved his life.

Philologists will be interested in the spelling of "brainwashing" here without the hyphen, although the title and text have it hyphenated. The public, the final arbiter in language, took the word I gave it and removed the hyphen, to which I willingly accede.

This was the first book to use the word, and it should, therefore, receive the credit for putting it into our language.

EDWARD HUNTER

Arlington, Va.
June 15, 1962

CONTENTS

BRAIN-
WASHING
IN
RED
CHINA

"BRAIN-WASHING"

"If God Himself was sitting in that chair we would make him say what we wanted him to say." —Interrogator's boast at Budapest, while questioning Robert A. Vogeler, American businessman, who later "confessed" and served seventeen months of a fifteen-year sentence for alleged espionage. Quoted by Vogeler.

—New York Herald Tribune, May 1, 1951.

AHOY! THE BRAIN!

I STARED AT THE YOUNG MAN SITTING IN FRONT OF ME. HE was thin and nervous, with long, narrow bones. His face was straw-colored, and his hair, naturally, was intensely black. His slanted eyes were deeply set in drawn skin. Evidently in his late twenties, he was very much Chinese, in spite of his new European clothes. He wore an open shirt, slacks, and sneakers.

We were in Hong Kong in my top corner room in a detached part of the Correspondents' Club, from which I had two grand views. The nearby mountain seemed to elbow in at my side window, and from the front I could see not only the grounds of Hong Kong University but the busy harbor still farther down the slope. Trim little river boats came and went on strict schedule to Portuguese Macao, thirty-five miles away. Other ships sailed, but rarely, to Canton in Red China, through the gap between the mountainous islands. Communist China was much too close for comfort.

3

I caught myself staring at the young man and hastily resumed my note taking, writing hurriedly to catch up with his last phrases. He was Chi Sze-chen (phonetically, Mr. Gee), a student who had recently graduated from the North China People's Revolutionary University, which is a few miles outside Peiping, and is the biggest and the most important of China's political indoctrination schools. He was telling me what he had gone through. The story concerned something wholly new in China—"thought reform," "self-criticism meetings," and the processes of Communist Party indoctrination in general as practiced in Red China. The plain people of China have coined several revealing colloquialisms for the whole indoctrination process. With their natural facility for succinct, graphic expressions, they have referred to it as "brain-washing" and "brain-changing."

Brain-washing became the principal activity on the Chinese mainland when the Communists took over. Unrevealed tens of thousands of men, women, and children had their brains washed. They ranged from students to instructors and professors, from army officers and municipal officials to reporters and printers, and from criminals to church deacons. There were no exceptions as to profession or creed. Before anyone could be considered trustworthy, he was subjected to brain-washing in order to qualify for a job in the "new democracy." Only then did the authorities consider that he could be depended upon, as the official expression is worded, to "lean to one side" (Soviet Russia's) in all matters, and that he would react with instinctive obedience to every call made upon him by the Communist Party through whatever twists, turns, or leaps policy might take, no matter what the sacrifice. He must fight by all possible means and be ready, too, with the right answer for every contradiction and evasion in Party statements.

The interview already had lasted a couple of days, about ten hours a day, and continued for several more. My dictated notes, exactly as I had jotted them down, filled three fat notebooks. From the typewritten copy (sixty pages, double space) I went over it all again, sentence by sentence, with Chi. He took the opportunity to fill gaps in the chronology, to recall incidents he had forgotten, and to expand on subjects he had glossed over. I tossed question after question at him, probing to bring out and verify his exact attitude on each point as well as to learn his precise experiences.

It was at this point that I stared so sharply at him before resuming my note taking. A peculiar feeling had come over me that certain passages in his description of brain-washing recalled some previous experience of my own. It couldn't have been during my years as an editor and newspaper correspondent in China. Revolutionary universities had been in existence only since the Communists took over the government, and Chi was the only student of any such Communist Party institution that I had interviewed so far. Nor could I have read the details, for this was the first such interview. Yet I couldn't shake off the impression that I had heard this before, at least certain essentials. Not the details, perhaps; it was the state of mind, the environment, that was not wholly new to me. I tried to pry beneath forgotten brain layers in my own head to search for what it was that made his words, and particularly the weird unnatural feeling they gave me, so familiar.

Then I remembered—not one, but two past experiences. A few months previously, before I had left America, a friend of mine had had a nervous breakdown. Lack of sleep had driven him almost to the point of suicide. His wife had arranged for him to be treated in a most modern sanitarium, where I visited him occasionally. Actually, it was what used to be called bluntly an insane asylum or even more crudely a crazy house. It was equipped to handle any case involving the brain, from the simplest temporary upset caused by fatigue or frustration to blabbering idiocy. The hospital grounds were more like a vacation spot, and the large staff included psychologists, doctors and surgeons who knew the clinical uses of hypnotism, and some of the leading psychiatrists of the nation—kindly, inquisitive men with great patience and long medical experience.

One psychiatrist seemed to be walking on air one morning. He had just won a glorious victory—the fight for a man's mind—and he felt that he was now able to recommend his patient's release. He had had a tough fight, not a physical contest but a mind struggle, a brain doctor's battle to fill a gap in the torn mind of his neurotic patient. There had been a painful family scene in this man's childhood that the doctor knew about, although not from the patient. Unless the man were able to place his unhappy incident in its proper perspective, to fit the pieces together to make his mental mosaic whole, he could not be considered safely cured. Nobody else could do it for him; he had to do it voluntarily. There was no valid reason for the patient's concealment because he had disclosed far more revealing details. His "cure" could come only by frankly recognizing facts—by "being frank," by "mind reform." Those were all terms the Chinese student, too, was using in our interview. The doctor could easily have mentioned the incident to his patient and have explained the connection between it and his present condition, and the patient would have readily, even eagerly, agreed, but there would have been no cure. The patient had to bring all this forth himself, voluntarily, out of the dark recesses of his own mind. The psychiatrist explained all this to me, for he was happy and proud of the battle he had won to give a man's mind back to him.

This particular morning, while walking with the doctor on the rolling grounds of the asylum, the patient had blurted out what had been stubbornly hidden in his mind for so long. The doctor told me how he had suppressed his excitement while the patient spoke naturally, intent on his recollections. He had done so voluntarily; there had been "no force" applied, a point the doctor stressed as the key to the cure.

It was this that I was recalling as I listened to the young Chinese relate his experiences in the North China People's Revolutionary University. The feelings that had come over me in that most modernized institution while talking to the psychiatrist were the same as those I felt as I listened to Chi's story: the same disquieting sense of probing into dan-

gerous fields. Chi's experiences in North China had been similar to that of the patients in the American institution. It
was as if that most advanced mental hospital with its staff of
psychiatrists had stopped treating the insane and had begun
treating only the sane, without changing the treatment.

The second experience had occurred at an Overseas Press
Club dinner in New York City that I had attended just before I left for Asia. Our guest speaker was Angus Ward, former American consul general at Mukden, who had been arrested by the Reds with several members of his consular staff
and held for several months before being released and deported. At dinner I sat on the dais with other American correspondents who had served in Asia. Ward spoke to us about
the lengthy questioning he and his associates had undergone
while under detention. He made one brief statement that
seared itself into my mind. While no hand was ever laid on
him physically, he said that if his Chinese interrogators had
questioned him for only a couple of weeks longer, in their efforts to persuade him to sign a "confession," he would have
confessed to anything they wanted. Not only he but the
others, he was sure, would have done so "voluntarily." Evidently these new questioning techniques would have so
shaken them out of their normal minds that probably they
would have believed their confessions and, if brought to trial,
would have "freely" admitted their fancied "guilt." If his Chinese interrogators had been only a little more skillful in the
questioning techniques, developed by Soviet Russia's secret
police, or if his interrogators had been the Russians themselves, he was sure that he and his compatriots would have
made a full confession within the time he was questioned. In-
nocence or guilt had nothing to do with it. "I suppose it is only
a question of time, with the setup they have there now, for
the Chinese Communists to acquire this additional skill from
their Soviet Russian tutors," he commented.

Afterwards, when I chatted about his talk with others, nobody mentioned these remarks, and they were not published.
They were too bewildering and were regarded by the very

nice ladies and gentlemen, the guests who constituted the bulk of his audience in the luxurious hotel dining room, as sheer rhetoric; they couldn't connect this tall, strong, and handsomely hirsute diplomat, so nattily attired, with anything so out of this world. The terrible significance escaped them. Such things were completely beyond the comfortable, decent framework of their comprehension and experience and sounded not only unrealistic but impossible.

That probably was why the anecdote with which Ward followed up his personal account seemed just like another strange story. While he was stationed in Moscow, before his China assignment, Ward said that an officer of another embassy was arrested, held for some months, and then brought to trial on a charge of rape. The trial was quite cut and dried; the man confessed, was duly found guilty, and was given a sentence that was commuted to deportation. When he returned to the embassy to get his passport to leave the country, one of his colleagues asked him: "How did they ever force you to confess?" The reply stunned the embassy and effectively shut off any possible protest. "They got the goods on me," he said.

The man actually was guilty! He admitted it! With the formalities completed, the disgraced government employee left Soviet Russia. A few weeks later, however, an embassy official told the ambassador that he had been looking over the records of the case, which showed that the man couldn't have been anywhere near the place where the rape took place. He was in another city at the time. Yet, safely inside the embassy he had confessed in front of them. They were simply bewildered.

A few months later the embassy received a letter from the deported man in which he wrote that he vaguely recalled that, while in the embassy, he had told someone he actually had been guilty of rape. He was writing to say he couldn't have been guilty. He now remembered he had been in a different city when the crime took place! Although he couldn't recall details of the period because there were still big gaps in his mind both about it and about what happened at the trial, he was sure he was innocent. He had been in a trance.

As I interviewed Chi, I had a growing feeling that all these matters were closely linked. Only the preceding week I had met a chap in Hong Kong who had been one of the consular employees arrested with Ward. He told me that among those seized was an Asian who did odd jobs about the consulate. The Communists tried to persuade him to sign a statement that he had witnessed all sorts of criminal activities by the American consular authorities. He was a simple man, much devoted to his family. The Communists, in their efforts to turn him voluntarily against the Americans, kept his wife from visiting him and then one day told him, with a great show of sympathy, that she was dead—killed in a fight with an American consular officer who had been one of his most trusted friends. The poor fellow, unable to conceive of anybody so evil as to say such a thing as a ruse, believed it. When he was freed eventually and came back to his consular associates, he was in a daze. His wife was there, waiting, but he couldn't recognize her. He couldn't believe that she was still among the living. He just stared in bewilderment, out of his mind, repeating, "You can't be my wife; my wife is dead." Gradually, as the days passed, the haze wore off and he recognized her and the cruelty of the hoax.

One recollection led to another, all of which at the time had seemed isolated instances. What I had regarded just before I left America as only a social evening with an unusual twist now appeared to be not such a joke at that. A group of friends had taken me to see a hypnotist entertain. His act had so impressed us that several of us went to see him perform for three days in a row. I saw him point to a stranger in the audience and tell a young lady in a trance that this was her escort. He told her that she had never met the man who actually had accompanied her. When she woke, she smilingly walked off the stage and sat down, not alongside her escort but alongside the chap she didn't know. When her real friend came over, she stared at him, waiting for the stranger to introduce her.

Another time the hypnotist told a man that in exactly half an hour after awakening from his trance he would get up and go about the salon ostensibly selling fish. This ridiculous order had slipped my mind when, in exactly half an hour, I saw the man fidget in his chair, suddenly rise, look about him quizzically, and then walk from table to table selling fish. When he came to me, I jocularly ordered a quarter's worth. The exactitude with which this man lifted a mythical fish from a make-believe basket, weighed it on nonexistent scales, then handed it to me and took my quarter, was unforgettable. No Barrymore could have acted the scene more perfectly.

The hypnotist called this "post-hypnotic suggestion." The thought went through my mind that, if this could be done in a salon among friends, why couldn't it be done anywhere else to achieve any other objective that a party, social or political, might desire? At home in America we might regard such things as great fun, but apparently they were being taken seriously by other countries, and their possibilities were being tried out. The Chinese masses were right in coining the phrases brain-washing and brain-changing. There is a difference between the two. Brain-washing is indoctrination, a comparatively simple procedure, but brain-changing is immeasurably more sinister and complicated. Whereas you merely have to undergo a brain-cleansing to rid yourself of "imperialist poisons," in order to have a brain-changing you must empty your mind of old ideas and recollections.

Brain-changing is something for sensational public trials. Cardinal Mindszenty in Hungary is supposed to have undergone a brain-changing. *Reader's Digest* spent a fortune and exerted every journalistic resource it possessed to find out what actually happened to Mindszenty to make him confess. Evidently, in a brain-changing, a person's specific recollections of some past period in his life are wiped away, as completely as if they never happened. Then, to fill these gaps in memory, the ideas which the authorities want this person to "remember" are put into his brain. Hypnotism and drugs and cunning pressures that plague the body and do not necessarily require marked physical violence are required for a brain-changing. China evidently was not so "advanced" as yet. She was using brain-washing, and when that didn't work, resorted to the simpler purge system. But in time she will use the brain-changing process, too.

As I listened to Chi talk, I became convinced that these remembered incidents and bits of incidents, seemingly so far apart, fitted with what he was telling me to form the rough outline of a pattern. They all had something to do with controlling the brain. Our age of gadgets and electronics had discovered the brain, and we were learning how to manipulate it. This was something drastically new, like the splitting of the atom, that had come upon this earth in the middle of the twentieth century. Such discoveries can be utilized, like primitive fire, for good or for evil, to help bring our earth closer to paradise than man has ever expected or to destroy it in an ultimate holocaust. We had known vaguely about the geography and the resources of the brain before, as we had known that there was much more to matter than met the eye. But the brain, like matter, had been a divine creation that could not be tampered with without paying a dreadful price. Here the Biblical adjective "awful" is more appropriate.

The discovery of ways in which the brain operates has led to the discovery of how to control its movements, a tremendous new field of science. My journey to the East had coincided with fascinating stories in the press in America about the construction by our mathematicians and mechanics of a mechanical brain that by use of electronics could compute in a moment what Einstein in his prime, with all his genius, might have needed many years to compute. Surgeons now are capable of extremely delicate brain operations that only a few years ago were literally impossible. Man has learned not only some of the theoretical processes that go on in a man's head but also how to direct his thoughts, and to do this in a "democratic group discussion," in a "self-criticism meeting," on the operating table, or in the hypnotist's chamber. The whole field of psychology has broadened to embrace everything that influences thought and attitude, from the first crude publicity put out for a movie actress to Ivy Lee and psychological warfare, and the whole wide range of activities that lies within—in effect, our entire field of modern communications media, from public-opinion surveys to aptitude testing. And it is used by individuals in private and public life, by small firms and big corporations, and by political parties and governments.

The politicians of the world have been quick to seize upon these discoveries in the realm of the brain in order to advance their own objectives. Initially, they worked primitively in the field of propaganda. Then the vast possibilities of psychological warfare, what we call a cold war, dawned upon them. Cold war as a term is unfortunate in one respect. It sets up a line between cold and hot war that exists only on the writing table, not on the field of battle. What actually is meant by cold war is warfare with unorthodox weapons, with silent weapons such as a leaflet, a hypnotist's lulling instructions, or a self-criticism meeting in Red China.

Or—the courses of training given in the North China People's Revolutionary University. Let us return there.

"WHAT DO YOU THINK?"

A FEW SIMPLE QUESTIONS BY CHI WHILE HE WAS A STUDENT in Tsing Hua University in Peiping* resulted in his transfer to the nearby North China People's Revolutionary University, where he was to spend nine months. This was a few months after the Communists had made this ancient city

* Peiping and Peking are the same city. Peiping means northern peace, and is the name of the city under Nationalist China. Peking, meaning northern capital, is its imperial dynastic name, which the Communists restored for its prestige value when they set up their capital in the ancient city. Peiping is used throughout this book, except for the actual name Peking University.

their capital. Educational reform had already begun, with group discussions taking up the greater part of the school day.

Wall newspapers, single sheets written and made up by hand in each class and posted on the wall, were one of the boasts of the new administration as a people's achievement and evidence of the democratization of the press. Factories, government bureaus, organizations of every variety, and villages now had their wall newspapers. These were supposed to be the medium through which the people might freely express their hopes and worries without the constraint of a capitalist society. There were no paid ads.

China's relations with Soviet Russia and the United States were frequently discussed in these papers and meetings. The effort to alienate the Chinese from America and to make them lean to Russia's side was already under way. Chi, intensely patriotic, wrote an article on the subject. "I believed the Communist slogan, 'for freedom and democracy,' and so thought there would be no danger in expressing myself openly," he told me.

He asked, in this article, why Soviet Russia at the end of the war, if it really were following a policy of peace, had taken most of Manchuria's machinery into Siberia, even going so far as to dismantle complete factories and to move them into Soviet Asia. Also, why did Russia continue to keep military forces in Port Arthur and Dairen? He agreed with the criticism of the United States for keeping its army in Tsingtao at that time, but asked whether there was any difference between this and Soviet Russia's occupation of Port Arthur and Dairen. He wanted to know, too, why the Russians had taken control of the Manchurian railways. The object of China's revolution included independence and territorial integrity. "Why then must we still let Russia hold our Manchurian ports?" he asked.

Many students gathered about the wall newspaper to read his article. A member of the Communist Party Committee of the university noted this special interest and brought it to the attention of the chairman, Wang Tang-man, a graduate of the wartime Anti-Japanese University in Yenan. He had been sent by the Communist Party, after the city's "liberation," to direct politics in the university. As was customary when a topic aroused such wide interest, Chi's question was distributed to all groups for discussion. Background information on the subject was distributed to the group heads at the same time for guidance. This was to the effect that, by taking the machinery and industrial equipment from Manchuria, Russia kept the Kuomintang from using the output to "fight the people," that by taking over the railways Russia was able to put obstacles in the way of Nationalist troop movements, and that by occupying the Manchurian ports Russia was protecting them from occupation by the Americans "in case of war." Moscow, the students were informed, was acting only to save the Chinese people from Kuomintang exploitation and American aggression.

"The students obviously were not satisfied with these replies," Chi said. "They continued to talk about the subject generally. The head of the Communist Party Committee finally called me to his office for a personal talk. He asked me to think over what I had done by bringing this problem up in a wall newspaper. 'Was it right to raise this question?' he asked me. 'Did you think about the consequences of its publication? How long have such ideas been in your head? You should never have raised the question in the first place.'

" 'The result is to destroy the fruits of the revolution,' he told me. 'The fact that such an idea could have entered your head means that there still are Kuomintang poisons in your mind.' He warned me to avoid any questions in the future that would give the discussion groups a bad impression of Soviet Russia. He hoped, he said, that I would make a record of what went through my mind during the group discussions. He told me to start a diary and said he would ask to see it.

"I didn't have to write this record of my thoughts because I explained them frankly for an hour and a half during the interview. The Party boss said he wanted to find out if my actions coincided with my thoughts. He asked me to tell him briefly how my thoughts had evolved since childhood, until I entered Tsing Hua. He took many notes as I spoke. He also asked to see all the personal letters that I had received from my people in Shanghai. My parents wrote only of family affairs anyway, so that didn't worry me."

Chi did have to keep a diary. A diary fulfills a distinct role in Communist circles. Elsewhere it generally is regarded as a most intimate possession, open to nobody's eyes except its owner's. A diary is the first confidant of boys and girls in their teens, into which they pour their aspirations, their disappointments and heartaches and hopes, for their eyes alone. A diary has always been considered as something wholly personal, where a person can express his most intimate thoughts, not to be revealed to anyone else in the whole wide world, except at his own will, and only such parts as he wishes to reveal.

This conception of a diary was completely contrary to Chi's experience under Communism. Observers have been amazed in Asia by the frequency with which members of Communist groups, particularly the leaders, keep diaries. The Communist guerrillas in the jungles of Malaya keep them, as do those fighting in Indochina's mountains and in the North Korean army. The practice is an extraordinary contrast to the usual Communist avoidance of anything that would give away a secret. Allied troops in World War II were discouraged from keeping diaries because of the important information which the enemy was able to gather when they took them from the bodies of the slain and from the wounded and the captured. For the Communists to encourage diary keeping can only mean that they have a most important Party use for it.

And so they do. The diary, more than any other medium, is the most intimate check the Party can consistently keep on what goes on in the minds of its people and it constitutes a means of personal control. A man's diary, under communism, is something which the Party's watchdog may ask to read at any time. That is the explanation of the many stilted phrases found in Communist diaries. They are written to be read not only by one's closest and most loyal friends but also by those entrusted with the responsibility of keeping the rank and file in line. The Communists aren't so silly as to believe that every sentence written in a diary under such circumstances is from the heart and truly expressive of one's innermost feelings. This is considered a bourgeois approach. The Communist approach is from a different standpoint, with a different purpose.

The person who writes a daily record of his thoughts in the framework of communist ideology, even if he starts out disbelieving, is sure by repetition to absorb part of what he is telling himself and ultimately perhaps the entire dogma. The Communists exploit man's inherent sincerity. Insincerity stands out in a diary; practically no one can successfully fake his true opinions over a prolonged period of time. The tone just doesn't ring true, and any experienced Party man entrusted with reading can soon detect the falsity in the notes jotted down, on the basis of which he can act. This is the theory, and it was being put into effect in the case of Chi.

"I began my diary a couple of days later," he said. "Now, wherever I went in the university, some student followed me. I knew him, but knew enough, too, not to question him.

"A few days later the Party Committee chairman asked the leader of our group to bring him my diary. Every few days for the next few months my group leader would ask me for my diary, read it himself, and then take it to the Committee head, who would give it a quick glance and then send it back to me, always without comment. This routine was intended not only to keep a check on me but to silence me. This is part of the Party's process of persuading students to reform their thoughts. When students failed, the authorities had other measures to shut their mouths.

"I was supposed to put my real thoughts into my diary. A record was always kept of what went on at group meetings, so it was impossible for me to falsify my role in the discussions. There were always long discussions, and each of us had to talk a great deal. This gave the secretary the opportunity to record everyone's thoughts.

"For the first few months after liberation these discussion meetings took up the whole university day and evening. The day began with a discussion meeting at six in the morning."

"Yes, six," he repeated, after I expressed incredulity.

"It continued to nine. After breakfast and a rest we renewed our discussions at ten, keeping them up until one in the afternoon. Then we were given a rest period, with more discussion following, from two-thirty to five-thirty." I looked up, but he continued talking. "After supper we gathered again between seven and nine for more group discussion. At nine-thirty, our minds in a haze, we went to sleep. This went on six days a week."

"Didn't anybody complain?" I asked. Chi nodded. Some students asked for a shorter discussion day, he told me. They got this reply: The People's Liberation Army often fought for three or four days without sleep; if these heroic soldiers could do that, students in their comfortable classrooms could certainly endure a program of mere study.

Party members obeyed ungrumblingly, but non-Party students got up a petition. They received no answer the first two times. Only after the third try did they receive a reply, which informed them flatly that the hours for discussion were intentionally long. You students have been fed with capitalist ideas and enjoyment of life, they were told. Compare yourselves to the farmers, who have to go out with the sunrise and only return home after the sun sets, doing a full day of strenuous work. Your hours of study are really very short in comparison with the work the farmers do; it is like comparing heaven and hell. When the troops are on the march, a peasant soldier is often seen with a book carried open on his back, with especially large letters, so the man behind can study reading. Imitate that spirit.

After three months, the grinding discussion program was relaxed. The morning was then given over to regular classes.

Discussion groups still occupied the whole afternoon, and the evenings were set aside for study. Unfortunately this lasted only a few days for Chi Sze-chen. He was among thirty-three students, including two girls, who received notices one morning that they had been transferred to the North China People's Revolutionary University. They were regarded as unreformable in a non-Party school. The Party directly operates the revolutionary universities.

The students left within the hour, by truck, taking only hand luggage.

SCHOOL BEGINS

CHI SZE-CHEN WAS VISIBLY ILL AT EASE THE FIRST DAY OR two of our interview. We went to the main dining room to eat, taking a table by ourselves on the porch. Peppi Paunzen, our Viennese manager, had everything just right, with splendid service in the European manner. Chi sat there like a guilty man. He spoke in a comradely way to the waiter and ordered Chinese-style food.

The Correspondents' Club had certain specialties on its menu, with a regular foreign type of tiffin and dinner which was comparatively inexpensive and extremely well prepared. Yet Chi passed over all of these for a simple Chinese rice dish. Only after we had been together for a couple of days did I find out why, and then only after hours of patient conversation during which he questioned me and my beliefs as intently as I did his. He felt that it was wrong in "China" (meaning Hong Kong) to eat foreign food.

My interpreter's patience and understanding were responsible in a large measure for overcoming his bias. We discussed with great tolerance the whole significance of his attitude, the futility of it, and how it merely perpetuated the petty prejudices and hatreds that we all wanted eliminated in order to establish a peaceful, friendly world. I was secretly amused, when Chi began ordering foreign dishes, to see how he enjoyed them—after all, T-bone steak is hard to beat in any language.

His course in the Communist Party University had left deep scars on him, which were evident in such incidents. He had abandoned the Communist way of life because his instincts were right. He felt that there was something essentially evil in it, working against the good of humanity, but he had nothing with which to replace it. This was his basic problem—and mine; mine in the sense that I was a representative of the democratic way of life for which I felt his instincts were yearning. He had come willingly, truly voluntarily, without any double-talk, and now was watching every move of mine and all those like me. Would I, would they, be able to point out the right path, the one that would satisfy his desires and do away with the guilt complex with which the Communist ideology had left him? I felt on that occasion that on a small scale this was a test of me and my whole civilization. I must help in whatever small way I could, by word and example; I had no right to ignore his plight or to be neutral regarding the issues. Somehow, I vaguely felt, the ultimate success or failure of our way of life will depend on how we individually deal with the multitudinous cases, such as his, of people who want to be on our side. The way we act as individuals is much more important than what the government says.

Chi was intensely patriotic. That was evident. Nor did he want to exploit his fellow man. What was evident in addition was that the only knowledge he possessed of how to implement his good motives consisted of the intensive drilling he had had in "the ideas of Mao Tse-tung," in Marxism-Leninism, and the numerous slogans and pat phrases with which this ideology had been drummed into his brain cells.

Before agreeing to see me in the Correspondents' Club at all, he had asked me repeatedly whether the Chinese staff could be trusted. Could I guarantee that there weren't any Communist agents among them? Of course I couldn't be completely sure, but I pointed out that most of them had been with the American newspaper corps for years, evacuating city after city with them as the Communists came in. Anyway, I was constantly inviting Chinese to the club for interviews and dinners. How could anyone tell who my guests were or what story I was after? That I persuaded him to come at all was quite an achievement. Hong Kong was crowded with Chinese intellectuals who had recently fled from Red China. They had all gone into hiding. They knew that Hong Kong had many Communist agents whose job it was to ferret out the identity of such refugees, to put pressure on them by penalizing their friends and relatives inside Red China, and to make it difficult for them to get jobs or to settle down in Hong Kong.

I was constantly hearing references to these people, but to meet them was another matter. Those who were willing to praise the Communists or to avoid discussing any controversial subjects were willing to talk. They had nothing to fear. The others simply could not risk their necks or the necks of their friends and relatives. Even the foreigners, the businessmen and missionaries and educators who had left Red China, were in this category. Each of them, before he had been granted permission to depart from the country, had to obtain a "guarantor"—actually a hostage—who signed his name and accepted responsibility for what the man leaving would say and do afterwards. One English-language newspaper in Hong Kong expressed its shock and frustration over the successful intimidation exercised in this way over foreign churchmen and educators who had been forced out of Red China. They knew the inside story of the crimes being committed against nature and humanity, but refused to speak for fear of endangering the lives of others left behind. This newspaper warned in an editorial that such tactics only played into the hands of the enemy and saved neither lives nor ideals. All it did was leave the field open to pro-Communist propaganda and so defeat its own ends. Was this Christianity? it pointedly inquired.

Chi consented to speak to me in the first place only because one of my closest contacts had been a friend of his for years, a friend who had facilitated his escape into Hong Kong and was now providing him food and lodging and helping him to find work. Even so, Chi had to be convinced that I would use the material he gave me in a manner that would "help China." He had to be assured that by talking to a foreign correspondent he was not being treasonable to his own people.

We therefore had a long, patient discussion over American aims in China and what Americans wanted there. He had to be shown that his aims and mine were parallel and that by giving me the firsthand facts he would be indirectly benefiting all peoples, including his own. A new comradely slant to internationalism had to replace the narrow Stalinist internationalism that had been taught him.

The young man who acted as my interpreter was a Catholic civil engineer who himself had only recently fled from Red China, leaving relatives behind who were virtual hostages. I had met him through a mutual friend, the only way in which such contacts can be made under present circumstances. He couldn't allow his real identity to become known any more than Chi. When I introduced them, I had to be careful not to use their correct names.

Each understood, of course, that the very formal, polite introductions were white lies; it is amazing how soon people under necessity become accustomed to such things, and it is one of the first consequences of the cold terror imposed by any police state. To record the new sets of conventions and forms of etiquette that developed would require, were she present, a completely revamped Emily Post. If I had tried to hurdle this obstacle or any one of the numerous similar obstacles that stood between me and my interview, I simply would have had no interview. A whole chain of such subtleties are involved in understanding the Chinese. Not until each of the two had convinced himself personally that it was safe to disclose his true identity to the other did he do so.

I had to take my cue from them. Before they reached this point, however, they had made innumerable cautious approaches into each other's character and connections, coming to know each other's personal likes and dislikes, even sex habits, before they felt safe to entrust each other with their true names. Privacy under such circumstances becomes a matter solely of safety. Nothing else is private. I was startled by their frankness on anything except their personal identities. My interpreter took Chi to an American movie one night to help him relax. The next morning Chi came late. He had been unable to sleep. "The scenes in that movie were so erotic I had a sensual dream," was his casual excuse.

There were about 8,500 students at the North China People's Revolutionary University when Chi arrived. Forty-six wooden, two-story barracks, each divided into twenty-four rooms, covered an area three miles in circumference. Of this area seven acres were parade grounds, used now in place of an auditorium. The barracks had been a training center for the Japanese and later for Gen. Fu Tso-yi's 207th Regiment. The gun emplacements were still there. On the way from Peiping, Chi's truck passed Yenching University, where American money and tolerance had been exploited in such a way that we unwittingly provided probably more minor administrators for the Communist government bureaus of China than had any other educational institution in the land.

When the truckload of transferred students reached the gates of the Revolutionary University, it was greeted by students who themselves had arrived only the previous week. They came out beating drums, shouting slogans, and doing the *yang ko*—the short, prancing folk dance based on the way a coolie walks while carrying a heavy load on his shoulders—which the Communist Party has made its dance symbol. They surrounded the truck and walked with it through the gate. The escort brought water for the parched arrivals and helped them carry their baggage inside. The new students were received like heroes and taken to a bathhouse

inside one of the barracks to bathe in water that happened
to be warm that day and to rest.

Older students and party members were waiting ceremoniously at the entrance to welcome the newcomers and to ask
them if they were willing to enter the Revolutionary University. The arrivals just as ceremoniously said that of course
they were glad to come, for certainly they would be better
taught here than anywhere else. Wasn't it, after all, operated
by the Communist Party itself?

"With their help, we told the older students, we were sure
we would all become Communist Party members in a short
time," Chi recalled. "We were given lunch at one-thirty, an
unexpectedly good lunch with *manto*, a popular dish of meat
and dumplings. 'We're lucky you came,' one of the older students said. 'This isn't the usual food. Life is very hard in the
university. Be prepared for it.'

"A group of students then showed us about the university
and took us for a walk around the campus. They escorted us
to the exquisite Summer Palace nearby, where the Dowager
Empress used to enjoy herself. When we returned at about six
in the evening, we sat down to the same good food and then
saw a movie. It was about the May Day parade in Soviet
Russia. We went to bed about nine-thirty.

"When we woke up the next morning, we were shown
where to wash at wells outside. Then we went to breakfast.
We had breakfast every morning that first week, but after
that no more. From then on we had only two meals a day. After breakfast we were divided into classes and groups. I was
put in the second department, second class, fourth group."

The students were divided among four departments: one
for students sent from other universities for ideological reform;
another for intelligence personnel of the Military Revolutionary Committee of the Communist army; a third for members
of the various liberal groups and parties (that these had been
anti-Kuomintang and had cooperated with the Reds made no
difference); and a fourth department for Party members accused of bungling their tasks or doing poor work. There was a

fifth department, too, directly under the principal, called the Study Department. However, it wasn't for study *by* the students but for study *of* the students—of their thoughts. Each of the four departments was divided into ten classes and each class into nine groups of twenty-three students. The faculty numbered four hundred and fifty, including about one hundred and twenty young women. The men were from twenty-eight to forty years old and the women between twenty-three and twenty-eight. One faculty member was assigned to each group but not as a professor or even a teacher. He was always a Party member who brought his own stool and sat aside listening and taking notes, not intervening except to settle points in the discussion. Actually he was not even a faculty member, but a Party member who had slipped up somewhere in the past and was himself deemed in need of a measure of mind reform. While indoctrinating others, he reaffirmed and strengthened his own indoctrination.

Chi, the interpreter, and I had quite a discussion on how to class this individual. Commissar was correct but vague. He was more a moderator than a teacher but had greater authority than a moderator.

"How did the students refer to him when they talked among themselves?" I asked, expecting this to settle the question.

"When we spoke about him among ourselves, we always referred to him simply as Comrade, or as the able Party member," Chi informed me. This was obviously one of those safe compromises which evade the issue. Comrade was the term used in referring to anyone in Red China, from Mao Tsetung, who headed the government, to the farmer in the field. Able Party member was also a vague term, but there were certain specific meanings to it that gave it significance. The term able Party member is used quite generally. He can be the political commissar of an army detachment, a class leader, or he can fulfill any of the innumerable watchdog posts with which Communist Party members are entrusted.

About twenty students were assigned to a room in which everyone slept on the floor. Each student was given a small stool on which he put his name and which he carried with him. Each brought his own blanket, but was given about five pounds of straw to help keep warm in the winter, for it gets bitingly cold in North China. Every room had a small coal stove, but only one catty (1 1/3 pounds) of coal was allotted each day, and this had to be used up the same day and not saved for a colder period. Conserving coal was considered the same as creating private property. "We shivered in those rooms, and our hands and feet almost froze," Chi said.

"Meals soon became routine—two a day—always a plate of vegetables and Chinese millet (*kaoliang*), without any tea. We drank only well water, which we boiled. Every two weeks we had a meat course, two ounces of meat each. We were not allowed to buy anything even if we had the money. That was considered the same as capitalism. A few who thought they were underfed bought eggs in the neighborhood, but were criticized for having bourgeois ideas of enjoyment. So they stopped those small purchases. Many of us became ill, mostly with stomach troubles and coughs. There was a doctor, but he seemed to know little about medicine."

The Revolutionary University was directly under the Party's North China Department. The principal was Liu Len-tao, a member of the Central Committee of the Political Department of the Party. A graduate of the Yenan Anti-Japanese University, he was fat, a six-footer, and had been a guerrilla in Shansi Province during the anti-Japanese warfare. The only professor was the writer Ai Tze-chi, the leading political philosopher of the Communist Party and its recognized authority on the indoctrination movement. He came only once a week, usually on Tuesday, when he spoke lengthily to the entire student body gathered on the open parade ground. Everyone brought his own stool. Ai spoke before a microphone, and four loudspeakers broadcast his words. The lecture was often broadcast to learning groups elsewhere.

When Chi's group was formed, its leader ceremoniously suggested that if anyone suffered any inconvenience in the university or had any complaint whatsoever he should inform him of it. Many students, he explained, were not used to the type of training they would get. The students replied, just as ceremoniously, that they hoped he would help them follow the same hard life he led. The first morning, after introductions all around, there was a brief free talk in the group, just a chat, with no organized discussion.

"Our actual studies began that day at ten in the morning, when the whole student body went out to the parade ground where Ai Tze-chi gave us a lecture entitled 'Labor Creates the World.' He told us that our ancestors were animals and that we must never forget our lowly origin. We could no longer be parasites; we must undergo a hard life and help labor advance. He talked for seven hours straight.

"We sat on our stools and took plenty of notes. There was nothing to drink or eat, and though we felt very weary we had to take copious notes, because we knew that after the lecture each group would spend the rest of the week discussing the lecture, and we had to prove that we had listened to it very carefully.

"When the lecture was over we checked up on each other's notes to see if we had missed any points. We were supposed to read them over three times and to be sure that we had grasped the theme of the lecture. We were supposed to ask ourselves what the speaker wanted us to extract from his mind. When we had any doubts about his ideas, or when there seemed to be some contradictions, we were supposed to raise those questions in our group discussions. This was one of the main purposes of the discussions. Heated arguments often ensued over the exact meaning of some particular phrase."

Ai's lectures always lasted from four to seven hours. He gave a nine-week course on these subjects: "Labor Creates the World"; "Idea Formation and Class Property"; "The Class Foundation"; "Internationalism"; "The History of the Chinese Communist Party"; "The History of the Chinese Revolution"; "Modern Chinese History"; and "A Brief History of the Imperialist Invasion of China."

A number of students in their first discussion said they doubted Ai's statement that "existing matter determined thought." The group leader said these doubts were absurd. "The reason we fly is not that we have planes," one student persisted. "We made planes so that we could fly." The leader said, "No, the airplane had to come from some form and not from nothing. What, then? Man saw birds fly, from which he got the idea he might fly himself, and so he built an airplane."

A student said that this was not the same thing, because airplanes aren't made like birds, with animal organs, but out of engines and machine parts. "An engine is the invention of a human being, which proves that labor can create anything," the leader retorted.

He then ended the discussion with the smiling remark, "If you don't believe that labor creates the world, then we'll make an experiment, right out in the open fields."

FIELD EXPERIENCE

The group found out what was meant by a field experiment the very next morning. All the groups found out. Each was given a small plot of land to farm. Production contests were started at once and continued for two and a half days. Then, after half a day of rest, the farm work was resumed on a new schedule that went on unchanged for three months. Field work took place daily from ten in the morning to one in the afternoon. Farm labor consumed a third of the entire university program.

In a production contest Chi's group won second prize, a pennant with the words "Labor Model." First prize was a pennant reading "Mao Tse-tung's Good Students." They were hung in the classrooms and could not be taken away. The crops were mainly spinach and cabbage, the mainstay of the university meals. Some students became ill from overwork, and others hurt their hands or legs. "Henceforth you will understand the sufferings of the farming class," they were told.

Two slogans were posted: "Every grain of cooked rice, every morsel of rice gruel, is the blood and sweat of the people"; and, "When you drink water, think of its origin; don't forget the farmer." The latter is a materialist version of the old Chinese maxim, "When drinking water, remember its source."

Students who belonged to the Communist Party kept their affiliation secret during the first two months of the course in order to obtain information on the background and ideas of the other students. "I couldn't talk frankly to my schoolmates, so I developed no special friendships," Chi said. "Nobody dared say what was in his mind for fear that a fellow student would report it to the university heads. Indeed, such disclosures were part of the requirements and were encouraged as part of the university's self-criticism program. The whole course was arranged so as to induce a student to reveal his deepest feelings and exact reactions.

"Real friendship could not grow up under such circumstances. All intimacy was artificial, with a calculated purpose. You could sense it in the atmosphere. Many students avoided me, too, because the news had spread that I had raised the Dairen and Port Arthur question at Tsing Hua.

"Our entire course was for the sole purpose of making us capable of being 'pure and reliable Communist Party members,' who could be trusted to remain unflinchingly loyal to the Party under any and all circumstances and in any environment.

"Even the students in the intelligence group received no technical training. They, too, were in the university just to 'reform their thoughts' and to form definitive 'trustworthy thoughts.' But their 'thoughts' must not interfere with their dependability under all circumstances. This was regarded as more important than technical training.

"After returning from field work, we usually had to write

a report on it. The university wasn't interested in technical details, such as how best to sow seeds, to water and fertilize, or till and weed, but rather in our personal feelings while at work and our attitude toward labor. We had no textbooks. Our textbooks were supposed to be our notebooks, which we crowded with notes. This was where we got the material for our group discussions."

When fall came the students were instructed to prepare for winter defense against thieves and bandits. The walls around the barracks had been destroyed during the Communist siege of Peiping, and the students were now sent out to repair them. This work lasted four hours a day for half a month. After rebuilding the walls, the students were shifted to road repairs. They were assigned an eight-mile stretch of highway between the West Gate of Peiping and the university. The entire student body worked at this and finished the job in a week.

"This was supposed to be an education program and was called reform by labor," Chi said. "We were supposed to learn the value of labor that way. We just worked. We weren't shown any modern farming methods, and the road repairs were the most primitive, using only shovels and rakes."

After the series of lectures by Ai Tze-chi and the field work, the groups studied the Communist press, taking up such subjects as the American White Paper on China put out by the State Department. This discussion was based on a summary of the report and an analysis of it in six articles by Mao Tse-tung, published in the *People's Daily*, a Party paper in Peiping. The groups were asked: "What was America's intention in publishing the White Paper?" The reply required was that it had a two-fold purpose—to split the Communist Party of China, and to destroy Red China's unity by attracting away the democratic parties that were cooperating with the Peiping regime. The commentaries by Mao were entitled: "Discard Fanciful Ideas" and "Prepare for a Fight."

Labor was not the only field experience given the students. At a time when the groups were discussing what was called productive power they were taken to a village one day to study farm reform techniques at close range.

"Two classes, including mine, went to this village, where a judgment table had been built in an open space," Chi said. "A landowner's wife sat on the platform, and about 250 farmers were gathered around it, both men and women. The woman's husband had fled from the village immediately after the liberation of Peiping. She was about forty years old, a farmer type, stocky and healthy, raised in the Peiping area.

"An able Party member called to her to stand up and then asked the public, 'How do you feel about the treatment given you in the past by this landlord's wife?' Some farmers spoke up, saying she had been all right, while others insisted she had exploited them cruelly. She was not only a landowner but a miser, said others.

"The able Party member then called for those who had suffered the most from her oppression to please stand up. Twenty did so. 'Those who suffered the most, please state their case,' he called out. A woman of thirty-five spoke up. She had had 1 2/5 acres of land, she said, but because of the landowner's miserliness had lost it all. Even so, she said, the landlord still wanted her to work for him.

"The Party man hereupon said that her complaint was patently true and sufficiently revealed the type of woman the landowner's wife was. There was no use asking anyone else to express any views, he added. 'Let us decide therefore how to punish this woman,' he cried out. 'Shoot her!' some shouted. 'Divide up her possessions!' others yelled. Still others suggested, 'Make her take off all her clothes.' Finally the Party man agreed that she should strip.

"The woman spoke up then, saying she would rather give away her family possessions. 'It's terribly cold; I'd freeze if I took off my clothes,' she pleaded, in a face-saving offer. The Party man only replied, 'Your property will be divided up sooner or later; your clothes must come off now, woman!'

" 'It is very disgraceful for a woman to take off her clothes in public,' the landowner's wife still pleaded. An impatient farmer threatened to beat her up. When he started a rush toward the platform, she terrifiedly removed her padded coat and trousers. The farmers were not satisfied. They demanded she strip off everything she had on. 'I can't; I'd freeze!' she kept repeating. A stone was thrown. The girl students among us sat with flushed faces and some began to cry quietly. The woman stripped to the waist. Still the farmers were not placated. 'I can only kneel to you and kowtow,' she cried plaintively, tumbling to her knees and striking her head frantically a dozen times on the boards. She began chanting Buddhist sutras, and during the next few moments agonized snatches of Buddhist prayers came to my ears.

"The farmers, their fury aroused, rushed to the platform. Their taunts quickly turned to stone throwing, cuffs, and kicks. The scene became a confused mass of shoving, screeching bodies around the bleeding, weeping woman's form. Soon she lay quiet—dead.

"More than a hundred farmers, including most of the women, had left before this final scene. Fewer than a hundred farmers and we 209 students remained, sitting tense and silent except for intermittent sobs among our girls.

"At our group discussion the next day this affair was discussed with the casualness of a laboratory experiment. The authorities criticized both the able party member and the girls who had broken into tears. The Party man was said to be guilty of 'tailism,' that is, the mistake of letting the people do as they wish, with the party worker staying a step behind.

" 'The party worker must know when the people want something that is wrong and he must stop them from doing what is not good for them,' the group leaders pointed out. 'The people need only capable leadership to make them turn over [change their allegiance to the Party], and then their strength is unbeatable.'

"The girls who had broken into tears were accused of warm-feelingism [sentimentality], of 'not knowing your friends from your enemies.' This kind of sentimentality, the girls were told, should be cured by self-criticism, for it was a dangerous defect in their characters.

"Before I had left the village, I had noticed a child crying over the woman's body. I found out later that this was her daughter, aged twelve. She became a beggar in Peiping. Some of the students suggested that she be raised by the government, but were told that this was impossible because she was daughter of a landowner and could not be included in the category of people."

Red China's organic law promises democratic rights to all the people, but in the *People's Democratic Dictatorship,* a written speech that ranks as basic law, Mao Tse-tung has defined and limited this right. Only "the working class, the peasant class, the petty bourgeoisie and national bourgeoisie," says Mao, can be legally classified as people, but not the "landlord class, the bureaucratic-capitalist class, and the Kuomintang reactionaries and their henchmen representing these classes." Obviously, almost anyone can be classified on either side of this dividing line, among the people or among the outcasts, according to Party whim.

After graduation, a number of the students who were ordered to engage in farm reform work tried to avoid this assignment, Chi said, and he was sure it was because they couldn't get that village scene out of their minds. They were transferred to Inner Mongolia, where they were assigned to farm reform anyway. The authorities felt they could be better watched and trusted there because the Mongols are considered a different race than the Chinese.

THOUGHT SEDUCTION

The backbone of the Revolutionary University's course was a personal investigation into the views and attitudes of every member of the student body. This was the medium for and the test of idea training.

Idea training began with the study of a subject called Idea Formation and Class Property. The big capitalists, the students were taught, aimed only at increasing their profits. The little capitalists tried to improve their lives, to progress, in order to achieve a secure, enjoyable existence. The workers aimed for security, just hoping to keep their jobs without interruption. Farmers did their duty, which is farming, but cared only for their own crops, and had a narrow perspective.

The university authorities asked the students to analyze their own ideas on the basis of those four points and to write a complete report on their thoughts. When the reports were handed in, the university used them as the basis for a personal inquiry into the views and attitudes of every member of the student body. This enabled the authorities to probe into each student's personal history as interpreted through the Marxist-Leninist doctrine of historical materialism.

The first part of the inquiry went back three generations, into how each student, his parents, and grandparents lived, and how they supported themselves. The students were asked to write about what they were taught at home, what they were taught in school, and then to describe their personal relationships in society. This had to be followed by a description of their preferences in general and what kind of people they liked to associate with.

After all this data had been assembled, the authorities figured that they had the thought processes of their students fairly well dissected. Then they did a clever trick. They compared the first report the students made on their personal views and attitudes with the details they had given in the report on their family backgrounds.

The announcement was then made in a dramatic manner that this checkup showed that half of the students (about 4,000) had deep-set contradictions in their lives. They were told that this proved that in the former capitalist society in which they had been reared they had been dark people, that is, sinners. In China's new democracy, they must cleanse their minds of all remnants of their evil past. The process through which this had to be done was by confession—the frank admission of their sinful, contradictory pasts in open congregation—publicly—through the medium of self-criticism. This was perverted evangelism and, along with quack psychiatry, constituted the two pillars of Red China's reformation program. The students were asked whether they preferred to be master or servant, and were told that if they wanted to be the master this showed that they needed to reform their thoughts, which could only be done by revealing their dark pasts.

"If you don't reveal your wrong thoughts and bad deeds," went the warning, "they will be an intolerable burden on your shoulders. They will become heavier and heavier, until the time comes when you no longer will be able to bear their great weight." They were cautioned that this burden of thoughts would surely become overwhelming, so the only way to become a new man was by revealing one's bad past, unhesitatingly.

"Surely the students didn't take this seriously!" I exclaimed. "Didn't they consider this kind of reasoning as a corny joke?"

Chi looked at me with the utmost seriousness. "A great struggle went on for the thoughts of the students during this period," he said. "This was a great struggle, truly a struggle of one's spirit. You must not underestimate it if you want to understand what took place. You must remember the environment in which we have been living." His sincerity was evident. He continued.

"The intensity of this personal struggle in our minds, and for our minds, can hardly be exaggerated. This was especially so in the case of anyone who had been a sympathizer with or a member of the Kuomintang, who had worked for the Nationalists, or who might have been an intelligence agent for the Chiang Kai-shek regime.

"In such a struggle, the question would come up in a student's mind in this way: If I reveal that I was a member of the Kuomintang, what action will the authorities take against me? If I don't confess, will it influence me in a bad way in my future work?"

Chi was speaking fast now, and I had to slow him down. He seemed to be living again those tense hours. "During this internal struggle, many students found it impossible to relax at all," he went on. "Some could not sleep the whole night through. When a student was restless at night this way, or couldn't sleep, someone sleeping near him would be sure to notice it. The next day the agitated individual would be asked why he hadn't been able to sleep peacefully.

"'What were you thinking about last night? What kept you awake?' he would be asked in a sympathetic tone. 'If you don't feel like revealing it in public, tell it to me.'"

This was the point in the interview when I suddenly had that feeling of having heard this before, but couldn't remember where, until I recalled my visit to that most modern mental hospital. If what was practised there was psychiatry, what Chi was telling me about was surely quack psychiatry. No wonder this gave me the eerie sensation of a world turned inside out, a world more horrible than a tale by Edgar Allan Poe, and one which made the ghastliness of a Grand Guignol fantasy seem normal.

"There was no escape from this questioning," Chi went on. "Even when you lay down at night you were watched, and your movements would betray your innermost thoughts. The fact that you couldn't hide even in sleep tormented you and made you even more restless."

Special agents conducted such questioning. Chi's attempt to tell me what these people were called led, as so often under such circumstances, into a maze of semantics. There were plenty of ways of translating it, but each time some essential point would be left out or the words would lend themselves to several interpretations. Doubletalk, which is so handy for propagandists, thrives in such situations. The translator favored the term "thought-seduction worker," and this seemed to fit best. The man's job was to coax forth the intimate thoughts, the secrets which the students struggled to keep to themselves. It could also be translated as "thought-revealing worker," but it was actually more penetrating than that. The Chinese characters *chi fah* meant more than just to reveal; they conveyed the sense of enticement, of seduction.

The difficulty we had finding a translation that would be completely true to the original phrasing and would also convey the correct nuance of the original demonstrates one of the main reasons for the confusion and misunderstanding over what is taking place in foreign countries. Editors naturally insist on simple specific language that is understandable within the framework of their readers' lives. Yet there are many words or phrases in one language that simply have no equivalent in another. To provide such a snap translation may be a clever bit of writing, but only at the sacrifice of accuracy. We are given an approximation, but not what the original exactly meant. Totalitarians have not hesitated to take full propaganda advantage of this search by the politician, the reporter, and the headline writer for the happy graphic comparison.

An inflexible rule in group discussions was that everyone had to participate. "After the weekly lecture," Chi said, "if you didn't speak up, and at length, to show your own point of view and thought processes, when you went for your rest period afterwards, you would be asked, 'Why did you have no opinion to contribute to your group?'

"If you replied that you had no questions to ask, you would be told, 'This means that you accept the whole idea of the lecture. If you accept it, this must mean that you understand it. Then why don't you speak up to help others understand? If you don't understand, then why don't you ask questions?'

"So everyone talks. Whether what they say represents their own ideas is irrelevant. Talking, you can't keep from exposing your own mental processes, and talking helps you indoctrinate yourself.

"A subtle pressure is used against a person who does not enter the discussion to the extent desired. In self-criticism sessions he is called a lagging-behind particle, a backward element, someone without responsibility for the People's Revolution.

"Students became miserable under such pressures. When a lecturer said something that contradicted his main point, you didn't dare bring it up, even by a hint. You asked only super-ficial questions and accepted the ideas handed down to you.

"There was no escape. After each lecture, the groups of twenty-three would meet separately to agree on the speaker's main idea. Then each group would break up into small sec-tions to confirm the group findings by discussing the lecture in detail so as to rationalize all points that seemed to conflict with the main idea. The object of breaking up into smaller groups, we were told, was to give each person the opportunity to find the correct answer by himself.

"Often, too, a group would be encouraged to challenge an-other group, sending it a ticklish question of political dogma to solve. If this group succeeded—success meant always ex-plaining away any contradictions—it published its conclusions in the wall paper, taking credit for it. This was called a learn-ing contest.

"If a whole class of nine groups couldn't solve a problem, the class head would summon all of them together for a class meeting. Always, by the end of the meeting, any ideas among the students that were not politically orthodox were sure to succumb to those of the university authorities.

"A problem was not considered solved if one person re-mained in a group who did not say that he was convinced. Opinions had to be unanimous.

"When the entire class met, at a certain stage in the dis-cussion questions could no longer be raised opposing the line laid down by the class leader. This stage was reached when it seemed possible that if discussion continued an oppo-site opinion might make headway.

"The class head, practiced in detecting such dangerous mo-ments, halted discussion by a simple tactic. When a student wanted to speak, the system was that he raised his hand and stated whether he opposed or favored the view taken by the previous speaker. The instructor always could choke off one side by saying, 'Wait until the other side talks.' Then, after allowing only those who agreed with the Party viewpoint to express themselves, he could announce the desired conclusion as that of the whole class and declare the meeting over. This was frequently done.

"A student had no right to speak once discussion was declared over. This was called maintaining discipline at a meeting. Anyone who tried to speak up would be criticized for disobedience. Where political opinions are the issue, disobedience becomes a very critical matter, affecting one's entire future."

Even so, the psychological pressure exerted by this skillfully devised technique of creating a hypnotic state of fatigue and forcing a person, while in this trance, to repeat again and again, lengthily and in his own words the political dogma demanded of him, was not over yet. This was only the preparatory stage. The main pressures were yet to come under critical, hypersensitive group conditions.

"After this initial period of mental struggle and mind reform, we were given back our reports and asked to rewrite them in accordance with the new thinking we had achieved through our intensive self-criticism program," Chi declared. "This was called our thought conclusion."

"The students became terribly upset and very unhappy during this period. Girls often broke into tears, weeping aloud under this constant probing into their thoughts and the internal struggles brought about in their mental systems. But they weren't the only ones to collapse. Men did also. They wept more than the girls, it seemed, but they were under greater pressure. Girls had fewer social contacts, politically speaking, and so comparatively less pressure was put on them. Some tried to escape from what seemed an insoluble problem by leaping into the quietude of Kwan Ming Lake within the grounds of the Summer Palace. Some tried other ways of committing suicide.

"The Communists taught that everything that a Kuomintang member had ever done was against the people's welfare. One student couldn't bring himself to understand how he, himself, had mistreated and exploited the people. He was no capitalist; he was just a plain workman. An idea-seduction worker told him that if he didn't confess in the group that he had worked against the people's welfare he would be sent to the People's New Life Labor School at Peiping, where he would get even more strenuous idea training and greater assistance in self-criticism.

"Idea training at the People's New Life Labor School consisted of six months of study and hard labor, and, if the results were unsatisfactory, the student would be kept on. Only if he did well during this period, he was told, and his ideas came closer to those of true workingmen could he be released.

"The student was horrified. He knew that the People's New Life Labor School was the same as a forced labor camp. The only difference was that you had to put yourself into a state of mind of agreeing that you were going there voluntarily to improve yourself. This requirement created a new mental struggle, for the simple fellow felt that this was all wrong and became greatly agitated. He apparently saw only one outlet—death—and committed suicide in our placid, inviting lake.

"There was another student, a graduate of the economics department of Nanking University, who had been employed by the United Nations Relief and Rehabilitation Administration in Nanking to gather statistics. He had been closely attracted by the American way of life and firmly believed that the welfare of the workers and farmers in the United States was being protected. He couldn't see why China had to lean to one side, as demanded by Mao.

"The university let him know that he was reactionary and stubborn, was suffering from America-fascination, and that he was doped with Americanism. He was warned that his state of mind would lead him to become a traitor, a hateful compradore, and an antirevolutionist. He was transferred to a college in Sinkiang Province to till the soil. This was a college only in name; actually it was a forced labor camp.

"The student protested that this was not reform, but a war of nerves intended to make him confess what he hadn't done. This was the same as 'mopping away the truth, forcing one to do what he doesn't want to do,' he declared. One night he swallowed an overdose of sleeping tablets, but was discovered and sent to the North China People's Hospital in time to save his life. Upon recovery he was immediately shipped to a labor university in Chahar Province to continue his idea reform under even more strenuous conditions. Two thirds of the time was spent in hard labor, and one third in classroom activity of the group discussion and self-criticism type.

"A special name was used to describe this period of intensive inquiry into our attitudes; it was called inspection of ideas, and at its conclusion, seventeen students were sent to the People's New Life Labor School."

RECREATION

Recreation was a serious matter at the North China People's Revolutionary University. Idea training could never be neglected during a single waking or sleeping hour. An able Party man and a thought-seduction worker were always present, as a team, the one to direct ideas into desired channels, the other to check on whether it had been accomplished.

Sundays were rest days. No trips or picnics were organized, and the students were permitted to wander about in small groups, but no farther from the university than one li (a third of a mile). "Even in such short outings we could not forget our idea training," Chi said. "We had to watch what we were saying at all times.

"We had movies every Sunday night. These were usually Soviet Russian movies, sometimes a Chinese film, but always propaganda. A typical film was *The Fire of Wrath,* with its message that a Communist Party member never surrenders.

There were never any American films or films from any other country.

"The screen was placed in the center of the parade grounds, with seats on both sides. About two-thirds of the student body attended, half of whom had to sit behind the screen. When you see a film from behind the screen, it isn't funny; it's just confusing.

"Our recreation was as calculatingly organized as our studies, and with the same objectives, as part of the university program. The university often sponsored evening parties, and you were obliged to attend whether you wanted to or not. You were expected to appear very enthusiastic when the date for such a party was announced. Otherwise the thought-seduction worker would casually remark that you didn't seem very happy about it, saying, 'Why not? Be frank.' And if you didn't appear to be enjoying yourself at the party, he would casually ask, 'You don't seem very pleased. Why not? Be frank.'"

Try this some time. Make believe you are enjoying yourself, do it over and over again, and you are liable to end up believing you are enjoying yourself. This seems to be human nature, and the Communist authorities were evidently exploiting this trait for political purposes. Coué created an entire philosophic system on the repetition by rote of the maxim, "Every day, in every way, I am getting better and better." This was the tactic which, in effect, the discussion groups were using for their political dogma, only making it mandatory and changing the end of the sentence to: "I am believing more and more." If you weren't really enjoying yourself, so what? Others would think that you were, and they would be influenced accordingly. Then they, in turn, would influence you. This, too, seemed to be human nature, a facet of mob psychology.

The evening parties took place about once every two or three weeks. As soon as the date was set, the Culture and Amusements section of each group would begin to make plans. Everyone would be invited to help prepare a program.

The evening often included a short play. Three or four students would be asked to act out a situation of topical interest, based on what appeared in the newspapers. One such living newspaper dramatized the situation in Korea. General MacArthur was shown sitting high and mighty on the stage, and President Rhee was portrayed abjectly crawling in and asking for help.

Another such living newspaper was put on during the famine period in North China and was intended to show how the United States was hoodwinking the world with its relief programs. A magician, dressed to represent America, came on the stage. He had on a khaki uniform and a cardboard high hat decorated with the stars and stripes. Of his two assistants, one represented China and the other Japan. The magician entered smiling, carrying gifts of milk and bread in his left hand while he held two pistols in his right. He handed the pistols to his assistants and began ravenously eating the food he had brought. He took a flag with the dove of peace insignia on it from his pocket and addressed the audience, which was supposed to represent the peoples of the world. "See the word peace on this flag?" he called out. "Watch while I set fire to the flag. You will see eternal peace instead. But first close your eyes." He set fire to the flag and, as it was about to be consumed by flame, cried out, "Now, everybody, open your eyes!" At the same time he held out an atom bomb and shouted, "This is what I'm going to use to bring the peace." With this, the act ended.

In another living newspaper Stalin was portrayed in a uniform without medals. He came on stage leading seven small brothers who represented the countries in the Soviet orbit in Eastern Europe. Stalin, who was the tallest, bowed and left the stage to the seven others, who were dressed to represent their nationalities. These seven began to make friends with each other and began a conversation. "We were cheated when under the rascals' rule," said one, evidently referring to capitalism or imperialism. "Our oldest brother has beaten up the rascals, and now we can live peacefully," said another. "We must still watch out," still another warned, "for all the rascals haven't yet been killed. Probably they'll try to come back."

Suddenly a larger chap, not as large and broad as Stalin but huskier than the other seven, entered to the back-stage beating of drums and the blowing of horns. This was New China in a Sun Yat-sen uniform. All the seven gathered around him and welcomed him as "our most powerful brother from the East."

"Hurry, let's call out our oldest brother to join the party," they exclaimed joyfully. Stalin came out again, and all the eight now, including New China, gravely asked him what they must do to prevent the return of the rascals. "What do you think you should do?" Stalin replied, in the manner of a democratic group discussion leader. All the eight cried out simultaneously, "We will gladly follow your lead; you must give the order!" Stalin agreed, saying approvingly, "You are all good and true brothers and you shall have a brilliant future." With this the playlet ended.

"During the performance we were all highly amused by the grotesque acting and really had a good time," Chi said. "Even so, the inferior status given the Chinese representative did not go unnoticed, as was shown by the questions asked later in our group. We discussed the roles of the various countries in the Communist orbit. Some students asked whether under internationalism, when the form of countries disappears, our nation would still have to obey Soviet Russia. The answer that came to us was that the Chinese revolution was world-wide in extent. Our object is to liberate all those who are oppressed, we were told. When we succeed, we will all be the brothers and sisters of all the workers in the world. We will live as one big family. Why should we then divide ourselves up into countries? This didn't answer the main point, but we could not pursue the question further. The stage had been reached in this discussion when additional questioning had to cease."

There were also singing and folk dancing at the parties. The Chinese have many simple peasant dances, and these were put on, including the invariable Communist *yang ko* with its short abrupt movements, and the folk dances of all countries in the Soviet orbit. There were no American dances, and the hula was excluded on a moral basis as creating lascivious thoughts and not being serious. "Our songs were all Communist tunes, and the only foreign songs we sang were those translated from the Russian. The *Marseillaise* was never heard, and the *Internationale* was sung only on formal occasions. The *Marseillaise* was excluded as belonging to a petty bourgeois revolution. We were taught that such a tune, no matter how inspirational, cannot represent the proletarian revolution, and anyway it had lost its revolutionary qualities," Chi explained.

"We played games, but they, too, had to be serious. They had to have revolutionary significance or at least to be educational. In principle, everyone had to join the games. If you weren't present, it would be noticed, and someone would meet you as if by accident and ask, 'What were you thinking about, Comrade, that made you give up your recreation?' Or 'You missed a lot; we had such fun!' This made the approach seem natural, but the next question would be of the usual thought-seduction kind. This sort of questioning always created a vague uneasiness in you, a sort of fear, and rather than undergo it you made a point to be present and to be noticed.

" 'You're not antisocial, are you?' a comrade would tease with a smile. To be antisocial was a serious matter; it meant you were stubborn and reactionary, and those traits were antirevolutionary, which would lead to more arduous idea training and perhaps your transfer to a stricter thought-reform institution."

Even the games played were purposeful. One was called Scatter-Names, or Union Is Force. The students all wrote their names on slips of paper and handed them to group leaders, who then distributed them haphazardly. Everyone therefore got a card on which was written somebody else's name. Each pinned the name he got to his back, and then the leaders cried out, "Everybody find his own name!" Each student then would dash about trying to locate his own name and, as soon as he found it, would grip the other person's back. The latter, if he hadn't found his own name yet, would have to go on searching, with the other clinging to him. Soon there would be long snake lines until everyone was in a shouting, squirming, single line. When unanimity had been achieved, and everybody had located his own name, the whole assemblage would sing in unison, "Union Is Force." The game, which always came at the end of the evening, was considered a good means of getting people acquainted with each other.

In another game thirty-one students were divided into two teams, with the extra man sitting in the center. A player, after discussion among his own team, would whisper the name of someone on his own side to the umpire. This detail was significant; the team as a whole did not actually pick the name, but the player selected chose it himself by the approved form of group discussion. Then the other side had to figure out whose name had been picked by the others. If they did so correctly, the student sitting in the center would cry out *p'ie*, the sound of a gun, meaning that a killing had been made. The player named correctly was then out.

"Although this sounds simple," Chi said, "it was amusing how much skill it brought into play. There were times when everyone on one side would be killed before anyone on the other side. I myself have been on a team that was wiped out. Each side would think up tactics and strategy, trying to detect who was most active on the other side and who most inactive. The game, obviously of a military character, was appropriately called Probing the Enemy's Intelligence."

Everything for the Front was the name of another military game, in which forty or fifty students were divided into two teams, each representing a village at the front. Two students were named to represent the Red Army and, one at a time, would shout out the name of some object supposedly needed by the Red Army. Each team would compete to get it to the front first. "Needed—a shoe for the left foot!" might be one cry, and the two teams would race to get it to the front. Whichever side got it there first won a point. A great deal of good humor was brought into the game by asking for unusual objects. "Needed—a white hair!" might be the cry, and then everyone would rush about searching each other's heads for a white hair, which would be promptly torn out and rushed to the front.

There was even an arithmetic game in which there were two teams of fifteen players each and an umpire. Ten students on each side would represent a number from one to ten, and the other five players would represent the symbols used in arithmetic: plus ($+$); minus ($-$); division ($\div$); multiplication ($\times$) and equals ($=$). The umpire would shout out an example, such as two times four minus eight equals zero, and each side would rush to line up in this order. The team to do so first was the winner.

SEX

After the first couple of months the university began to encourage the boys and girls to mix freely. Before then, they generally had been kept apart, except as they normally met in the day's work, and were not permitted to engage in any romancing or sex talk. The girls slept in their own barracks. "When we took a walk in those first couple of months, the boys went in groups, or the girls, but not mixed," Chi said. "Even on Sunday, which was our day off, we couldn't go out on mixed parties.

"All this was changed in our third month. We were now considered politically mature enough for boys and girls to mingle. Now we could not only mix, but talk all we wanted to about sex. Before, if a girl or boy walked about and chatted in friendly fashion with a member of the opposite sex, he or she was criticized for it in the next discussion group meeting. All such criticism was now dropped.

"Now we could go out on mixed parties on Sundays, and couples even began to be seen walking out alone. Most parties were made up of several couples. Nobody paid any attention any longer to how far the students went in their sexual relations, or even whether they had sexual relations. Whether a girl became pregnant or not was her own business. The Communists didn't care, and this attitude soon became known to everyone.

"Seventeen girls, so far as I know, were pregnant at graduation time. Most of them asked for permission to marry, and I am sure the boys wanted to marry them. Some told me so. The authorities refused point-blank to give permission for any of them to marry. The university pointed out that it was unlikely that any of them would work in the same locality after they were assigned to their new jobs following graduation, and so marriage would only handicap their Party activities.

"The girls asked, 'Who will be the father of my child? It is shameful to have a baby without a father.' The university answered that this was a feudal idea. When they asked, 'What shall I do if a boy is born?' they were informed, 'Your child will be the people's boy and will be raised by the government.' They were told they didn't have to worry.

"One of the girl group leaders had two children, both boys, who were being reared in Peiping at a nursery home run by the Party. I accompanied her there one Sunday by special permission. We went by bus. She had not been married, and her two children, aged three and one, were sons of the people.

"I just called her Comrade, the way we all addressed each other. She was twenty-six, stocky, with a fresh complexion and an oval face. She came from Hopei Province, where she had graduated from the Military and Political University at Shih Chia Chuang. She was a farm girl who had become a Party member quite young and knew nothing else but Party work. She never told me the details of her past.

"She made a curious remark to me one day. 'If you would cut off your relations with your father,' she said, 'perhaps our political affections for each other could be better.' Whether this implied a willingness to marry me, or what, I never found out. The relations between ourselves and our relatives were controversial points in our group discussions and personal struggles at that time.

"During this period of inspection of ideas, many sons were advised to cease all communications with their parents. A landowner's son was told, 'Your father belongs to the exploiting class, while those who have undergone idea reform do not belong to the exploiting class.' The suggestion was made that he eliminate such antisocial relationships from his life. This constituted both a warning and advice.

"Efforts were made to discredit family connections generally. This was during the class-distinction period and coincided with the complete right-about-face in the attitude of the university toward the mingling of the sexes. During the class-distinction period the students were told, 'You must fight against your family and reveal what your family did in the past.'

"The authorities made an intensive inquiry into my family ties. They wanted me to cut myself off from my father, to fight against him."

This was the turning point in Chi's own attitude. Except for the incident of the wall paper at Tsing Hua, which had been provoked by his inquisitive, essentially fair nature, he had accepted Communist claims at face value.

"My father is only a small merchant and didn't earn enough to support the family, so my mother had to go to work too," he told the university authorities. "As for me, I have been wandering since I was nine years old. I feel that my father himself has been exploited and I've spent my childhood and youth half in work, half in study. In my thoughts and feelings I simply can't cut myself off from my family and fight against them. If I have to, I can only ask myself what meaning is there to life in this world and why was there a revolution.

"My father and mother now are very old," he had pleaded.

BRAIN-WASHING"   49

"They have little work and are almost unable to engage in any business. On what or on whom are they going to depend in their old lives? Their sole ambition was that I could work and earn some money with which to support them. If I now cut off my relations with my family, it means that I want them to starve to death.

"If the university insists, then I would rather be an anti-revolutionary. I will do anything the government wants me to do, but I will not, under any circumstances, separate myself from my parents. I will accept any punishment the university sees fit to impose on me rather than do that."

The university assigned a faculty member to have a detailed talk with him about his family situation. "I told him that my family lived in Shanghai and led a life probably poorer than that of the working class or farmers, having no piece of property they could call their own. If the university didn't believe me, I said it certainly could send someone to Shanghai to investigate.

"A Party member was sent, and on his return reported that my family's condition was not as poor as I had made out. 'His parents are much better off than the farmers,' he told the university. 'At least they dress much better. If they have no money, they can borrow some from relatives. His father and mother, although over fifty, are still able to work.'

"He reported that my parents could be sent to North China to work on a farm, and that it was not necessary for me to support them. I was therefore told that from then on I must understand that I was a son of the people, and not of my father.

"'In the future you must work for the people, and thoughts about your family must not be permitted to arise,' I was instructed. The university authorities said they trusted that I would reconsider my position and let them know my decision. I told them I would do so and I kept telling them this until graduation.

"Because I refused to break relations with my parents, the Communists sent policemen to neighbors of ours in Shanghai to gather information against them. I learned of three such instances. They also asked about my past activities. They could find nothing against us. From then until I graduated, some able Party member would come to me every once in a while to discuss my parents with me and to try to persuade me to make the break.

"They asked me whether I considered my country or my family the more important. Weren't the lives of the 475,000,-000 people of China more important than the lives of a few persons in my family? I just didn't reply. Actually, I couldn't see how my father and mother could be considered outside of the Chinese people. Weren't they Chinese too? The object of the revolution seemed to me to be the improvement of the living conditions of everyone, and I believed that the benefit brought the nation by the revolution should coincide with the gains made by its people.

"If everyone severed relations with their relatives, it seemed to me that this would only add to the chaos in China."

His was not the only such problem. Many students were married, and had been separated from their husbands or wives by this training course. They keenly felt the pressure against their family ties. When a married person entered a Revolutionary University it usually meant that he was separated permanently from his wife, because he knew that after graduation he almost surely would be sent to work in some locality where the other couldn't go. The Communists tried to persuade such persons to ask for a divorce. They based this demand on the reasoning that once a man has gone through a course in idea training, while his wife continued living or working somewhere else, their ideas would not be alike when they resumed living together. They would have different viewpoints on life. So a divorce was recommended as the only way out.

Married students were told, "This course is giving you a different political foundation from that of your wife. There can only be two alternatives. If you resume living together, either you will influence her, or she will influence you. Unfortunately, experience has shown that for the most part it is always the person who does not participate in idea training who influences the other."

The students asked why old thoughts should decisively influence new thoughts and overwhelm them. The answer they got was: "After spending twenty or more years in the old society, you can't expect idea training to cure your mind of all that evil past. Remnants of it will still persist in your memories, and this is what makes it possible for you to suffer a relapse and return to your old way of thinking."

A number of the married students were persuaded by this sort of logic to divorce their wives or husbands. Chi said they were a pathetic sight when they finally sat down to write home for a divorce. The able Party member and the group leader would encourage them during such periods of intensity. "You are doing right," they told them. "Don't weep; be a man."

GRADUATION AND ESCAPE

The discovery that his family had been put under police surveillance in Shanghai shocked Chi. Thereafter he was very careful to say only those things that he thought the Communists wanted him to say and he no longer raised any questions that might be interpreted as counterrevolutionary.

Graduation day either sent a student to a job that the Communist Party had decided he was fit to handle, to a stricter institution for further mind reform, or kept him back in the university. Even so, the students were told that graduation after the normal six-month course was only the first step in mind reform because theories were learned in school and had to be translated into practical life in the outside world. The Revolutionary University was considered a bridge from the old, decadent life to the new life.

No special oral or written examinations are required. A student's final revision of his self-criticism paper constitutes a thought conclusion thesis that largely determines his fate. What are called Democratic Examination Councils are set up, one for each student. Each council is composed of eleven members: the leader of the student's class; the head of his group; other ardent supporters of the Party in the group, known as positive elements, which include the chiefs of such group functions as culture-amusements; and three reliable individuals from other groups who know the applicant. The councils are established and perform their functions in the last two weeks. Chi was a member of eleven such councils. Their findings are recorded on a democratic examination form entitled "Administrative Agreement Group's Opinion." The class head has to sign it and then turn it over to the principal and department heads for their signatures.

As in all group meetings, findings have to be unanimous. Sometimes, before an opinion is recorded, others in the student's group, or in other groups, are brought in for consultation, and sometimes the applicant's entire group joins the discussion before a decision is reached. There are no marks and no formal examinations into a student's knowledge in any particular subject. All that matters is one's revolutionary reliability. There is a space allotted for remarks above the signatures. Whether the student is graduated, kept over, or transferred to another idea reform institution is recorded below the signatures by the class head or higher authorities. The class head does not write in the remarks section when the student is to be graduated, but only when there is something unfavorable to report.

The student himself has to appear before the council, where he is called upon to participate in the discussion. "He often defends himself, as I did," Chi said, by "reminding the group of some special revolutionary achievement or some example of revolutionary ardor. As it was, I was lucky to squeeze through. The list of my defects was much longer than the list of my good points. Indeed, I was judged to have only one good point, which was described on my form as 'a positive attitude toward the laboring class.' This was judged sufficient to pass me even though the remarks section of the form said I was a backward element.

"I was found not steady in my political stand and it was felt that I hadn't sufficiently grasped the principles of the revolution—Marxism-Leninism. This simply wasn't so. Their conclusion was based on my refusal to cut myself off from my parents and was interpreted as a failure to meet the requirements of a relentless class war. It was considered as giving overemphasis to my own personal situation and showing an unrevolutionary interest in one's own profit. I was called stubborn. Another opinion, which at the time I feared would destroy me, was that some old ideas were still in my head, not yet completely eliminated. This, too, was probably an allusion to my attitude regarding my parents.

"The final verdict added up to individualism on my part. I don't deny it! What I learned during my training course in Communism was largely responsible for it.

"Three students fled before graduation. One ran away because his wife was ill, and the university refused to give him permission to visit her. Another fled for the same reason that revolted me, the demand that he fight against his own father. The third student merely felt that Communist ideas were nonsense, so far as we could learn. Two other students had been sent to the New Life Labor School for thought reform. You rarely mentioned these cases. Of the original twenty-three students in my group, eighteen were present at graduation ceremonies."

Gen. Chu Teh, Commander-in-Chief of the Red Army, gave the principal graduation address, which lasted three hours. Talking before a gathering of what he presumed to be thoroughly indoctrinated Communists who would participate in the Party's future, he frankly outlined its global program. He discounted fears that the United States could not be overthrown, and in a very succinct manner outlined the strategy by which, he said, the Asian and European hemispheres would work together as a pincer to crush the United States, utilizing and fanning racial antagonisms for this purpose. The Chinese did not have to worry about American obstacles to Communism, Chu Teh said, because "America is lame; one of its legs is held tight in Eastern Europe by Soviet Russia."

"With the union of 700,000,000 to 800,000,000 people, achieved by bringing Soviet Russia and China together, we can smash in the tiger's head," Chi heard him boast. "When we succeed in smashing the tiger's head in the Far East, then we can return to Eastern Europe and cut off its legs. We are on the eve of the destruction of American imperialism." That speech was given on March 11, 1950.

Chu Teh outlined the military program of the Chinese Communists. "Communism constitutes one entity—a united country," he told the graduates. "Capitalism, in spite of the fact that the capitalist countries have the same general ideas, is like the blowing sand. Countries such as India, Burma, and Indochina are striving to learn from the experience of China. Burma and India formerly thought that China's revolutionary tactics were wrong. But now they are learning that we were right. So these countries are coming to know that to start a revolution you have to gather a revolutionary force, and for this you need the farmers. In India and Burma it will be easier to create a people's race revolution because those countries were under imperialist oppression."

This allusion to a race revolution,* with its fearsome conno-

---

* Sun Yat-sen, in his *San Min Chu-I* (*Threefold People's Doctrine*), the bible of Nationalist China, says China is made up of five races: the Hans, the Manchus, the Mongols, the Moslems, and the Tibetans. Wong Tu-Chien, a member of the Commission of Nationalities Affairs in the Communist regime at Peiping, in an article in the English-language *People's China* of April 1, 1950, entitled "China's Policy on National Minorities," wrote: "Although 95 per cent of the 475,000,000 Chinese population are the Han people, the national minorities, which comprise only five per cent of the total population, however, hold a rather special and significant position. This is because they are numerous in race and living in extensive areas throughout the country." Race and nationality are frequently considered alike among the Chinese, both legally and socially. The five-barred flag of the first republic was designed to represent these five races. The three principles in Dr. Sun's work, the ideological basis for which he derived from a little-known political treatise by an American

tation, was startling to me but not to Chi. He had heard it often. Later I was to come across it frequently in Communist Chinese indoctrination textbooks and in the standard school books put out by the new regime. They frankly referred to China's "national racial revolution."

Here, in Chu Teh's talk, he was referring to an anticipated "people's race revolution" in Southeast Asia and the Middle East, clear evidence of Communist policy to arouse and exploit latent racial feelings between the white and yellow races.

Inside China, and in the areas of insurgency in Asia generally, the Communists have given a yellow-race-against-the-white-race coloration to the struggle. This was all the more callous and irresponsible in China itself, for there the people have been brought up to consider themselves a race, distinct from the other peoples of Asia.

How did this propaganda twist affect Soviet Russia? Wasn't this just as much a threat to her as to Europeans generally? "Oh, no," said Chi. "Everyone knows that the Russians are Asians. Didn't Stalin himself say, when he met the Japanese envoy before World War II broke out, that he, too, was an Asian?"** Indeed, while the West interprets the risings in the East as mere nationalism, in the minds of most Asians nationalism is confused with race. The national revolutions in Indochina, Indonesia, and elsewhere were started as part of a racial movement, encouraged by underground means for half a century by the Japanese ultranationalists as part of their Pan-Asia movement. The Communists, when

dentist named Maurice Williams, were: nationalism, the people's rights, and the people's livelihood. Nationalism here was actually racial nationalism. The Chinese were then a subject people to the Manchus, and the initial struggle was for the equality of races. The Communists have used this racial confusion completely opportunistically.

** "You are an Asiatic; so am I," said Stalin to Japanese Foreign Minister Matsuoka in the Kremlin, during the convivial Kremlin negotiations that resulted in the signing of the Russo-Japanese Neutrality Pact in April, 1941 —a treaty which protected Japan's flank and enabled her to put her energies into preparations for a Pearl Harbor against the U.S. The depth of racial feelings in Asia to this day is evidenced by how frequently I still heard Asians refer to that remark by Stalin, the Georgian.

it became evident that Japan was to be defeated, quickly moved into the race field in Asia, and in numerous instances worked together with the Japanese agitators. Whether this was farsightedness on the part of the defeated Japanese extremists or infiltration on the part of the Communists is purely academic.

In his graduation speech Chu Teh went on to tell the students, who were about to go out themselves on their assigned missions, that many Communist students from Southeast Asia and the Middle East were coming to Red China to learn how to succeed as the Chinese Communists did and how to coordinate policy.

"Many students have already come to North China from those countries to study our experience," he said. "Some have come to learn our experience in the economic field, others in politics, and still others in the military sphere. Some have already taken an active part in our work in every part of China. They are learning from experience by working alongside us in China.

"They will have much to offer to the revolutions in their countries, and meanwhile we have many men working in their lands. I am speaking frankly before you because you are all standing in the same front line of the world Communist revolution. Our men working in those countries do not have any titles, but they hold very important posts. If America wants to start World War III, all of Southeast Asia will be under the leadership of China. This I can guarantee."

Graduation certificates were given to the four departments for distribution to the classes, and right afterwards the students were notified where they would be sent to work and in what capacities. The selection was according to each student's qualifications and his receptiveness to idea reform.

"If you were fit for the military, you were sent to an army post," Chi said. "If you were not an active person, you might be given an office job. I was ordered to go to Tihua, capital of Sinkiang Province, to join the Sino-Russian Petroleum Co. I had studied some Russian in Chungking near the close of

World War II, and so the Party decided that I could be made into an interpreter.

"If I were to escape, it had to be now. A few nights later, I left the university and walked to the outskirts of Peiping, where I went to the home of a friend whom I had known at Tsing Hua University. He gave me shelter for three days. The next morning his cousin went to a small, suburban railroad station to buy me a ticket to Shanghai. I went to the station just before the train pulled in.

"I wore ordinary trousers and a singlet and carried no baggage except a blanket given me by my friend, as it was still very cold. I had discarded the plain Red Army uniform we wore at the university. I had no money, for the university had not given me any for the trip to Sinkiang. The Communists had not even given me my travel permit for Sinkiang, but had merely arranged with the railroad station, informing me when to show up for the train trip.

"When I got to Shanghai, I went to my uncle's home in the western district, and he informed my parents. He hid me for twenty-seven days. The third day after I reached Shanghai the police came to my parents' home to inquire about me. My family told them they had no idea where I was. Two days later several police broke into their house at a very late hour. I wasn't there. Some time later, early in the morning, two police dashed into the house. I wasn't there then, either.

"After I escaped to Hong Kong, I learned that the police again had paid a surprise visit to my parents. My father was summoned to the police station and had to sign a guarantee that, if I returned home, he would surrender me to the police at once."

"LEARNING"

LEARNING

"LEARNING" IS WHAT HAPPENS IN BRAIN-WASHING. THE word doesn't mean what it used to mean in China or any-where else. The Communists have given it their own double-talk definition. In the Party lexicon it no longer means learn-ing in general but political learning. And political learning in Red China means the study exclusively of Marxism-Lenin-ism and the ideas of Mao Tse-tung—these two alone.

Learning is the function of democratic group discussion meetings and of self-criticism meetings, where brains are washed, and these are held as a special indoctrination course in a room set aside in a factory or office building while the learner keeps his job, or in schools and institutions of higher learning, as in the Revolutionary universities of the sort Chi-Sze-chen attended.

Democratic discussions drag on interminably. This is part of the technique. The same topic is gone over again and again and again, until the mind of the student rings like a phono-graph record that has stuck at a point where it soporifically sings something about dialectical materialism, tailism, or pro-ductive relationship. And the student has to be able to get up and talk interminably and "correctly" on all of these, as hap-pened to Chi. The meetings constitute the machinery for the intellectual conquest of the Chinese. Through them the Party is creating, in general, a docile, believing, obedient public and, in particular, its trusted agents. These may be sent out on any mission—as watchdog and thought-seduction worker in home, school, or factory; picking up a rifle and going to the battlefield; making believe that he is a non-Communist and infiltrating into enemy ranks to sow discord or to engage in rear-guard action.

The wearing-down tactics used in learning and democratic discussions are carried over into every field of endeavor into which Communism extends, and it extends everywhere in China. These tactics were utilized even in realms so far afield as the sale of Communist government bonds. A simple example was the usual procedure by which quotas were reached in Red China's 1950 Victory Bond campaign. A couple of tax collectors would visit a shopkeeper, farmer, or houseowner and ask for some specific amount of subscription, say, 500 parity units.*

"I could never pay that," the comrade would cry out. "Why, that's more than the Kuomintang took. I just haven't got it."

"Well, sign for it anyway," he will be told. "You'll raise the money somehow."

"But that's silly. How can I? That's more than my income for the next six months."

This discussion would go on politely for, say, four or five hours. Then the tax collectors would politely say good-by.

That wasn't the end of it. They would return the next day for a new democratic discussion. The theory was that these subscriptions were voluntary, and so no force could be used, only democratic discussion. The second democratic discussion would go on longer than the first, perhaps up to six hours.

* A parity unit is the standard of measurement for calculating the official value of money in Red China. Salaries are sometimes calculated in this way. A parity unit is the prevailing total cost of 1.333 pounds (one-hundredth of a picul) of rice, 14.1 inches (one-tenth of a chang) of white cloth (cotton), one catty (1 1/3 pounds) of coal briquettes and one catty of oil (vegetable). The Chinese Red dollar is called the jen ming piao (jmp, or people's currency). At Shanghai, on May 31, 1951, for instance, the rate was JMP $3,880 for one Hong Kong dollar, of which there are about six to an American dollar. A parity unit was calculated as worth JMP $5,331, or about H.K. $1.37.

Anyone who believes that this is impossible simply doesn't understand how a democratic dictatorship works. Democratic dictatorship is the amazing name Mao Tse-tung coined for his form of government. A contradiction in terms? No, not at all, to Mao's way of thinking. He defined it as democracy for some, but dictatorship for others—"democracy among the people and dictatorship over the reactionaries."

The discussion with the tax collectors wouldn't be continuous. They would talk, sit about, chat about the evils of the American capitalist system and how lucky China was to have Soviet Russia to guide her. And of course every patriotic Chinese wishes to express his appreciation tangibly, doesn't he? And a tangible way is, of course, the Victory Bonds, isn't that so?

The harassed victim would raise his ante by, say, twenty per cent, which was still below the figure set. The tax collectors would politely say good-by.

They wouldn't return for more than a day. Instead of this bringing peace of mind to the intended subscriber, it only brings mental anguish, because he hasn't subscribed yet and knows that he won't get off that easy.

Sure enough, at perhaps three o'clock in the morning, when he is fast asleep, he will hear a loud banging at his door. Terrified, he will leap out of bed and ask who's there. "It's only us," he will hear, in polite tones. He will by now be able to recognize the voices of his two tax collectors.

Possibly the fleeting temptation will come to our prospective subscriber to call the intruders the descendants of particularly vile varieties of turtles, but, if so, he will suppress the desire, welcome his guests, heat some tea, and resume democratic discussion. This may go on until dawn or later.

By now, patience will have worn somewhat thin, and there will be circuitous references by the tax collectors, with plenty of quotations from Karl Marx, Josef Stalin, Mao Tse-tung, and Liu Shao-chi, to backward elements and lagging-behind elements, as the Party expresses it. This means people whose brains need washing or perhaps people who are so reactionary and decadent that they can't be trusted with whatever enterprise or business they are engaged in or even be allowed to remain in their own profession.

So a settlement will be made, a little less than originally demanded perhaps, but nearly the amount that had been asked.

How is such a levy paid up? Often it isn't; the subscriber just liquidates his possessions and joins the unemployed, flees into the hills to become a guerrilla, or escapes to Hong Kong or tries to.

INDUSTRIAL DEMOCRACY

DEMOCRATIC GROUP DISCUSSION EXTENDS INTO EVERY FIELD, and so it is only natural that industry should also participate, along with educational institutions, government bureaus, and agriculture. Indeed, the industrial phase of the reformation was what the workers found most attractive in the Communist program. They were promised privileges such as they had never before possessed in China. Soon spokesmen for Chinese Communism at home, and their foreign sympathizers, began to talk about the unparalleled enthusiasm with which the new system of industrial reforms was being put into effect. Workers were setting their own pay standards and their own working hours by democratic discussion. Capitalist monopoly could no longer stand in their way, depriving the working class of the just profits of their sweat and toil.

This put a new responsibility on the workers to preserve and protect the people's property, for the new basic law of Communist China gave all such property to the people and distinctly recognized the workers as the vanguard of the people. Naturally, inasmuch as the industrial plant, that labor had created along with everything else, was now being given back to the people, it was only to the advantage of the workers to produce more in order that all of the people would have more to share.

News was not slow to come out that the workers were showing their satisfaction and appreciation over their new status by guarding the tools of production from thievery and corruption. The Communist press was full of instances of workers tracing missing parts of machinery that had been removed by the Nationalists to hamper the new Communist state in reviving industry; of workers achieving almost miraculous repairs to damaged equipment; and of other workers, who had taken advantage of the turmoil of civil war to steal parts, returning them of their own free will.

There was no doubt that the workers took the promises given them seriously, believed the simple economics being taught them, and were doing their part to make the new system work. The Communist press, too, was full of stories containing evidence that the workmen now understood that they were working for themselves and not for "monopoly capitalists," and were giving tangible proof of their loyalty. The proof was invariably the same—the detailing of instance after instance of workmen lengthening their working hours and slashing their wage scales.

This sounded almost too much to expect of human beings, but I attributed my skepticism to the imperialist poisons in my unwashed brain. These dispatches always stressed the voluntary nature of the sacrifices being made by the workers. I decided to find out just how this all came about. Those who participated in this gave the same details no matter whether they had worked in a textile plant, on a university faculty, in a government bureau, or in any other enterprise for which workers were receiving regular stipends.

Lee Ming's experience was typical. He was a young member of the Chinese Customs who was in Hong Kong only for a few days to visit his relatives before returning to Red China. I was introduced to him by his brother, a pharmacist, who had mentioned him to me some time previously.

"My brother is a Communist," the pharmacist had said. "He has been deeply stirred by the Communist practice of deciding things by democratic discussion."

Here is the personal experience of Lee Ming, as he related it to me while riding in an automobile in the winding mountain roads of Hong Kong. He was so afraid of being spotted with me that there was no house in which we could settle for a visit. A friend took me for a drive, picked him up at a designated street corner, and after the interview let him off first.

"Our staff was called to a discussion meeting to hear a report by the customs officer from Peiping," Lee Ming began. "He gave us a thrilling speech on the new spirit that had spread throughout the land and explained that our progress was still being obstructed by the remnants of Chiang Kai-shek's forces supported by the American imperialists.

"He said a wonderful thing had happened. While he had been talking to some of us before the meeting, he had heard some of us suggest that the customs staff give up its annual bonus this year so as to stimulate national production. Perhaps someone might want to present this idea in the form of a resolution.

"I hadn't heard about this. On the contrary, we had been eagerly awaiting our regular year-end bonus, an accepted part of our salaries in China, so we could settle outstanding debts. We had made our arrangements accordingly. Nobody said anything. 'Let us have some democratic discussion on the matter,' the speaker said. He explained again the difficult position of the Peiping government, caused by what he described as the need to counteract the warmongering intrigues of the United States in China. All we had to do to convince ourselves of this was to read any of the newspapers, he said.

"Finally someone did get up, but he opposed the suggestion. How could we give up the bonus, which actually was a part of our wages? this man asked. He explained his own situation; he would have to sell his furniture if the bonus was not distributed. He could borrow no more, and there was no other way to make ends meet. Encouraged by his frankness, others got up to speak, all in the same vein.

"The delegate from Peiping then mentioned, in a significant manner, that the Peiping headquarters of the Customs

Department would be much disappointed if we did not voluntarily give up the bonus. He no longer said that the first time he had heard this suggestion was from ourselves. He now took the line that this was what was expected by our Peiping chiefs. I was stunned by the casual way in which he switched his argument. He said our Peiping chiefs would be much embarrassed if we failed to prove our sincerity in this matter. This meant only one thing to us. They had received instructions from even higher authorities.

" 'If this is a government order, we can do nothing about it,' one of my colleagues declared. The delegate said no—no pressure was to be used; this was purely a voluntary matter. And he abruptly closed the meeting with the announcement that we would resume democratic discussions in a week. Meanwhile, he said, we should all think about this so that we might understand the need.

"I was puzzled when I talked it over with my wife that night. I felt good just the same. This was democratic discussion. No force was being used; what a change from the unhappy past!

"In the interval before the next meeting each customs employee who had attended our meeting was visited in his home by the Peiping delegate. He was quite frank in pointing out that Peiping wanted us to pass a resolution giving up our bonus. I asked whether we could refuse. He avoided making a direct reply, explaining again the blessings of democratic discussion and how wonderful it was that we could now voluntarily reach decisions affecting our own welfare. Before action could be taken, we would all have to come to an agreement. This was not the unfair, unprincipled procedure of America, with its majority pressures. Here everyone had to be convinced.

"So you can understand that I went to the next meeting with my faith in Communist practices unspoiled. I was seeing it operate under my own eyes. At this second meeting several employees promptly arose to say they had become convinced that we should give up our bonus. Nobody else joined them, and the discussion became quite heated.

"The meeting was closed rather abruptly again, with no announcement this time. I thought the matter had ended there, and we all felt good. Democratic discussion had come through the test unscathed.

"You can understand the shock it was to me when I picked up the newspaper next day and read, in black and white, that the customs employees had decided to give up their year-end bonus. The speeches of the few who had been persuaded to speak in favor of the cancellation were quoted; nothing was said of the opposition. No mention was made that there had been no vote and that so few of us had approved while so many had disapproved. I was terribly shocked.

"When I asked my superiors how we could be put on record in favor of an action we opposed, they said that it couldn't be helped. The Peiping government had decided. I still couldn't understand why, on such a small matter, such important people should come to a decision.

"Democratic discussion, I learned, was the privilege of agreeing to what had already been decided, but without the right to disagree. Self-criticism meetings were the same. They were intended to criticize any failure faithfully to fulfill orders sent down from above by the usual chain of command, and not to criticize the orders.

"The next day another shock awaited me. I read that the staffs of other customs stations throughout Red China had decided to take similar action. Stimulated by the thrilling example we had set, they had promptly called discussion meetings to do likewise. They were just as voluntarily going to approve the stand we had taken! I have friends in those ports. They let me know how much they, too, were opposed to this measure.

"Everywhere the routine was identical. Customs employees were visited in their homes and pressed to approve the decision before democratic discussion took place. The meeting was called only after a few persons had been persuaded by various means to agree. Then the approval of these few was recorded as representing that of everyone.

"This wasn't all, though. Soon the newspapers began to tell of other industries following the glorious lead of the customs staff. Then something new was added. At these meetings, we were told, patriotic Chinese were demanding that their wages be cut and that their working hours be lengthened. Industries were competing with other industries in this, we were informed; this was democratic competition the people's democracy way.

"Now I understood the importance that the Communist government has set on recording our approval. We were to give the pay cut a democratic appearance. If only the government had frankly ordered us to drop the bonus and accept the slash, and told us why, I could have understood it. But not this hypocritical way."

QUESTIONNAIRES

FREDERICK GERHARDT LIVED IN THE MIRAMAR HOTEL, ON the Kowloon side of the harbor, across from the mountainous island that gives Hong Kong Colony its name. He was a pharmacist who had developed quite a lucrative business with drug concerns across the border.

"I just got a phone call from an old friend I haven't seen since I left Tientsin," he told me when I met him by chance on Queen's Road. "He'll tell you all about life on the other side of the bamboo curtain." He uttered the last phrase in a derisive manner. I accepted the invitation and joined him for tea at the Dairy Farm. Now, after looking over my notes, I can't tell which made the more illuminating account—the details of life in Red China, as pictured by Dr. Nathan Bloch, or the remarks between him and his friend.

"When are you going back?" was the first question Gerhardt asked him after he had introduced me.

"I'm not going back," Dr. Bloch replied. "I saw the rise of the Gestapo and it makes me sick to see the rise of another Gestapo."

This was said in a matter-of-fact manner, without heat. Dr. Bloch told me how he had arrived in Tientsin in 1934, coming to China to get as far away from the hated Nazis as a human being could go on this earth. He had opened a dental parlor, studied the language, and settled down for what he confidently expected was to be the rest of his life. On the way over to see him Gerhardt had told me how deeply his friend had entered into Chinese circles, making many close friends among the Chinese people, particularly in academic and professional life.

"I am going to Canada," Dr. Bloch said. "I shall start anew there. I am only in my early forties."

Gerhardt looked glum. "There's an appointment I ought to go to," he mumbled. "If you have to go anywhere, Nathan, I'll be glad to drop you off."

"Do you mind explaining what you mean?" I asked Dr. Bloch, ignoring the interruption.

I was the first person to whom Dr. Bloch had a chance to open his mind since his arrival in Hong Kong. He had not spoken openly to anyone for many months. He seemed full of suppressed ideas and obviously had had no opportunity until now to express himself frankly. This was to be a different sort of frankness than the much glamorized frankness of the self-criticism meetings.

"In Tientsin the police came into your flat any time of day or night, with every sort of personal question to ask you," he said. "'Where were you last night? You were seen buying a bottle of wine. Where did you get the money? You were seen buying two chickens in the market. Did you have a party? Who was there? What did you discuss? When did your meeting take place? Was it a meeting? Why did you hold it?' They questioned not only me like that but everyone else.

"They wouldn't string the questions out in that fast manner, but make a long awkward show of it, beating around the bush, hesitantly, shamefacedly. Yes, shamefacedly. I don't know of an instance when the man doing the questioning didn't apologize at the same time. 'I can't help it, you know,' he would mutter. 'They tell me what questions I must ask. It's not me, you know.' And they would shake their heads disapprovingly. And I knew they were unhappy. Such inquisitions are not the Chinese way. They are caught in a trap now."

"Do you think you ought to be saying all this?" Gerhardt broke in. "You know it isn't safe. The British could withdraw your visa. You know how the British are here."

Gerhardt had a point there. The British in Hong Kong were discouraging anything that might jar relations with Red China, that might interrupt the prosperous trade then going on through the British colony with the Communist regime.

Dr. Bloch looked worried, but I promised to keep the interview under wraps for some time, until I was sure he was out of the colony. He then resumed his story.

"I know how it feels to realize suddenly that someone is outside your door, and to open it, and to see a man almost stumble on his face into your room," he said. "The Communists often sent Chinese agents snooping that way.

"Tientsin is full of policemen, who walk in pairs, and watch outside shops, and when they see a woman come out, with a bit of meat and a head of cabbage perhaps, they stop her to ask where she is going with all that food and how many parity bonds she has bought. With these, the so-called Victory Bonds, the government tries to balance its budget and to beat inflation by the simple procedure of swallowing up the bulk of the currency.

"And it succeeded, at least temporarily. How can there be inflation when so much money is sponged up by the authorities? The Kuomintang could have beaten inflation that way, too."

He went on to tell about the incessant questionnaires, and those sounded like a written version of self-criticism. He mentioned countless tax stamps that had to be bought to obtain permission to do almost anything.

Gerhardt laughed. "Sure, that's a nuisance," he chuckled. "It's a nuisance here, too. Every country does the same thing. When you pay a bill in Hong Kong, you have to put on a government stamp. It's the same everywhere." And he laughed again.

His friend was in no laughing mood. "No, it's not the same; it's not the same at all," he exclaimed, and it was evident that this apology was no joke to him. He had lived through it. "How can you compare the simple, fast procedure of going to an office and paying a small fee and getting a license, or of attaching a small tax stamp to a business contract, to the daylong repetitious applications required by the Communists, often dragging out into months or a full year; of having to get permission from not just one bureau, but a dozen, and of any official who decides that he, too, wants to have his say; and to be under the horrible fear that any one of these, for any reason or no reason at all, might say no? Then you have to go through this all over again, for all the permissions you have already obtained, and all the promises, are futile."

"We all have our troubles," persisted Gerhardt.

"There is no such thing as standard pay, low or high," Dr. Bloch went on. "Many of my Chinese friends were enthusiastic about the Communists when they came in. Indeed, they helped bring them in. They were educated men and women who took jobs as technicians or in the government. They were proud of the low pay they were receiving. They wanted to feel that they were doing their part to bring about a new order. I felt that way, too. You know that, Gerhardt. Well, it soon became evident that the low scale of pay was not merely a matter of need. Through constant questioning and snooping the Communists find out how much a man possesses, and then they set his salary just low enough and put his quota of government bonds and other taxes just high enough to take what he has away from him within a matter of months, except what he needs for bare survival.

"Then you are a slave of the state. Then they don't have to worry about you any more. You have to work for them. Then they see to it that you get enough pay to subsist; they raise your wages if necessary, after you have become completely a hostage, when you belong to them, body and soul. You call that idealism? I call it the exploitation of idealism."

I wrote fast to get it all down. "Oh, come now," Gerhardt declared. "You don't want to take such extensive notes. This isn't an interview, you know. It's just a social meeting. A social conversation. We're having tea. Won't you have some more cake?"

Dr. Bloch went on, his pent-up feelings demanding an outlet. "How can you explain the great support which the Communists have among the intellectuals and the students as well as the workers?" I asked. "Everybody talks about that."

"Everybody knows about how it was in the beginning," Dr. Bloch countered. "Feelings have changed. The students have turned, too, but it's the coolies who have come to hate the Reds most. Now it is too late to do anything about it. The Communists have created their own check and balance, making everyone dependent for his livelihood on keeping the next man in line.

"They have devised the most skillful, diabolical method of making them do it themselves," he remarked. "They have invented a method of making each man the keeper of his brother's thoughts. They are doing this through what they call democratic discussion and self-criticism, with the threat of purges hanging over the heads of nonconformists."

How often had I heard these details! The tea lasted almost three hours. Gerhardt finally insisted that he just had to make the appointment he had so suddenly remembered. Apparently the interview had not proceeded as he had anticipated. Apparently Dr. Bloch had changed his point of view since the last time the two friends had separated—one to live inside the bamboo curtain, the other outside.

THE "WHITE CHINESE"

THE "WHITE CHINESE"

A MUTUAL FRIEND TOLD ME THAT HARRY CHANG WAS IN town. He was a Shanghai-born Chinese who spoke fluent English, a Catholic, and one of those whom the Communists, by a subtle racial smear, were calling "White Chinese." They were killing two propaganda birds with one stone by that label.

The term White Chinese made people think of the pathetic flood of White Russians into China at the time of the Russian Revolution, with their extremist yearnings for a medieval past of special privileges and unlimited monarchy by divine right, and their fantastic impracticability in matters of money. Also, it brought up the contrast of these Chinese with the white man and portrayed them in a ridiculous, subservient manner. In case this connotation was missed, the Communist press kept the racial allusion alive with grotesque cartoons and biting articles. This chorus was kept up so incessantly that before I left the Far East, Chinese who impressed me highly by their physical and moral fortitude were jocularly referring to themselves, in a self-conscious and apologetic manner, as White Chinese. The subtle smear with its insidious connotations was getting them down.

I was anxious, therefore, to make a comparison of the effects of learning and self-criticism on the White Chinese as well as on the "real Chinese" of the Chi Sze-chen type. So I was mighty pleased to find out about Harry Chang's arrival. He was as Westernized in his characteristics as Chi was not. He was a young man, too, quite typical of the Western-educated Chinese. Obviously his point of view, and how he had been influenced, was of the utmost importance. He represented another big, vital leadership segment of the Chinese people. He had just come out of Red China "on a mission," I was told, and was returning in a few days. He already had had his brains washed, but apparently the washing hadn't been done too thoroughly because he agreed to see me.

Our meetings were not casual affairs; they had to be arranged with the utmost caution and preparation to prevent his discovery in the company of so unwashed an individual as myself. He was too well known in newspaper circles to come to the Correspondents' Club, so we met in the home of our mutual friend.

"If they find out that I'm seeing a foreign correspondent, specially one I knew before, it'd just be too bad for me," he remarked at our first chat.

"I'll make every effort to hide the fact that I'm seeing you," I promised.

"What worries me most is the uncertainty," he said.

"Uncertainty about what?"

"About whether they know that I've seen you or not."

"So what?" I exclaimed encouragingly. "If they don't know about it, you have nothing to worry about, and if. . . ."

He looked at me sadly. "You'd be a hard man for brain reform," he said. "You have such bourgeois conceptions. No, it isn't as simple as that at all. If it were merely a question of whether they found out or not, I'd forget about it. But what I have to figure out is whether to tell them right off or not."

"I don't follow you."

"Well, it's this way. Soon after I return to Shanghai,

just as after all my trips anywhere out-of-town in China, some police will stop at my house to ask some questions. It's always that way now with everybody. They'll talk very friendly, say that they hoped I had a successful, pleasant trip, and by the way, what did I do and whom did I see?

"If I tell them the truth, and there is nothing incriminating, they'll say good-by and that's that. If I tell them the truth, and there is something incriminating, I may get into trouble. But if they know something that I don't tell, I'll get into worse trouble."

"What will they do to you? Throw you into prison? Beat you up?"

"Oh, no, they'll probably not do that," he replied. "If that was all they'd do, I wouldn't mind."

"Huh?" I was puzzled.

"No, what they'd do would be to send me to learning. I'd be given a brain-washing. Oh, I don't ever want to go through that again."

I couldn't help laughing, he was so deadly serious. Also, I remembered so many other Chinese whose reactions were similar.

"Begin at the beginning, and go slowly, so I can keep up with you," I told him. I expected an illuminating account, but I didn't anticipate the basic document on human nature that he was about to give me. Often he could not have spoken too fast if he had wished; he was too choked with emotion. Certain parts he intentionally falsified, to cover up for some relative or friend; he told me about these later. The structure of this story was true and laid bare his state of mind.

There was a tone of contempt in his voice as he told of the victory parade by the Nationalists in Shanghai, almost on the eve of the Communist capture of the city. Truckloads of students and workers paraded through the main thoroughfares, showering the populace with leaflets promising that Shanghai would become a second Stalingrad rather than fall. Two days later the city fell.

"For two weeks, four students had been hiding in my

apartment," he told me. "They left on the eve of the Communist entry into town. My brother-in-law invited them into my home, telling me that their own part of town was too dangerously near the front lines. I never suspected that they, or he, had any Red tendencies.

"I was assigned by my newspaper to interview the Communist soldiers as they entered Shanghai. I found them very polite. They said they hadn't slept for three nights. They didn't enter anyone's home, but slept on the pavement. They were even reluctant to take a glass of water, and if you pressed, they would insist on paying a few coppers for it, saying, 'This is the people's property.'

"The public was very much impressed by this, especially as everyone had been so terribly fed up with the Kuomintang. I, too, was deeply impressed, and began right then and there to wonder what was so bad about those soldiers.

"When I came home for dinner that night, I was surprised to see that the four students were back. They were sitting at the table with my brother-in-law. My wife had prepared something special. We drank, and my brother-in-law said a toast to the liberation of Shanghai. This astonished me, but my brother-in-law explained that the students had been working for the Communist underground. I had thought that they all were just liberals.

"My newspaper soon closed up. I was not a union member and was given only three months' severance pay instead of the five months that the others on the news staff received. I had been led to believe that we all would get the same. This made me awfully sore, and naturally I told everyone. My brother-in-law made a great deal out of this. 'That's American imperialism for you!' he exclaimed. 'Take them to court!'

"I thought to myself, now we have a people's court where I can sue even an American. The court wants no money from me. That's pretty good.

"The idea of going to court to get my money calmed me down, but I hesitated about doing so because I still had my doubts about the Communists.

"My Christian education made me ask myself, what is money anyhow? So I swallowed my loss. This was a bit of a struggle. To sue or not to sue ran through my head like a refrain. The man who had deceived me would get his due some day, I finally told myself, and so I didn't sue.

"The workers were really happy when the Reds took the city. We're the boss now, they said. When I went back to the office after the settlement to get my things, the Communist workers asked me, 'You haven't taken any office equipment, have you?' So much in all of this depended on mere whims that it scared me; it was actually so undisciplined. The Shanghai *Evening Post* strike was a test case. I read in the papers that the employees were getting what was called sympathy from labor organizations throughout the city, including the textile workers. They paraded in sympathy and contributed flour and rice.

"The strike was in the form of a sitdown. This confused me. One moment I'd be thinking that the Communists didn't seem to be so bad after all and the next moment I'd say to myself that there should be some more proper system of obtaining money, not this way of just setting any figure and getting it by threats.

"This was the first time the workers could act like this in China. They put the American editor, Randall Gould, under a nerve treatment. They beat gongs and drums in front of his office and wouldn't let him sleep. He was a prisoner this way in his own office for two days and two nights. No food was allowed, and he couldn't even go out to the toilet. If he had left the room, he would have been beaten up by the aroused throng.

"The workers demanded a fabulous sum. I noticed, however, that what they finally got was fixed by the union's attorney when the authorities decided the affair had achieved its purpose."

This was to show that the new regime could humiliate the powerful American colossus. The Japanese had done much the same thing a year before Pearl Harbor when they stripped foreign men and women indiscriminately during routine searches at railway stations, bridges, and the like.

"I was now without a job," Harry resumed. "What was I to do? I had foolishly shoved the million Communist dollars that I had received as severance pay into a bank, instead of changing it into American dollars which would have given me a fancy profit. Even so, I was able to live on the interest. This amounted to 50,000 Chinese Communist dollars every three days—twenty good American dollars. I was sitting pretty, and even bought a Parker fountain pen out of my surplus. I rented a room in my apartment to a Chinese family at forty American dollars a month, and they paid me six months in advance. Yes, if I had been satisfied to be without a job, I was sitting pretty.

"My wife suggested that we get private tutors to perfect our knowledge of written Chinese. Instead of perfecting our Chinese, what we really did was to study Mao Tse-tung's book, *New Democracy*. We thought that we could accomplish two purposes that way. I was soon calling the book the 'New Hooey.' My teacher was really quite anti-Communist, but so long as he got paid he was indifferent over what he was teaching and patiently explained everything in the book.

"I did not approve of what I read. I found the doctrine vicious and thought it degraded human beings to the level of animals. I had hot arguments all the time over this with my brother-in-law. I still thought he was only a leftist. He was very subtle and quiet. When I'd lose my head, he'd be cool and calm. He never talked unless it was necessary. I wouldn't know when he came into the room, his step was so soft. He was younger than I and devilishly clever. My wife didn't like my arguing with him.

"I was surprised over his attitude toward religion. He denied the existence of God and the existence of a soul in man. I told him his destination was hell. He laughed and said that when the Communist state had been properly rigged up people would be so content that they would have no need for religion. He said that only man's material welfare needed to be cared for because he had no spirit. Religion, he said, was an imperialist weapon.

"A comfort-the-soldiers drive was held at that time at the French Park. People thronged to the park by the thousands, and business was good. All gate receipts went to the army, as well as the proceeds from donated goods. The people seemed very happy.

"The best actors and actresses sold donated objects. The best movie stars were there. Opera groups performed on specially built stages. Even the Shanghai Municipal Orchestra was there to entertain the people. Paper fans sold at 1,000 Chinese dollars each. They were white, so you could fill them with autographs. I just drank beer and watched, thrilled. It impressed me very much to see actors and actresses become waiters and soft drink vendors.

"Darn it, I thought, under Communism actors come right out and mix with the people to help the soldiers. That's democracy, all right. All people mixing together. I saw how happy the soldiers were, how courteous and appreciative. They rolled on the ground, wrestling like pups.

"The number of foreigners and Chinese who mixed together, sitting on the grass, especially impressed me. There was no trace of racial discrimination. There was only an atmosphere of warmth in the air. I was deeply affected. Hell, I'd say to myself, after all, what's wrong with the Communist Party? At least I can now call China my own. These foreigners can't kick me around. That impressed me more than anything else.

"My inferiority complex was gone. For once, while I don't feel superior, I do feel just as good as you, I'd say to myself. I felt very happy. I felt free. I left the park, but returned the next evening to see the same affair all over again. My wife came with me this time. We had an extremely good time. We enjoyed everything and especially the happy faces all about us.

"The two visits I made left me deeply influenced. After I

went home, I sat down quietly, trying to figure things out. Communism, as I had just witnessed it, seemed totally different from what I had thought it was. The atmosphere in the park was good, the people were happy; foreigners and Chinese mixed wonderfully and naturally without restraint on either side, everything seemed good about it. I just couldn't figure out what was actually wrong with Communism.

RELIGION

"One evening," Harry continued, "I went to a Communist-sponsored play about the farmers of Honan Province. The play troupe was employed by the government and formed a group known as a cultural team. Its job was to act, sing, or dance, usually for the troops.

"Tickets were hard to get and every performance was packed. Standing room was sold to eager customers who insisted on seeing the play. The title, literally translated, would be 'Blood, Tears, and Revenge.' I was impressed again, this time by how every performance was packed. I had expected any Communist-sponsored show to be poorly attended.

"The main characters were an old farmer and his family. A young man took the part of the old farmer and did the finest job of acting I have ever seen.

"The play began with the old farmer singing a prologue about the unhappy plight of the Honanese farmers under the notorious rule of Gen. Tang En-po. The audience was deeply moved. The play showed how the ill-treated farmers made their way from the Kuomintang areas into regions that had been liberated by the Red Army. This brought tremendous applause from the audience, especially in the grand finale when the stage was bedecked with red flags.

"Many in the audience, including myself, couldn't keep from crying. There was a tremendous wave of sentiment, and tears streamed from our eyes when we witnessed the spirit among both the actors and the audience. I never saw a more touching play. I stood up with the rest of the audience and clapped with real sincerity. Everybody left the theater with smiling faces, and for a moment all these people seemed to be long-lost friends. The mark of equality was everywhere.

"As I left the playhouse, I told myself, I'll work for the people now. Let them send me to any village, and I'll gladly go. China is a free China today, and a new China. Right then I thought I'd write a pro-Communist book. The next day I took my brother-in-law to the play. He was very pleased and said to me, 'Now you, too, are enlightened.'

"But I really wasn't. I still distrusted communism because it was a materialist doctrine. I told my brother-in-law I'd do anything for the Communists if they would just abandon their purely materialist philosophy.

" 'Impossible,' my brother-in-law replied. 'Marx is based on dialectics. We leftists view things in a materialist way, for man is essentially an animal, gifted with intelligence, but without a soul.' 'In that case,' I said, 'I'll never be a Communist, but I still want to work for the people.' 'You can work for the people and still maintain your beliefs,' he told me. 'The government that is forming in Peiping will never deny you the right to believe whatever you want to believe.'

"This sounded like democracy again. I asked, 'Will we really be free and have freedom as they have in America?'

" 'Oh no,' he said. 'The American people have no freedom. There is only freedom for Wall Street.' He said the average person in America was being exploited every day.

"The fateful July 7 arrived, commemorating the 1937 Lukouchiao [Marco Polo Bridge] Incident, a memorial day known to the Chinese as the Double Seventh. Many big parades were planned. They were the first such since liberation. It rained as it had never rained before. Many sections of the city were inundated. The main parade was called off, but some others went on just the same. The participants marched through flooded streets. They didn't care.

"I went out in the pouring rain and watched, amazed and

stirred. I saw how happy those people were, trudging of their own free will through the water. Later I found out it was not entirely so; some sections had received orders to parade. Anyway, the postponed big march took place a few days later. It rained again. Again I was much impressed. These are the people themselves, I said to myself. They can't be all Party members. They are just workers, students, and simple folk. I applauded and cried out, 'You guys are wonderful; you even parade in the rain.'

"'Yes, we do, because we're happy that we've been liberated,' they actually shouted back to me. This tugged at my emotions; things always seemed to tug at people's emotions in those days. There was such love for the common people as had never before existed. Formerly, we had only the gold exchange and business. I felt that Shanghai at last was being transformed from a purely commercial city into a much less commercial place. This made me very happy.

"My interest in reading Communist-sponsored newspapers mounted as the days went by. I was very happy to learn that a new cabinet had been lined up for the new government at Peiping, which would include several political parties. This impressed me a great deal because I had always been led to believe that the Communists were dictators, and that once they took over no other party could exist. I thought to myself that the people at last had a government made up of representatives from all walks of life. It occurred to me then that this was democracy.

"Red Army Day was proclaimed, and the new Red Army flag was unveiled that day. Again it rained cats and dogs. The soldiers were drenched. They didn't seem to care. The parade went on.

"Several days of holiday were declared when the Central People's Government was officially formed. Parades, parades, parades. They were always accompanied by rain, firecrackers, and the hustle and bustle of people everywhere. The way this festival period was organized made me think that I might really come to like the Communists. Maybe they were really good. My biased opinion of them had perhaps been just the evil of American propaganda. Maybe the Americans themselves were really the bad ones, really the imperialists. That's the impression everyone in that environment gets after a while.

"I began to think that this thing, religion, might be all nonsense too. Maybe, after all, the Communists are right when they say that religion is the opiate of the people, that it is an instrument of the imperialists and the capitalists to keep the poor classes quiet. My faith began to waver.

"But, curiously, the fact that it rained cats and dogs during every parade staged by the government seemed significant to me. There was something ominous about that rain, because it happened not only in Shanghai but in Peiping and Tientsin too. Chinese friends of mine, who obviously were not pro-Communist, told me it was the work of heaven, because heaven was angry with this new crowd that didn't believe in God. I found myself watching to see if it rained on each of these parade days. The Communists said it was just a coincidence, but they did agree that it was a confounded nuisance. The rain, however, didn't stop me from wanting to know more about the Communists, as I was beginning to like their ways more and more. I entertained the thought again that religion was all nonsense.

"I became a little happier. An odd feeling that I had never had before came over me. I thought I was a new man. I myself had been liberated. At least, I had rid myself of the evil influences of capitalist society. This thing has created a new meaning in life for me, I told myself. I had some goal in life to achieve. I knew that this was not just a natural phenomenon but an international affair. I now felt that I had to do my best for the liberation of the entire human race.

"I joined the Shanghai Commercial College. This had the same name as a real business college then operating, but it was Russian, and taught Russian literature, conversation, and grammar. Everything about it was Russian. In Chinese, its name was Soviet College of Commerce. No commerce was taught, but it was called a commercial institution because it was privately owned and was run along commercial lines. At the same time, it got a subsidy from the Soviet Club. The school also taught the Soviet Constitution. Some students on their own studied Stalin's *Dialectical Materialism Simplified.* The faculty was all Soviet, but composed of Russians who had lived in China for many years. Previously, it had been a school for Soviet children. The Chinese were admitted only after Shanghai's liberation.

"I thought that by knowing Russian it would be easier for me to get ahead in the future because there would be much closer cooperation with Moscow. I wanted to learn the language in the hope of being sent to Russia some day.

"The school also taught singing and dancing—Russian folk dances. Soon after entering, I began to be a leader in all fields. Mine was the first class in which Chinese were admitted. I was a member of the students' council, chief of the entertainment committee, and I was named prefect—class captain—of my class. Since ours was the first class, we beginners were really the seniors. We started off with eighty students.

"Then I began to like the Soviet Union. I liked its way of life, although I didn't know much about it. It was supposed to be a socialistic state, so I thought it must be very good. Our teachers all told us how wonderful their country was. I really believed them. We learned how to sing Russian national songs. We all called each other *tovarich,* comrade in Russian. This tickled me, as it seemed to bring closer cooperation between the students.

"When the anniversary of the October Revolution, a big Soviet Russian holiday, was approaching, the headmaster asked me to arrange a nice program, with singing and dancing. I was captain, too, of the hallway where we all ate in the evening. Afterwards, I was called on to play the piano— American jazz for dancing! They wouldn't listen to any other playing. Soviet teachers of both sexes liked jazz very much. I was a little irritated by this, for we were celebrating Soviet

Russia's national day, and I felt that we should not be playing imperialist songs.

"I became very popular overnight, especially with the girls. My wife didn't like this and suggested that I spend more time at my lessons.

"Stalin's birthday, too, was a big day. We had great fun before dinner decorating the China Textile Union's Hall, which we had specially hired. The affair started at six in the evening with dinner and drinks. The speeches came first. I sat on the presidium with the Russians and led in yelling slogans.

" 'Long live Joseph Stalin, leader of all the proletariat in the world!' came first. Next I yelled, 'Long live Mao Tse-tung, chairman of the People's Government!' After this I cried out, 'Long live Sino-Soviet relations!' and then, in succession, 'Long live the Soviet Union!' and 'Long live the People's Government of China!'

"Each slogan was followed by three tremendous hurrahs. The entertainment included Russian folk dances and singing songs such as *Cantata to Stalin* and *The Song of Our Country*. The 'our country' was Soviet Russia, which seemed proper to me under the circumstances. We sang the Soviet and Chinese national anthems.

"Then we had Western dancing until eleven-thirty. Afterwards, my entertainment committee, several Soviet teachers, and the entertainers all went to the Soviet Club, where we continued the merry-making until morning.

"While in the Soviet Club, I was aware of a wonderful feeling of internationalism. The Russians patted us on our backs, gave us drinks, and expressed great admiration for Mao Tse-tung. Everybody toasted 'bottoms up,' and you turned your glass to show you had drunk it all. I yelled slogans there, too, and everybody joined in. I danced with I don't know how many Russian girls.

"Somehow, it was very difficult to get near any real Soviet Russian, male or female. By that I mean people who had come from Soviet Russia recently. I only saw two at the Soviet

Club party, and they breezed in and quickly breezed out again. The Soviet military attache came for a few minutes and seemed to look us over with an amused smile.

"Following these two celebrations I began to like the Russians immensely and felt that China and Russia would get along very well. The local Soviet citizens showed great respect for us Chinese and were always pleasant and willing to extend a helping hand. I was then convinced that Russia had to be a good place, because its people were so nice, and that all this talk about the iron curtain was all lies. I said to myself that there had been much too much anti-Russian propaganda and that this was intended just to dope the people so they wouldn't realize how good Russia was.

"My lessons in Russian improved. I was getting happier and finally decided that religion was altogether the bunk. We don't need any religion. Why, we are happy as it is. These people were doing something, I now felt, whereas the Church had done nothing. From that day on I didn't go to church any more, although two or three months back I had used to stop in at church each morning.

"At last I had rid myself of the poisonous thing called religion. I was convinced that religion was selfish, that it contributed nothing toward helping mankind. So Marx was right after all when he said that religion is the opiate of the people. Little did I realize that this was going to be the start of a whole string of troubles for me.

"So, at last, I had given up my religion, something which I had held sacred and had cherished all my life. How I was able to do it in such a short space of time was amazing. Either this Communism thing was really good or I had been a darned fool who had become a slave to some master mind."

INDOCTRINATION

"Christmas came, and for the first time it held no meaning for me. I just used Christmas as an excuse to have a party. The idea that Christmas was to commemorate the birth of Christ appeared irrelevant. A little nostalgia accompanied this, and Christmas seemed a little on the empty side. My mind went back to the old days when our whole family would gather around the piano and sing hymns and carols. There had been a certain amount of warmth in those Christmas parties. Now that I had thrown my religion overboard, I sensed that something was obviously missing. Had I thrown away something true and beautiful for something that might be really poisonous? Was I still wavering? Time would tell.

"In January, I read an advertisement in the official Communist paper, *Chi Fang Pao,* or *Liberation Daily,* about an indoctrination school in Shanghai literally called the New Democracy Youth League's Higher Learning Institute. It promised to help get jobs for those who joined. I signed up. The only charge was the fee for the application form, $500 Chinese. The Russian school was costing me 120 parity units for a 4½-month term. I attended for two terms, except for the short course at the indoctrination school.

"The course was called Seven-Day Learning. I applied at a neat little building on Avenue Haig. Applicants crowded the office, which overlooked a large, green field. A Chinese school certificate was required to enter, which I didn't have. The war had so upset my family life that I had been moved from place to place. I brought a letter of introduction from my brother-in-law to the 'in-charge,' and she fixed me up at once.

"Still I did not realize that my brother-in-law was a Party member, although I was beginning to have strong suspicions. I received a membership card in the school and was told the students would gather at the McTyeire Girls' School the next morning to listen to a lecture.

"The lecture started at nine in the morning and continued until two that afternoon without a break. A minor Communist official gave a talk entitled 'The Importance of Learning' —political learning, of course. When the lecture ended, we stayed where we were, without refreshments or lunch, and then until three the speaker showed us slides on 'The Evolution of Society.' These slides combined Darwinism with the theory of a class society. We were then divided into groups of ten each, and released to go out to eat and rest up before resuming at five. Each cell of ten students was assigned a meeting room in some Shanghai building.

"My group went to a Chinese school. We held a democratic discussion on what we thought about the afternoon's lectures. We were told to ask ourselves whether or not learning was important. In these group discussions, no matter how hot the debate became, the conclusions reached were always in agreement with what the Communist speaker had outlined to us.

"Actually each group numbered eleven, because a leader was always assigned to us. The man in charge of our cell was a member of the New Democracy Youth League. Each group had one such participant who was not a student, who seemed to be just a listener, except that he always was equipped with notebook and pencil, and we frequently saw him jotting down notes. He never spoke during class. He created an eerie feeling. Most in our cell, composed half of boys and half of girls, had joined because they thought they would be able to get a job this way.

"We met the next morning in the same school, but were allowed to decide our own meeting hours. We settled on nine to twelve. This was called the democratic method of doing things. What was obligatory was that there had to be three hours in the morning and three hours in the afternoon. Our subject the second day was 'How to solve the livelihood problem in Shanghai.'

"I became the semi-official mouthpiece of the Communists without realizing it. Students would bring up opposing points, and I'd argue and usually win out. Discussion on any subject could not end without everyone agreeing. It had to end with all believing. If anyone remained in disagreement, the subject was postponed until the next cell meeting.

"I began to suspect that they were all yesing me because they suspected that I was a Communist Party member. They thought that what I said, therefore, was in the nature of something obligatory to them, something to regard as gospel truth. If they didn't believe that way, they thought they might lose their chance to land a job.

"I began to feel very happy about this, because I thought it meant that I had the makings of a good politician, that Communism had taught me how to say the right things at the right time. I was pretty good at this and I actually believed that Communism would give the Chinese people a brand new society in which there would be no starvation or even poverty.

"The first offer we got of jobs took the form of a movement in school to recruit a number of us for the Red Army. This wasn't necessarily for the front, but for clerical work and other such military posts. We were asked if we wanted to join the 9th Regiment of Gen. Chen Yi's 3rd Wild Battle Army; the usual translation in English is guerrilla army. We knew that this regiment was intended for the invasion then planned of Taiwan (Formosa). I suppose it later went to Korea.

"All the students looked up to me and said, 'You're progressive; you lead the way by joining the army.' I said that I felt the need first to learn more, and so couldn't join the army right off. By learning more, I said, I would be better able to judge the correct way to work for the people. I would have the correct proletarian viewpoint. 'This is the only way you can truly work for the people,' I heard myself telling them. 'Your views must be based on Marxism-Leninism, because Marx and Lenin stood on the correct proletarian platform.'

"When someone in the class said, 'I can't join the army; I have my family to support,' I heard myself telling him that he stood on the wrong platform. I told him the correct platform was to be able to discard luxury and, better still, 'You can discard your family for the cause.' I thought that this was the right thing to say. I think that I was saying what I really meant.

"Other morning lectures, which we discussed in the afternoon, were 'Social Evolution' and 'Was Humanity Created by Monkeys or by God?' I took Darwin's viewpoint. Some argued against me, and said men were not evolved from monkeys at all. I proved it to them. I began to be cool and calculating myself—cunning. I would say good-naturedly, 'You know that piece of bone in my dinner? That used to be your tail.' I soon won them over. They all agreed.

"I suppose some agreed with reservations in the back of their minds. The young, silent fellow with the notebook, who just sat and watched, was very pleased with me. I know, because he spoke to me once after the meeting, saying, 'Keep up the good work. We need more people like you.' Naturally I was flattered.

"Graduation day came after seven such straight days of lectures and group meetings. To my own astonishment I didn't show up. The first real conflict was starting in my mind. I asked myself if I had become so hardened that I could even discard my wife and my home, where I had been truly happy? Was this the right thing? Could I be sure?

"I decided to sit down and think things out properly. The thought of leaving my wife had occurred to me theoretically, but to actually do so was another matter. I only thought about that later. Of course, I never mentioned this to my wife.

"Am I a confounded theorist? I asked myself. Would I actually go out into that field, in a tiny village, and work for the people under the hot summer sun?

"Yes, I suppose I could do it, I told myself. I went to bed. My wife was almost asleep. She's an awfully sweet kid, I thought. That really got me. I asked, and felt a stab in my heart: am I going to give her up for something I'm not sure about? Then I started to wonder if it wasn't true what I'd been hearing, that, after all, the Communists do finally get around to breaking up the family with their mind enlightenment program. Suddenly it dawned upon me that probably there was something pretty horrible about the whole thing.

"I thought of my wife, and then I thought of the people. I thought my place should be with my wife and that it would be downright unfair if I left her flat for a cause that left some doubts in my mind. In that case, I shouldn't have married her in the first place. The fact was: I couldn't bear to think of leaving my wife because of my strong love for her.

"I remembered the angry retort I once made to her brother. You might not have a soul, but I have, I told him. In bed beside her I felt as if she had a soul, but now I didn't. Had I lost my soul? I couldn't have, because I never had had one. Had I or not? I suddenly felt that maybe all that I was doing was utterly wrong, so utterly wrong that it appeared to me as something right. How confused and upset I was! What actual torture I was going through!

"Then I went back to the Russian-language school. Here the extreme leftist business in me came out again. I found that it was easy to be one when you are comfortable. When you have to go out into the fields, it might be something else again. Of course I didn't realize that all this time I was getting more of the Communist enlightenment into my system. It gradually gets into you without your realization. You begin to talk like them.

"I began to lose friends because they didn't think the way I did—the extreme leftist way, the way I considered the only correct way. I wasn't the least bit irritated over the thought of losing them. I wasn't, because I thought that those poor fools didn't know what they were missing.

"My brother-in-law reprimanded me for not trying to help my friends become enlightened, which was the correct attitude. He told me to self-criticize myself, a method of expression which in the old days I would have referred to as examining my conscience. I did so and agreed I had been wrong. I apologized and said I would try to make others think the proper way.

"My brother-in-law was well pleased. When I returned to school, what arguments I had trying to convince my colleagues that Communism was good! Many just didn't agree whereupon I promptly spoke up like a veteran Communist Party member, without being aware of the fact. I became very insulting. I'd call my friends reactionaries and running dogs of American imperialism because they always seemed to speak highly of the United States.

"This irritated me most, because by then I had developed an extraordinary and artificial hatred for America, which I considered to be probably the worst country in the world. I now always criticized American motion pictures as a weapon with which to dope the minds of youth. Communism had taught me to hate anything that obstructed its cause. As a result, I became bitter, conceited, full of hatred. 'We Communists this' and 'we Communists that' became my attitude. I became so arrogant that people would shy away from me except for those in the progressive crowd, which naturally stuck together.

"Some time later I saw another notice in the paper from the indoctrination school. The announcement said that those who had joined the first course could re-enroll in a new six-months course without paying any additional fee. I enrolled, but attended only on and off. The course was indefinite; the idea was that you stayed on until you landed a job. During this period they didn't accept any more students. There were other schools of the kind; they were all really just job placement bureaus, some of which were run by the newspapers. All we had were lectures on Marxism-Leninism and the ideas of Mao Tse-tung. There were altogether about 1,000 students, double those in the first course.

"We met in a branch of the New Democracy Youth League. Each day we ourselves set the time for our next meeting—the democratic way. The lectures lasted six to eight hours without any break for lunch. We again divided up into cells, but we all stayed in the same building, which was full of little rooms and cubbyholes. Each cell meeting lasted the usual three hours.

"The school had no teachers of its own. They were all invited speakers, usually the principals of People's Revolutionary universities or minor Communist officials. One lecture was beamed to us by radio from the North China People's Revolutionary University, and was a talk being given by Ai Sze-chi on 'The Evolution of Society.' This was one of the two main subjects we studied and one to which we returned again and again. The other main topic was dialectical materialism.

"Our only textbook was Mao Tse-tung's *New Democracy*. Our constant theme was America's imperialist aggression, how hateful America was, and how America was the enemy of all progressive peoples around the world. I soon was attending only a couple of times a week, then once a week—just to show my face, to keep on the roster for a job.

"Some were already getting jobs. A group was picked and sent to Mukden to work in the Sin Hua bookstore, and others were sent to the Military Political University at Nanking for further indoctrination. When graduated, they would be attached to a national defense unit or become Red Army officers. Some of the girls were transferred to People's Revolutionary universities."

What he was telling me made it evident that getting a job didn't mean the same as it meant in a non-Communist society. It didn't mean getting work somewhere for wages or pay. Getting a job, as the term is used in Red China, means simply solving your living problem. Whatever way you accomplish this is called getting a job. This was merely an extension of the old Communist Party practice of providing board for its staff, and when they got a job outside, collecting what was more than they needed to live on. Party functions are supposed to reward the worker by giving him the satisfactory feeling of contributing to a good cause. Now, in providing jobs in Red China, these workers weren't being paid wages; they were merely being supplied a place to sleep and sufficient food and clothing to keep them going. Where they did get a regular wage, it was calculated not in accordance with what the work was worth, but what was required to live.

"In our group discussions nobody ever raised any serious objection to any point laid down in the Communist line," Harry went on. "Everyone only wanted to get a job, to be able to eat, clothe himself, and have a place to sleep, and we all knew that objecting to Communist theory was no way to solve one's livelihood problem.

"The realization suddenly came upon me that there was something different in the atmosphere. People in general were no longer as enthusiastic as before. Instead of suspecting that Communism was bad, this change in people's attitudes made me all the more determined to awaken the poor devils to the fact that Communism was the only answer and that the aftereffects of any revolution naturally could not be too encouraging. People must go through a tough time. They must work hard. That's the only way to achieve a better world. This was my argument.

"I went to more Communist plays, which usually were very moving experiences. I'd go with a group of school chums —progressive elements all—and we'd have a whale of a good time. I was no Communist Party member; I would have denied it if anyone had called me a Communist.

"About this time I received quite a shock. My brother-in-law calmly walked into the house wearing a political worker's uniform.

" 'Since when have you been a member of the Communist Party?' I asked.

" 'Oh, about five years.'

" 'What! How did you avoid being arrested?'

" 'We had a wonderful system. Usually it's the Party sympathizers who get arrested. We don't often get arrested.'

"He had put the lives of both our families—his own and mine—into awful danger, and this didn't seem to make any difference to him. I became very angry over it, but didn't display it to him. The Kuomintang, if it had found out that he was an active member of the Party, working underground, would have seized the whole lot of us.

"He, as a skilled Party operator, certainly knew this, and he hadn't hesitated to put us all in danger of losing even our lives, and it made no difference to him whether we were for or against Communism. He told me that he joined the Communist Party while studying in Chiao Tung [Commercial] University, a government institution in Shanghai.

"He came this time to say good-by. He was going to Peiping to work in Party headquarters. I was able to visit him twice, but he never told me what he was doing. All that he did say was that for years he had been doing underground work for the Communists in Shanghai."

ROMANCE

"May 8, the Communist-sponsored International Woman's Day, was a turning point in my life. I went again to a party at the Soviet Club, where we had a lot of drinks, and I met a girl, a Communist sympathizer. She was pretty and had a snappy figure. We danced. How we danced! The two of us danced the whole evening.

"We two had similar ideas, we agreed. She spoke only Chinese. At three in the morning we ended up cheek to cheek. You know, that is something in China. I saw her home. I saw her often after this, and always without my wife's knowledge.

"I had no conscience left; I didn't believe in it any more. We confessed our love for each other based on the principles of Karl Marx.

" 'What about your wife?' she asked me. She said that in her family everyone was a feudalist. Her husband was just a businessman. She said she led an awful life, and that she was suppressed and wanted to be liberated.

"'Now that the Communists have come in, there's a chance for me to be liberated,' she said joyfully. She was twenty-one and terribly earnest. She said she was very happy to have met me, as I gave her new hope. I felt very sorry for her. She seemed such a sweet kid. She had the same ideas as mine, and we got along very well.

"'What about your wife?' she asked again.

"'My wife is not enlightened.'

"'There's always the People's Court.'

"This simple statement stunned me, and it dawned on me that I had become so hardened that I had even gone as far as falling in love with another girl. I knew that I should not have done it, but the fact is that I was human. Curiously, this experience had an odd effect. I realized that I still had human feelings in spite of dialectic materialism.

"I saw that she was embittered, and I wondered whether all Communists and their supporters also were embittered, frustrated people. But what struck me as strange was that I wasn't frustrated; I had always led a good life. Was I a hypocrite without knowing it? I began to worry about this. Girls do complicate your life, don't they?

"These doubts didn't interfere with our affair. One day, after some drinks at a friend's house, I returned home drunk. As soon as I entered, I slammed the door, and then saw my wife and my mother standing before me. Drunk, I addressed my wife first, saying that I was sorry, but that hereafter I'd only be able to love her like a sister. I only could have blurted this out, all at once this way, while drunk. There was a hush. My mother spoke up coldly, ordering me to my room, and my wife, too. She merely said that our quarrels were not to be in front of others.

"My wife cried all night. She was terribly broken up. 'Have you another woman?' she asked. Then something really happened to me. I told her that I had another woman, but that it was all over now. I told her to forget about it. I had been silly. I lied remorselessly.

"The next morning my wife said, 'I'm leaving. I won't

come home for two weeks. This will give you time to think things out.' As soon as she had left, I felt like a free man. I could do just what I wanted.

"My wife came back that same morning, after having been away only two hours. She had sense! I told her what a heel I was, but I was lying again, for my mind was on the other girl.

"What I couldn't understand about myself was that I wasn't feeling any sorrow over the fact that my wife, the sweetest person on earth, was in such a state of sadness. I tried to understand, but was completely at a loss. I figured out then that I had done something cheap, and I decided to have it out with the other girl.

"As soon as I saw the girl the next morning, I told her what had happened. To my amazement she gleefully replied, 'Good. We shall be liberated.'

"'What's good about it? My wife is brokenhearted.'

"'Oh, your wife is probably just pretending,' she answered. This phrase shook me. I realized that this was an awfully inhumane attitude to take. Am I like that myself? I asked myself. I felt tears in my eyes, and those tears were real. I said to myself, there is something topsy-turvy about this whole Communist system. Are they all so cruelly calculating? I had better find out before I make another move.

"But I kept on seeing the girl, and I kept lying to my wife that everything was now all right. Then something inside me began to hurt. I became nervous and jumpy as a cat. I came home all hours of the night, drunk. I thought that by being drunk I could solve the problems that were fermenting in my mind.

"I stopped going to the Russian-language school, because when I went there I couldn't study anyway.

"Each morning I grabbed my textbooks, and then instead of going to school, I just walked aimlessly about, block after block, kind of running from myself, fooling myself that everything was O.K. I became terribly agitated and restless.

"Then I raised one question for myself to answer. What is truth? I asked. I told myself I'd never be able to reply if I kept on seeing this girl. Sometimes I sensed the cause of the throbbing pain in my head. I began to show less interest in Communism, and I began to suspect that my suffering was due to the fact that I had thrown away gold for dust.

"This heavy chain I was carrying, this beating about all sorts of places, almost drove me crazy. Sometimes I wandered into some back alley, into some brothel, trying to find the answer there. This complicated matters even further. My conscience began to hurt more and more.

"I tried praying, but that didn't give me much comfort. I began going into church again. Gradually I found myself going back to my old surroundings because they appealed to me more and more and because I felt that here were the people who were truly happy and were really human beings, whereas I had almost reduced myself to the level of a beast. Communist ideology had taught me to believe that I was only a beast, anyway.

"This was the semifinal, but I was still slightly wavering. Now I began to understand why, after their great initial enthusiasm, the sentiments of the people during the past few months had steadily become more and more deflated, and why the happiness which I had witnessed and which had stirred me so deeply, was fading away so fast.

"Communist ideology, I now learned by myself, through my own simple experience, had forgotten one thing—the wants and desires of human nature. I came to the conclusion that man is more than just an animal, and that Communism, with its barren philosophy, is designed only to enslave him.

"All about me I saw how little children were being indoctrinated every day in Communist ideology. I shrink from imagining how these little children will be when they reach my age, if communism is allowed to last that long.

"That I myself was nearly caught in this hideous web gave me the shivers. How I nearly threw my wife away for some cheap little girl with tinsel thoughts filled me with horror. I went back to church, and this time I felt my old self surging back into me, and my long-lost soul seemed to rejoin my physical body. With more or less a peaceful mind, I was resting better now, and then I reconciled myself with my wife. This experience made me appreciate her all the more and brought us closer together.

"I decided to go to Peiping, to the capital of Communist China, to convince myself once and for all whether Communism was or was not all wrong. Perhaps this constant vacillation sounds ridiculous to you, but to understand it you have to visualize the atmosphere of living inside Communist-run territory, where values are so upside down and where every word you read or hear presents your normal way of thinking as the abnormal, as the unreal, as bad; and where you have to talk their way, in a convincing manner, in order to get a job; and to hold it you have to keep on talking this way, every day, after you've gotten it. It's enough to drive anyone mad. Emotions reach terrible heights and agonizing depths in such an environment.

"When I arrived in Peiping, everything seemed to be going along well. The people appeared to be happy. I questioned some of them while sitting around and chatting. 'Tell me, do you feel really happy now?'

"They hedged about answering, and then, in one way or another, remarked 'You know, we northerners are very good at hiding our feelings,' which made me think that they were not half as happy as they might appear.

"I met a number of Communist government officials. I saw that they were well fed, that they drank a lot of beer, had nice girl friends, nice cars, and preferred the company of Soviet Russians. But they all seemed so embittered, so cold, so utterly without a heart, that in them I saw myself as I had been a while before. This was an ugly portrait.

"I remained in Peiping for a few weeks and saw everything that I felt I ought to see. And always I had that sense of something missing in the Peiping of today. Peiping had become a city without warmth, without soul—unlike the Peiping of the past.

"Then I took a trip by myself to the Great Wall of China, past the Green Dragon Bridge, and stood and looked about me. There at last I could witness, without any Communists around, the grandeur of Mother Nature. I walked about on the top of that wide, wide wall for many hours, admiring the mountains, the people, the goats—all of God's world.

"With all this in my mind, I now knew that there was no doubt that dialectical and historical materialism and the whole ideological baggage of Communism cannot and will never succeed. As I stood on that Great Wall, I couldn't help admiring the genius of man, which alone was able to construct such a masterpiece of engineering 2,000 years ago.

"I returned to Shanghai with my mind completely at ease. I promptly severed all relations with the girl. I came to a final conclusion about Communism. Communism is allied with treachery and violence. It tends to hypnotize the human race into believing that wrong is right."

Harry Chang thus concluded his story. He was leaving in a few days. He had come to Hong Kong to buy some radio equipment that a government office needed and had taken the opportunity to sound out a few close friends on whether he could land a job. There was nothing he could get that would pay him above subsistence for himself alone, let alone enough to support his wife. And what was he to do with his parents in China? He had no alternative but to return.

Never before had I heard such a perfect description of what it feels like to be behind a political curtain, bamboo or iron.

THEORIES

INSIDE THE GROUP

THE TEACHING ESTABLISHMENTS OF CHINA WENT THROUGH a uniform system of reform when the Communists took over. The difference was in degree; some underwent the process sooner than others, some to lesser or greater degree. Ho Yuen was a schoolteacher from Hanyang in the interior. He helped the Communist army take over his city. Let him tell his story.

On their entry into the city, the Communists announced that no changes were to be made in ordinary school practices. There was to be the utmost freedom of education, but of course without reactionary abuses. So, after a few days of celebration over the arrival of the liberators, Ho went back to his classroom.

Ho had been an enthusiastic participant in the celebration. When the Red Army held its victory parade, Ho went out to help, going by auto and speaking over a loudspeaker, praising the discipline of the Red Army, drawing attention to its superiority over that of the beaten Nationalists. "This shows that the Red Army is a real People's Army," he cried out, "for see, all this is American equipment that came from the Nationalists."

His first impression, he frankly told me, which he said was the same as that of the rest of the city, was that this new Chinese army was the best in the world and could tackle any other country's. That it was Red was secondary, that it was Chinese was an invigorating thought. "Everyone was very excited and believed that China from then on would be able to stand on its own feet, freely making its own decisions," he said.

The occupants of his car had been taught a song, but at the last minute were instructed not to sing it over the microphone, as it might excite the suspicion of the democratic non-Communist groups who were cooperating with the Reds; for the song frankly didn't recognize any other party. Here are the words:

> *Without the Communist Party, there will be no China.*
> *Without the Communist Party, there will be no China.*
> *The Communist Party works hard for the people.*
> *The Communist Party plunges ahead headlong for the people.*
> *The Communist Party tries to save the nation.*
> *It points the road of liberation to the people.*
> *It leads China to light.*
> *It persists for eight years in the war of resistance.*
> *It improves the livelihood of the people.*
> *It establishes bases behind the enemy.*
> *It carries out democracy which brings all welfare to the people.*
> *Without the Communist Party, there will be no China.*
> *Without the Communist Party, there will be no China.*

The theme, that there could be no China without the Communist Party, didn't upset Ho. He felt that this was merely their boastful way of expressing pride in the contribution they were rendering to China. He pooh-poohed the interpretation that the words were meant literally by the Communists, that it denoted a rule-or-ruin policy. He found out, but too late.

When Ho returned to his school, he found only half of his class. The rest were still out celebrating. Afternoon sessions were converted into discussion groups. A young man in his twenties arrived from Peiping to become adviser to the principal in administering the school. Actually he took charge, as head of the school's Communist Party Committee. His first activity was to summon the entire school population (faculty, clerical staff, servants, and students) to a mobilization meeting for learning the new democracy. He addressed them all, saying, "Mao Tse-tung's principles are the only ones that can bring about China's reconstruction. If you don't agree with Mao, you don't want China to become strong, and this means that you are a personal-doctrine man." This was a serious matter, for a personal-doctrine man is Communist idiom for individualist, and there are few things that Communists condemn more vigorously than individualism.

He then asked how many of those present were willing to study the principles of *New Democracy* and the ideas of Mao Tse-tung. One third answered in the negative. They were asked why in this way: "Don't you want a strong China? Don't you want to live a better life?" Someone spoke up and asked what was the use of learning the principles of Mao's *New Democracy*. "We don't want to become officials; why then do we have to study politics this way?" The young chairman replied that the existence of imperialism and capitalism in the world made it necessary to fight them, and "so we have to learn."

"If we attend such classes," someone else asked, "are we sure to succeed, and be able to fight the imperialists?" "Yes," he was told, "if all the people join, our power will be unlimited."

Someone else spoke up, saying, "We can do what we are told. Why learn such principles in detail?"

"If you don't accept Mao's thoughts, you won't be able to rid yourself of your own reactionary thoughts. "If you do not study them, you will not be able to achieve a better living because a superior-to-classes viewpoint does not exist in Communist areas. We believe in classes."

Superior-to-classes viewpoint was another phrase in the

Communist lexicon and meant another anathema—not a person's denial of the existence of classes, but his attempt not to be included in any of them. The meeting made it plain that the recommendation that everyone proceed immediately to the study of Communist ideology could not be opposed, and neither could the desires of the Communist Party.

The students and the school staff then were separated, and each divided into small discussion groups of about twenty persons for daily meetings. Several times a week the whole student body and the entire school staff, from principal to sweepers, would meet separately, and on occasion all met together. The chairman nominated group heads from a list prepared beforehand. He called out a name and asked all those in favor to raise their hands. There were never any opposing votes, although the number of abstentions increased as the meeting dragged on—from nine to three in the afternoon without a break. By coincidence, those who were named on the list were the ones who had been the most enthusiastic over the entry of the Reds; henceforth they led the meetings and set the tone for the discussions.

Ho said he made several remarks at the meeting. Once he pointed out that he wasn't too concerned about the political aspects of the situation, but wanted China to be strong and respected. The students studying to become engineers agreed with him, and said that this was why they believed they had to concentrate on engineering and science instead of on politics. In order to save our country, we must have more and better engineers and scientists, they said.

The chairman said no, that this was not the correct approach. "If you don't have clear thoughts, the point of the gun that you produce will be pointed backwards, at you," he said. "So, your first task must be to learn how to make use of science and engineering."

Students aspiring to be engineers or scientists generally were regarded as backward elements by the Reds.

At the close of the meeting everyone stood up to sing *The Red Orient*:

*The Orient is Red, the sun rises, China sees the birth of
    Mao Tse-tung.*
He fights for the welfare of the people.
Hoo-lee-ya!
He is the great savior of the people.
*The Communist Party turns like the sun; wherever it
    shines, it brings light.*
We follow the Communist Party.
Hoo-lee-ya!
We shall be liberated forever.
Chairman Mao loves the people.
He is our guide for the building up of New China.
Hoo-lee-ya!
Leading forward!

Ho knew several teachers who asked embarrassing questions in their discussion group. They did not appear in school after that. Ho knew of one in particular, a friend of his, who "evaporated." Soldiers took him away from his home and he never was seen again. Teachers didn't discuss these matters with each other, and neither did the pupils. A few days ahead the discussion groups would be informed what topics to take up at their next meeting. In the interval they had to study up on the subject.

Before the group meetings began, there was a meeting of group heads alone, at which they went over their membership lists to determine reactionary types who would be given special attention or even be transferred. The procedure at each meeting was for the group head to speak first, and then to ask each participant to stand up and speak, one after another, according to their seating arrangement. "We were told to express ourselves freely, and that attendance was voluntary," Ho said.

"We also had what was called self-criticism. Self-criticism meant that if you did not enunciate the Communist line clearly and ecstatically, you were called to order and corrected by others in the meeting. They instructed you—this was what was supposed to be democratic about it—to prepare your talk over again and to do better next time.

"Self-criticism meant, too, that if you failed to attend, your excuses were shot full of holes by someone in the meeting (a Party man, if others failed to do so) and you were frankly advised to watch your step. You always followed such advice—if you wanted to stay in the school, or with your family."

The meetings were supposed to be cultural. Books were studied and discussed. They were taken up by "popular consent" and by coincidence were always modern books, always on political subjects or with the proper "line" allusions. Mao Tse-tung's *New Democracy* naturally was the first such book.

In it Mao points out that the Chinese revolution "is a component part of the world revolution," that in the event of a new war that he assumed would be begun by the United States, China "inevitably would have to take sides," with the choice being between America and Soviet Russia, and that China's future progress depended on Moscow's help. His policy of "leaning to one side"—Russia's—is enunciated in this book, which he wrote in 1939, and one of his allusions to the United States is accompanied with one of the filthiest curses in the Chinese language. (See Appendix D.) A rewritten version of the book was put out in English for distribution in America, with drastic changes made in offending portions to make them sound palatable and even friendly to the American mind. Rarely has such a bold distortion of a man's words been perpetrated on so extensive a scale.

"You just couldn't say you had studied the book and get away with it," Ho said. "You had to stand up, answer questions on it, and explain specific portions, and you had to do so in the approved Party manner. Otherwise you found yourself out of school."

The first topic given the groups was the history of the evolution of society. "We discussed how capitalism was formed, and how capitalism would be destroyed, and concluded that only the Communists could replace capitalism," Ho said. "The lack of balance between productive power and productive relationship would bring this about. By productive power was meant the labor force and labor's tools, and by productive relationship was meant the class that controls the productive power and owns all the resources for production—land, mines, railways, banks, and so on.

"When the stage is reached when productive power is sufficiently confined and oppressed by the productive relationship, we were taught that there must be a revolt. Those under feudalism whose excesses brought this revolt about were the landowners; in capitalism they are the capitalists, and in a slave economy they are the slave owners."

He drew a diagram of this. This was not the first time I had heard about this from participants in group discussions, for everywhere in these meetings, in all of Red China, this is one of the main topics brought up, and the involved phraseology is the obligatory framework in which it is explained.

Ho's diagram was a grand illustration of the kind of quack scientific thinking being imposed on the Chinese. When persisted in for hour after hour, the result created a comatose state in which pat phrases, particularly if they contained long involved words and double-talk, were repeated and repeated until a curiously twisted ideology permeated the subconscious, like the one-track mind brought about by drunkenness. Here is the diagram:

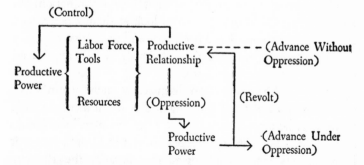

There was an ominous similarity in the logic followed and in the examples taught in these discussion groups throughout China, showing that they were centrally directed and devised in a manner to exploit envy and build up suspicion and hatred, and to focus these negative attitudes against the United States.

Economics is taught by simple catch phrases, in capsule manner. The assumption is accepted, as the basis for economics, that a certain supply exists of any specific object, and that if one person or group has more of it, then the others inevitably have less. That wealth is not static is ignored. That there can be improvement in the status of all by increased production for all is simply not considered. The inflexible form of Asian society generally, with the slight prospect it affords anyone to increase his holdings except by taking some from somebody else, lends itself to this twisted logic and distorted economics. Here, for instance, in Ho's words, is the form in which basic economics is taught; I have heard it in much the same words from many others, and have read it in indoctrination textbooks.

"In the United States there is one auto for every eight people. If we bring down this average, which is maintained at the expense of the Chinese and colonial peoples, then there will be more cars for us Chinese. If we could bring down the American standard to one auto for each 16 persons, then there would be enough for China to have one car for each 16 persons."

These statistics, of course, do not bear examination, but should a discussion group wish to look at them closely, such study would be considered irrelevant and indicative of a reactionary, stubborn attitude that obviously would require additional brain-washing to cure.

The United States is often discussed at such meetings as a glaring example of what is wrong and evil. "At a certain stage there must be a revolution in that entire country," the groups are taught. "The rate of production in the United States is high, but its markets are decreasing because the Russian-controlled areas of the world are increasing and already contain 800,000,000 persons. America, therefore, cannot get the raw materials it needs and cannot sell its output, and so its factories will have to close. The lack of balance that this will bring about between productive power and the productive relationship will cause the inevitable revolution.

"The workers of the United States will eliminate capitalism as a consequence of this revolution, and then the productiveness of American labor will belong to society as a whole and not just to the capitalists."

The conclusion reached in these first group meetings was that after the "inevitable United States revolution," Communism would take over in that country.

Someone asked, "Why is there no revolution of the workers now if there is so much production in the United States while its markets are decreasing?" Here was the answer given! "The American workers are blinded by the capitalists because the latter have so many ways to cheat them, by using trickery, such as insurance, the movies, the right to talk against the government, and various laws that assure the welfare of labor, such as retirement allowances. So the workers at present don't want to revolt. But all those welfare measures are cheats. They do not constitute true democracy. In a true democracy everything belongs to the workers."

Another reason given for delay in the anticipated American revolution was that the workers in the United States wanted to avoid bloodshed.

This whole line of reasoning aroused a lot of questioning. Someone brought up the point that the workers in America seemed to have a better life all the time because of such protection, and could demand raises in wages, whereas workers had no right to ask for pay increases in Russia. "Isn't the object of communism to raise living standards?" he inquired.

"American workers are being fooled," he was told. "They don't understand class distinctions. They don't know the cheating ways of capitalism. Communist principles are not allowed to be spread through the United States, so a general understanding of them cannot be obtained by the workers. The object of revolution is not just to raise living standards or to stabilize working conditions. The most important object of a revolution is the seizure of political power so that the workers can become the masters of the country."

Another question raised was: "If the workers in the United States get to understand Communism, there will of course be revolution, with bloodshed, but isn't it possible perhaps for the American workers to take over their factories without bloodshed?"

"There must be bloodshed in the United States," was the answer. "This bloodshed must come because the capitalists possess all the machinery of state—armies, government bureaus, and the like. The workers must first get hold of this state machinery before they will be able to enjoy the fruits of revolution, and to accomplish this there must be bloodshed."

This discussion ended there; there could be no further questioning. The next topic taken up was country and politics. "We were taught that the origin of a country was through the creation of private property," Ho said. "Politics was based on an economic foundation, and politics was the form of oppression or control by one class over another class.

"In order to obtain political power, economic resources have to be amassed. In order to amass these economic resources, the workers must engage in strikes and other such activity for increased wage scales and shorter working hours. This is the beginning of revolutionary politics by one of the exploited classes.

"At first, countries didn't exist. A country was formed by the accumulation of private property. Somebody asked whether the primitive model of a country wasn't a race or tribe, and was told no, that a country was simply a means by which a certain class oppresses another class. I asked whether a country wasn't actually a combination of land, property, and sovereignty, and was told no, that a country was formed by the army, the police, courts, and prisons.

"We were taught that originally society consisted only of family gatherings, which exchanged their own possessions, without any country existing. The rate of production was very low, and everyone had to produce in order to exist.

There had to be mutual production so there could be mutual existence. When the productive rate went up, this meant that the tools of production were improved, and there was no longer need for everyone to work. This was how the leisure class came into existence.

"Some people therefore started enjoying themselves. They scattered production in this way and soon obtained control over small groups, and these original capitalists created what we call a family society. They attained their status by engaging in primitive business in the form of barter, such as exchanging fur for fish. That is why, we were told, the term not to work means not to engage in labor, and doesn't mean not to engage in the exchange of the products of labor.

"The man who labors can become a primitive capitalist, and then his accumulated property will enable him to sit back and do nothing himself—just command others. This is the beginning of the leisure class.

"The younger people in such primitive groups appointed their elders to take care of tasks such as exchanging what they had for other necessities. The elders in this way got private property into their hands, little by little, and this was the primitive form that a country took."

As the discussion proceeded, Ho said it became evident that the Communists opposed, in principle, the idea of a country, and were breaking down such a conception in their ideology. They were urging patriotism, independence, and nationalism only as expedients; actually, they were aiming at internationalism. What they meant by internationalism was clearly brought out by other teachings in the indoctrination meetings, when Moscow was frankly named as the true center for all authority.

Our interview concluded, Ho told me how he was making ends meet in Hong Kong. He was sharing a squatter's hut on a hillside with two other schoolteachers. They found work from time to time doing anything from pulling a ricksha to tutoring some backward child so it could take an examination. Ho said he might have to return to China, or else starve, but if he returned, he vowed that he would find ways to express his true feelings.

I lost track of him after this.

THE THOUGHT CONCLUSION

The simple thesis or term paper, the climax of the school year in almost every American institution of higher learning, became in the hands of the Communists a weird confessional and a pitiless medium for thought control. Without writing an acceptable thought conclusion, as the thesis is known in Communist China, a student is completely barred from any sort of employment above that of the simple coolie. Its contents are supposed to be the individual's conclusive thoughts, the measure of his thought reform after engaging in group discussion and self-criticism.

A chap named Robert Liang gave me as vivid a description of this as anyone. He had attended Peking University, where for a brief spell years before I had taught a class in journalism.

Robert's thought conclusion consisted of his biography and a report on his thought development. These were used as the basis for judging his school progress, in determining what job he was considered suited for, and whether to let him join the Democratic Youth. The last was a Communist-run organization whose members were among the politically elect and given many class advantages.

"The biography had to describe our family environment from our earliest childhood," Robert said, "what sort of teaching our parents gave us, what sort of friends we had, the type of people we liked to play or associate with, what organizations we joined or refused to join, what role we took in them, and countless more such details.

"The thought development thesis took up from there. We had to outline our political ideas, how we came by them, and in what form we expressed them. This was a lay confessional, in which we had to expose the errors of our thinking in the old, so-called decadent society, and show how we progressed to New Democracy. Everyone in some way or another had to criticize himself for not realizing earlier that a Communist-led government would be the only salvation for China, and for that matter, for the world. Everyone had to throw everything out of his mind that he had cherished before, because it was bourgeois sentiment or feudalistic.

"During this period of writing, everyone in class appeared grim, nervous, foreboding. Those of us who lived at home had the added strain of having to write exhaustive and ruthless criticism of our parents, of their whole way of life, and of what they had done for us, and to do this in front of their faces.

"How could we discuss such things with them? How could we keep them secret? It made you feel like a traitor to your own family. Most of the students lived on the university precincts, and so were saved that part of the embarrassment.

"There was the added strain, too, whether you wrote at home or in the dormitory, of knowing that you would have to stand before the whole class to read your confession, and that the class would judge your thought development, and that you would have to reply to the criticism of any student and answer him to his own satisfaction. How you wrote didn't matter; content was all that counted.

"The ordeal when everyone had to read his thought conclusion aloud in class was horrible. What shocks we had during the reading! A classmate confessed that he had secretly helped the Nationalists. We had never suspected it. Others, whom we had regarded as merely liberal or even nonpolitical, told of the help they had secretly given the Communists. Some admitted that they had benefited from the graft collected by their fathers or other relatives while engaged in business or in an official post. Often these things had happened years before, but all of it had to be put down in black and white, properly denunciatory, and properly penitent.

"The whispered tenseness with which many students read

their papers showed the terrible pressure they were under. Voices trembled. I could tell from the voice of many that they were deeply shamed by the whole proceeding. Others appeared to get a singular satisfaction out of the whole affair. I couldn't sleep a whole week after reading my paper. Others couldn't, either; they told me so.

"Many eyes became moist during the reading, and boys and girls cried openly in class. Some students cracked up under the strain. A relative of my bosom friend lost his mind under the mental struggle he had to undergo.

"The worst part was when everyone had to pick flaws in the papers of others. If you didn't participate, this would be held against you. I have never known so efficient a way of prying into the lives of other people as to force a person to stand up and read a confession, and then be questioned by others who would try to find contradictions and omissions. These weren't laughing matters. The questions had to be answered fully and seriously.

"There was a strange atmosphere during the reading and criticism. Certain students were always among the first in finding faults in the papers of others and seemed to take a particular pleasure out of this. They would bring up every rumor or bit of gossip they knew, confident that instead of being blamed they would be praised for it as progressives and for correct thinking. Then there was a different, small group of students who appeared to take a special glee in exposing themselves, their closest kin, and their friends in public.

"Why had I gone out with a reactionary girl? Have you slurred over your father's membership in a Kuomintang organization? Did you omit reference to that time you told your friends you thought America was a progressive nation? Why have you not been frank about this and admitted that your mind was poisoned by imperialist American propaganda? Don't you think you ought to do your paper over again, giving special emphasis to the parts criticized in class?

"You have no alternative but to consent, and then to read your rewritten thesis once more to the whole class to show that you have sufficiently confessed the evil thoughts of your past. My paper was picked to pieces, and I had to admit faults I never dreamed of and criticize myself for overlooking them. I had to apologize and promise never to do it again. Then everybody leaned back contentedly.

"I was saved."

"THE QUESTION
OF THOUGHT"

SELF-EXPOSURE

CHINESE COMMUNISM HAS PRODUCED, IN A PLAY CALLED
The Question of Thought, a dissection of its own political
body. Indeed, it has done far more than that. If it had merely
exposed its internal organization, like the medical professor
who uses a skeleton to illustrate his lessons, it might have
been interesting but not nearly as remarkable. What the Red
regime has done in this four-act drama is to lay bare its technique and expose its purposes, just as though a brain surgeon
were capable not only of exposing the tissues of the mind but
the thought processes and reactions that go on inside them.
No more self-revealing human document has ever been issued
by any political organization.

An exposé, of course, was not the intention of the play's
authors or sponsors—just the contrary. Their intent was only
to extend the field of indoctrination—brain-washing—beyond the classroom and out to the public in general. They
did an extraordinarily good job in this. In fact, they succeeded so well that by studying this propaganda play the
observer can obtain a liberal education in how Chinese
Communism actually manipulates the people, and focuses
their efforts, as faithful and obedient disciples of Rus-

sian Communism, on a world crusade for war against the United States.

The sponsors of the play should have realized that such a public display of classroom indoctrination would necessarily reveal the strategy being used. What goes on inside a psychiatrist's office or in an indoctrination class can be kept secret or denied, but not when one of the four walls is removed and the proceedings are transferred to the stage. This is what happened here. Probably the Party didn't care; it has never been hesitant about saying what it wants to say to its own audience, confident that its message will sound so unreal to outsiders that they simply will be unable to conceive of such things existing in this supposedly civilized world.

The subject of this realistic drama is the procedure by which men and women undergo thought reform in the North China People's Revolutionary University. In it the essential facts in Chi Sze-chen's interview are confirmed by the Communist propagandists themselves.

The plot is a simple one. A group of intellectuals with unwashed brains are brought together. One is naïvely pro-American; another is a landlord's son. There is a former Kuomintang army officer, a subdued clerk, and a pretty girl whose head is full of frills and boy friends. There's sex, intrigue, and everything that Hollywood demands. Through the medium of democratic group discussions alone, this diverse group goes through varying periods of agonizing conversions until, in the grand finale, all have become true Communists, full of hatred for the United States and of eagerness to go to war against it—particularly the disillusioned former friend of America. They are full of love for the Soviet Union and fully indoctrinated with the conviction that the highest patriotism that a Chinese can show his own country is to support and defend Moscow.

Fantastic as this all sounds—fantastic and unbelievable—there it is in the play in black and white. The similarity of the political indoctrination process, as outlined in this play, to the methods used in psychiatry—a half-baked psychiatry that makes a quackery of the profession—I have already stressed. What the play conveys, in addition, is the other side of the Communist indoctrination coin—evangelism—a distorted evangelism that is cold-blooded and calculating.

The evangelism that is used as a model for conversions to Communism is the old-fashioned evangelism of Billy Sunday and Aimee MacPherson. This whole revival performance, so much a part of the American folk setting, with its usual long, long sermons, the far-fetched similes and extravagant parables, and the communal, uninhibited rejoicings over each sinner who is saved, is here adapted to political ends and parodied.

There is a similarity, too, to the mutual discussion aspects of the Moral Rearmament movement, but this is mainly superficial, for Frank Buchman's movement stresses the bringing together of people through a give-and-take process in which reason and compromise predominate. This is not so with thought reform as conducted by the Chinese Communists and as portrayed in this play. Here the similarity is closest to the old-time conversion down the sawdust trail in the pinewood tabernacle or in a plain wooden barracks where a flash of light opens the sinner's eyes to the true faith— Marxism-Stalinism—and the spirit of Nicolai Lenin suddenly enters his body. The Communists have their hell, too, for those who fail to heed the call, and if it is not as eternally drastic as the original, that is not their fault.

The play is a collective product, attributed to the Central Drama School* in Peiping, and the writing is credited to the "joint efforts" of three persons. This is a factory-made piece, set up according to specifications, and if there is anything wrong with the lines, there would be a lot of people to share the blame. Every participant therefore, has surely combed and brushed it to remove any bugs. This is mutual responsibility with a vengeance.

The Peiping drama group, like all other organizations in Red China concerned with the communication of ideas, is

_____
* See Appendix B.

under the supervision of the propaganda authorities, and the plays and movies it produces are developed by democratic discussion and self-criticism in which the writers are just a few among the many who go over the text. The technique was explained by Tsolin, one of the better known Communist stage and screen directors, in an interview published in Shanghai, which reveals why the text of Chinese Communist plays and movies are now attributed so often to just three writers.

"Immediately after liberation, writers began experimenting with the collective writing system in which a number of writers collaborated," he says in this interview. "However, it was found that work did not get on so well when too many people worked on the same script, because the job of getting organized and turning out the work was rather difficult. At present we have found that the best method of collective script writing is for three people to work together." This doesn't mean, he points out, that the text actually is the product of just these three minds. Oh my, no! They are only given the responsibility of doing the writing, but "the final product is really a collective effort because of the rigorous criticism and self-criticism" to which it is subjected. Indeed, he says, such meetings, at which texts "are literally torn apart" and "have to be done over," are "a matter of course." The name used in writers' circles for such meetings is quite illuminating—bombardment meetings.

This sharing of responsibility is why there can be so complete a disclosure of Communist tactics and aims in one normal-length drama. The play had to pass inspection by the whole school, with its corps of able Party workers and thought seduction workers, each of whom had to have his say, and all of whom have to be listened to and heeded under the unanimity rule.

This method of production is the reason, too, why the play is as corny as the most melodramatic road show of David Belasco's younger days. Everything that could be found in the current Communist political line is in it. It's as if a long,

long list of "points not to be neglected" had been drawn up and checked off as they were inserted into the play in the form of dialogue. Nothing was permitted to be missed—too many collective eyes and ears were involved—and each tongue had to be heard. The result is a true-blue humdinger, a thriller-diller, a super-colossal extravaganza in propaganda, a twentieth century ideological tear-jerker of the most skillfully manipulated psychological corn.

And it works! I have spoken to many persons who have seen the play and the movie made out of it, and without exception all of them were deeply affected. Whether they were for or against Communism seemed to make little difference; the play was good theater.

What was of particular significance was that this favorable impression remained with them all the time they were in Red China, until they went back to the cold text to determine what it was that had so mightily moved them. Then they were astonished and a bit crestfallen over the crudity of the artifices used and the coarseness of the propaganda for which they all, to some degree, had fallen. There can be no doubt that, if this were the case with educated Chinese who were anti-Communist, the impression on innumerable other Chinese must have been lasting. It must be particularly so for those Chinese for whom the play was primarily written— the marginal man who either was wavering between ideologies or who hadn't yet been cured by brain-washing. The objective is mentioned in the second act with the statement, "Win over the middle-of-the-roaders, and victory will be ours."

The effect of the play is enhanced by its seeming adherence to fact. The writers are themselves graduates of the North China Revolutionary University, and in accordance with the much publicized technique of art "merging with the masses," * the play was first produced by students of the university it portrays. No wonder it was put on so realistically. The scenes actually do present the agony of mind struggle and the pathological intensity of the emotions aroused.

* *On Literature and Art,* by Mao Tse-tung.

The realism of the drama was cleverly put across by giving the playgoers a real sense of participation, as if they themselves were sitting in on the discussion meetings that were taking place on the stage, as if they themselves belonged to the group of students chatting so earnestly in front of them. This, of course, is a highly successful propaganda device, for it has the effect of bringing all outsiders into an indoctrination meeting without their realizing it; indeed, they paid good money to come of their own free will.

There were frequent outbursts of frenzied applause at the performances, and when the curtain went down, clapping reached a prolonged crescendo. People in the audience climbed onto the stage and shook hands with the players, a signal for everyone on the stage to burst forth in some fiery revolutionary song in which the audience joined. That this happened at each performance was widely known and was apparently one of the reasons the people went; the audience looked forward to the thrill. If there were occasions when it didn't take place spontaneously, there were always able Party members present to give the impetus.

Friends of mine, still stirred, told me that no matter how much a person might be opposed to Communism, it was impossible in this environment not to have some good feelings for the Communists as individuals, if only in thanks for a welcome spiritual experience so utterly lacking in their normal life. This was quack religion, of course, and half-baked psychiatry, and also just plain consummate propaganda. The sight of strangers standing singing together, holding hands, was not at all uncommon in the theater. One student told me how he found himself standing alongside a group of weeping schoolgirls. One clasped his hand—they had never seen each other before—and asked him if his mind had been changed—in good old revival language, if he had been saved. He heard ecstatic exclamations all about him, in a Sinatra swoon-manner, but the words were so different: "My mind and thoughts have now been changed!"; "Nothing in the world is going to stop me now from working for the people!"; "We

must all see ourselves in the mirror of Marxism-Leninism!";
"We must repair our past faults!"

Nobody would dare in such an environment to break the
spell by uttering a wisecrack or expressing lack of faith. The
letdown would have been taken out on the "poor sinner" with
much violence.

During intermissions, members of the audience were heard
comparing each other and people they knew to characters in
the play, chiding each other jocularly for being a "White
Chinese" poisoned by Americanism, or for going out on
dates just for romance, instead of dedicating their emotions
to the people; or of being rough and dull-witted like the
ex-Kuomintang army officer, or guilty of leftist impatience.
The latter is a peculiar ideological error. Enthusiastic Party
people who take their ideology to heart and refuse to compromise their principles for tactical purposes are accused of
it.

The play was first produced for the public in August, 1949,
and soon was being shown throughout China. The play
troupe claims that this was the consequence of public acclaim
for the production, and if the reactions of those I met who
had seen the play were any gauge, this is probably true. There
was general agreement that tickets were difficult to get and
were sold out days ahead. At times, entire offices and organizations would buy up all the seats in the house for a night for
their staffs. This is a favorite propaganda device in Communist countries to bolster ailing propaganda plays, but in this
instance it is doubtful whether it was necessary. Box office
records were claimed for both the play and the movie. The
text was printed as a book and became a popular text for political studies in indoctrination classes. Countless discussion
groups read it as a model for themselves. Higher-bracket
Communist officials wrote their views of the play. While
these Red chiefs were generally well satisfied, some of their
comments indicated that they had some doubts regarding
certain aspects of its value to the Party.

They had two main criticisms. According to Party ideology, although the educated strata of society are called the precious gems of the nation, they are not considered capable of participating in the final phase of a people's revolution because of bourgeois inclinations. Communist theory regards the greatest stumbling block to the Chinese revolutionary cause to be these intellectuals, and intellectual in Chinese means anyone with any sort of education, even of a middle school.

Several other plays are known to have been written by top-flight Communist authors regarding the difficulties gone through by political officers in their efforts to reform the thinking of intellectuals. *The Question of Thought* does point out the great need and the great difficulty of changing the point of view of these individuals, but the Party people felt that it should have stressed this more, particularly the inherent selfishness and self-centeredness of the intellectuals.

The next criticism was far more important from our viewpoint. Details were found lacking on the process by which the characters in the play really came to change their thoughts. There seemed to be little actual reasoning in it, mainly a sudden, frenzied grasp of the truth. In this case, the play was accurate and the Party critics were wrong, although they probably had good reason for their apprehensions. The conversion angle is exactly the means by which the Party in Red China is exploiting the susceptibilities, desires, and idealisms of its much harassed and war-weary population. Only it is not in the interest of the Party to admit it.

Here lies the fundamental failing of the play from the Communist point of view. Few people who have undergone a hysterical, semimystical, semireligious experience would claim that there is much that is rational about it, any more than about any ecstasy. It just seems to happen, and to make it a public experience, through a drama, can bring an entire audience into its scope, but lays the experience open to serious clinical inspection. *The Question of Thought* constitutes, in this respect, a basic document.

"RUNNING DOGS"

We had been going over the text of *The Question of Thought*, this alert young man from Red China and I, and were going back over the emotions he had experienced to find out how they had been aroused. One trick showed up at once. The writers had softened up their audience to swallow the indoctrination by conveying the impression that the plot constituted fact, not fiction, and that the audience was seeing a documentary rather than a drama.

The young man had a keen mind and felt that he, of course, unlike most others inside the bamboo curtain, could see through the propaganda artifices of the Communists. Then, full of this confidence, he asked me a question.

"Tell me," he asked, "where is Eastern Illinois College?"

"Eastern Illinois College? I don't know of any college with that name. Where is it supposed to be?"

"The play didn't say, but just gave the name. Did you ever hear of a Professor Thomas?"

"No, who is he?"

"Well, I assumed that he was some well-known educator. He's supposed to be connected with that college. You see, in the play. . . ."

I recalled the scene. "Ye gods!" I exclaimed. "You're not thinking, are you, that that scene was taken from life?"

He looked sheepish. "I doubted it," he hedged, "but I wasn't sure. When you saw the play, it seemed as if a true episode was being reported."

Indeed, it was one of the highlights of the play, a flashback, a page out of the past.

In the scene a newspaper clipping is handed to Chow Cheng-hua, a snobbish and highly sensitive university graduate who utterly dislikes the disciplinary ways of the Communists, and as an individualist also harbors deep resentment against the Kuomintang. He sincerely adores America's material advancement. He is an accurate enough representation of an important segment of the Chinese intellectuals—those who had welcomed the Communist army into their city because they had lost hope in the KMT and trusted the fervent promises made by the Reds. Here is this dramatic scene:

(The lights surrounding the stage dim. Thomas, a white-haired and white-bearded man, a typical American professor who is principal of Eastern Illinois College, appears. A purple light centers on him. He speaks Chinese with an American accent.)

THOMAS. Yes, we want to set up some schools in China, but we must understand why we are doing this. Actually, any country that is able to educate the Chinese youth of this generation will be able to reap rich harvests, not only spiritually, but commercially and industrially. If America could have diverted a flow of Chinese students to this country thirty years ago, and if it could even have increased that flow, then we would definitely now have been able to make use of the most satisfactory and the trickiest, slickest methods of controlling the destiny and development of China. This is to say, too, that we can help and finance China by a process of spirituality and knowledge. (Laughs dryly, then immediately becomes serious again.) For the sake of increasing and expending our spiritual and moral influence, money can be expended, and speaking purely from a materialistic point of view, this would be better than any other method, and would also give us a richer harvest. We should finance China through education, and control China through education. Using commercial and industrial channels is better than waving the flag of war. (Laughs wickedly.)

(Light dims and the American disappears. Lights brighten and Chow is seen deep in thought.)

How could the young man sitting before me, intelligent and sharp, have ever believed that such an incident really took place, that this scene actually referred to a real professor named Thomas and to an actual university called Eastern Illinois? In order to find the answer, one has to enter the upside-down environment in which he had lived inside the Soviet bloc.

When all that a person hears about him, when all that he is able to get hold of to read, hammers out the same theme, then, when this individual goes to a theater and sees something like the scene described, instead of it appearing patently false, as it would at once under normal circumstances anywhere else, it appears perfectly logical and likely. This is because the setting has been so skillfully arranged—not only on the stage, but the setting of which the theater itself is only a part, of real life as it is lived in a Communist country. The play, the audience, and the streets and city outside were all part of the setting. Where was the dividing line to be found between play acting and real life, between fiction and nonfiction, between melodrama and a documentary? With this demarcation line destroyed, how could an ordinary citizen—or comrade—retain his sense of balance and discrimination? In a Communist society, the dissenter remains silent, living in a splendid mental isolation in which his feelings, possibly held even by the majority, seem to him to be held only by himself—abnormal, lonely ideas that are uncomfortable and too heavy a burden to carry.

People are most susceptible to propaganda when already in a high state of tension, and the emotion aroused by this scene was quickly used in the play to deal with what is perhaps the most difficult problem facing the Communists: how to break down the traditional family system in a manner that will split fathers and sons in hatred, and thus turn them in bitterness to the promising haven of Communism.

While the audience is still stunned by the Eastern Illinois College flashback, a group of indoctrination students are shown flocking in for a visit from another school. When they ask some questions, Chow, the former sceptic, now speaks up like a Party veteran. A boy asks his advice. His father used to be a landowner, and the Communists took his land away. Now the father was unable to make a living in the country any more, so he came to the city, where he "is pestering" his son for help. The boy asks what he should do about his dad.

Chow had the Party line answer down pat now. "You should tell your father nicely that he should go back and till the land and join in labor production."

The boy is still unconvinced that the right way of acting is to show his hungry father to the door. "The way my father sighs and groans about losing everything, I can't help feeling very sad and moved by the whole affair."

"To know and to understand can change feelings," says the new Chow. "Indeed, it is through knowing and understanding that feelings are changed. When I first entered this school, my feelings were skeptical. But after a while, when I began to understand, my feelings began to develop and blossom."

Here the Party puts a plug into the play for a policy which it was still concealing from the peasants—the intention to duplicate in Red China what has been the procedure in every country that the Communists have taken over in Eastern Europe, where, after a honeymoon period of so-called land reform, in which the peasants were encouraged by the lure of free farmland to serve as the backbone for the Red Army, all the land was taken away from them and collectivized.

Chow continues in his advice to this farm owner's son, "If we want to produce on a large scale, we will have to be like the Soviet Union in the future; we will have to build collective farms."

This policy is subtly brought out, too, when a lad named Wang Tsang-sheng, who has only attended primary school, tells his classmates he has "good news" for them. The good news is that he has written his parents a letter telling them that he has "learned a lot about revolutionary theories." This is just one of the numerous scenes in which the play takes on the coloration of old-time religious revivals, with everybody rejoicing over the saving of any lost soul. Revolutionary theories, as interpreted in the letter, consisted mainly of repeating excuses for everything Soviet Russia had done, including its looting of the industrial plants in Manchuria on which China was depending for its rehabilitation after its weary decades of war. Most of the letter is given over to support of such Soviet Russian excesses. Included in this remarkable letter is this passage: "The Soviet Union will definitely help us build and achieve a new democratic state. Isn't it already like that in Manchuria? From today onwards, all of China's farms will be like those of the Soviet Union; they will all enter the path of collective farming."

Plays such as *The Question of Thought* are seen only in cities, and so the Party does not hesitate to talk in this off-hand manner about a policy that would antagonize the farmers if it became widely known. The Party can depend on its controlled press not to carry the news to the countryside.

In scenes such as this the students are shown converting each other by a chain reaction set up by emotion engendered by different political issues. This bandwagon psychology carries over into the audience, particularly because the performance doesn't seem like a play at all, but like an actual indoctrination course in which everyone present is participating. The entire political indoctrination system is given a sugar coating. A timorous clerk remarks: "The political workers and the teachers are nice and courteous to us. The principal—why, he's just like your old man when he gives us a lecture. It's really so warm and intimate. And the way they always smile and sensibly say things that really have something to them really moves people. I have never seen anything like it before."

The Party, too, in this play, unwittingly explains its negative attitude toward romance in general as taking up time that it wants spent on Party activities, and it reveals its hesitant attitude toward marriage in general for threatening the undivided loyalty that it demands of its adherents.

The play opens on this note. As the curtain rises, a boy and girl are heard singing, *How Can I Stop Thinking About Him?* This dialogue ensues between a group of students:

Hey! Hey! Hey! This is the North China University, and it is a revolutionary place, so quit this "thinking of him and thinking of her" business.

I'll think what I like. What's it to you?

There's no class right now, why can't there be any singing?

When I say you can't sing, you can't sing, because this sort of sensuous trash does not belong to a place like this!

Forget it, forget it! Stop all this quarreling. Don't take it too seriously. After all, it is Sunday. What's wrong with a little singing?

What do you mean, don't take it so seriously? This is the question of what sort of airs you put on, a question of thought. We'll talk about it later during the criticism and self-criticism meeting.

In a conference of group heads, in one scene, a leader reports a real achievement. A student's girl friend has given him up because of his failure to show sufficient interest in Communist ideology. This so shook him that he became a model Party boy. Here is how the leader tells about it:

The change that took place in student Ting Kang is still more interesting. In the past, he was a scatterbrain. He didn't know anything about what a revolution is. Because his sweetheart is a progressive and managed to pass the entrance examination to enter this university, he followed suit. When he finally entered this school, he just talked love to his sweetheart, Miss Lo Ping-ting, showing little or no interest in learning, which finally reacted on his sweetheart. As a result, she gave him up. This gave him a terrific jolt, and so, because he wanted to show his own progressiveness, he began to work hard at learning, and showed enthusiasm in his work. After a period of time, he felt that this new way of proceeding had benefited him quite a bit. He realized that his new way of life was far better than how he used to live. He felt emotionally happier, and his thoughts were completely changed over. He was very thorough in his self-examination during our last self-criticism meeting. All this he told our group during one of our meetings.

In a bourgeois play, of course, this young man would be united in the arms of his lady friend, but there is no mention of this here. Now that he had the right political ideology, it apparently didn't matter whether they ever saw each other again.

There is a romance to this play, though, which runs as a theme and a lesson from start to finish, except that there is a difference between this romance and that usually found in conventional dramas. Here the play begins with the couple already sweethearts, and the denouement is the complete and successful smashing of the romance. Although this may seem ridiculous and unnatural to the mentally unwashed, the Communists by their frankness in portraying it this way cleverly arouse one of the main motivations of young men and women anywhere in the world—the strong appeal that the sacrificial has for idealistic youth. That this trick was successful was shown by the numerous instances related to me of how young members of the audience expressed their determinations henceforth to dedicate themselves "to work for the people"—double-talk in Communist lingo for engaging in purely Party missions that sacrifice self along with ideals.

Several of the main characters in the play are girls. One is the romantic Miss Yuan Mei-hsia. Another, the perfect example of a loyal Party worker of the approved type, is Miss Tsao, a class leader.

The first sight the audience has of Miss Yuan is of a giddy girl who has just come from a dance. The first sight it has of Miss Tsao is when she settles, Solomon-wise, a squabble between new students. Miss Tsao is always busy, and yet always has patience and time for additional work. Miss Yuan never seems to have time to do what is expected of her. "All you know is to play and have fun," she is admonished by another girl, Miss Kao Jieh, a member of the Student Council, who is described in the cast as an enthusiastic element. Miss Kao even condemns Miss Yuan for wearing her plain hat in a way that makes it look "quite pretty."

This enthusiastic element tells her classmates that Miss Yuan has stopped dancing and has given up high heels, but that, nevertheless, "we still haven't solved her thought problem. Her heart throbs have not been liberated. She still runs around with that Ho Tsiang-suei and talks love, lukewarm love." This is not considered gossip, or a hen party; it is democratic group discussion, and Miss Kao decides to talk it over with Miss Yuan, which she proceeds to do.

She tells the romantic young lady that she's not against falling in love, "that's anybody's privilege," but she goes on to explain what she means by this "from a comrade's point of view." She tells Miss Yuan that her attitude in the affair wasn't "serious enough," and that her feelings were not "developed on the basis of comradeship."

"You two have never had an exchange of views regarding learning and thought problems," she tells Miss Yuan. "You two have never had mutual criticisms or the like." Miss Yuan doesn't even know her boy friend's family ties, how he was educated, and what work he did. The meaning, in this setting, is not at all that he might be socially or financially unsuitable, but that he might be politically undesirable.

"What sort of a sweetheart can you call him when you don't even properly know the situation in his mind when he first entered this school?" Miss Kao asks.

With a touch of unintentional humor that escapes the audience in Red China, Miss Yuan, now "uncomfortable," answers, "I guess I never thought of those things."

"We women comrades must pay particular attention to such matters when we are working in the outside world," Miss Kao warns, "otherwise we will be carelessly tricked into something that we will regret for the rest of our lives." In this context, too, what is meant by one's sweetheart having "a good time with us" is his failing to be serious about his political thinking.

Miss Yuan becomes properly alarmed at this dismal prospect. In imperialist society she probably would have told Miss Kao to mind her own knitting. But not in an indoctrination school! Instead she asks Miss Kao's opinion of the fellow. "If he's no good, I'll break with him," she exclaims in desperation.

Miss Kao is a tolerant young lady in her way. "That's your own personal affair," she says. "I can't definitely say what he's like. But from now on, you should try to know and understand him more. Become good comrades first, then you can talk about being in love."

In imperialist society, too, the "definitely" would have sounded cattish. But here, comrade is the key word.

Lucky girl to have been so warned in time! Sure enough, Miss Yuan's boy friend, Ho Tsiang-suei, had a most wicked past. He had worked for the Americans! This, in the environment created by the play, sounds dreadfully wicked. But it's not enough to suit the playwrights. So they have him sent by the Americans to this very school to "wreck it." He had been put up to this by no less than the Sino-American Cooperative Organization.

That SACO was purely a wartime body formed by the Americans in their effort to help fight the Japanese and free as much of Chinese soil as possible from the conquerors, and that the North China Revolutionary University didn't exist until years later, aren't the kind of facts in which the Communist sponsors of the play were interested. If anyone in any of the criticism meetings that helped produce the play had mentioned this discrepancy, he would have automatically found himself classified among those "reactionaries and their henchmen" whom Mao Tse-tung declared do not belong in the legal category of "people."

Fortunately, none of the Americans who staked their lives, and the Americans who sacrificed their lives, on missions to help free the Chinese mainland during World War II ever suspected that their services would be interpreted in this manner, only a few years later, by Mme. Sun Yat-sen and the Yenan faction. They were then busily expressing affection for the Americans and unlimited gratitude for their help —in between suggestions that the United States switch its recognition to the Communists while the war was still on.

Few in the audiences who saw the play could know that this scene was patently and viciously false and a libel on both the Chinese people and the Americans. The documentary manner of the presentation must inevitably have convinced many impressionable youths.

The scene in which Ho confesses is a tear-jerker of the first water. Here it is:

HO. (Bursts out into tears after several minutes of being suppressed in an atmosphere of tension.) I am . . . a sinner, a criminal. I am one of those who should be dead . . . . I am one of those terrible Special Service agents! (Everybody shows surprise.)
EVERYBODY. Ho Tsiang-suei!
MISS TSAO. Student Ho Tsiang-suei, what is this all about? Tell us!
YUAN. You what? You really are a . . .
HO. I'm from the Sino-American Cooperative Organization. The Americans trained me for six months, and sent us to this school to try and wreck the program!
CHOW. Was it the Sino-American Cooperative Organization's Special Service Camp?
(MISS YUAN bursts out in tears and runs unhappily off the stage.)
MISS TSAO. Student Ho Tsiang-suei, it doesn't matter. Tell us all!
HO. My main job when I was sent to this school was to spread counter-propaganda, to create rumors, to start rows with everybody, create friction between fellow students, divide everybody, and destroy unity and start factions. My main job was to spread anti-discipline, antiorganization propaganda, and to spread incorrect isms of freedom and democracy.

Ho confesses how he was ordered "to spread love America and hate Russia views," and that he singled out Chow, the admirer of American ways, "without him knowing, and used him as a spokesman for my plans."

"Punish me," Ho pleads. "I'm not a youth; I'm not human."

The next big moment, as might be expected, is Chow's con-

version scene. He sees the light. The play is ending like a
revival meeting and also on a war note.

CHOW. (Cannot control himself; stands up abruptly and angrily.)
Leader, fellow students! What else is there for me to say? I never
thought, it never occurred to me . . . (Tears start trickling from
his eyes, but he holds them back strongly.) I have become what
Student Liu Ging said. "You think yourself high and mighty. You
have become the mental slave of the aggressive thoughts of the
imperialists; you have become the spokesman of the Kuomintang
thought." This is something that I never before realized in my life.
Ten, twenty years of slave education completely blinded my views,
prevented me from seeing the truth, and knowing and understanding things clearly. I was not satisfied with the Kuomintang,
but neither did I have any faith in the Communist Party. I
thought that people who are like us, who have been given foreign
education, we so-called democratic self-centerists, were the only
ones fit to save my country. I worshipped America's material culture and advancements, strongly advocated self-centerism. I could
not see the murderous blade lying behind the masks of the
American teachers and professors; I could not hear the guns and
bombs behind their musical films. Now I thoroughly know and
understand the entire situation. Three months of learning have
educated me; these last few hours of chatting have awakened me
and strengthened me; what else is there for me to say? What
Student Liu Ging said was right. There is no middle of the road
today. On one side are the imperialists and their running dogs, and
on the other side are the Communist Party and the people. To
want to become a free man, one must lean to one side, join the
actual struggle, join the organized body of strength!
    (Everybody is moved, and applauds.)
HO. I have sinned. I want to be sent to the war's most dangerous
sector, so that I may pay for my sins.
MISS TSAO. Good! Fellow students! You have all seen with your
own eyes what the Kuomintang reactionaries do to youth, how
they push youth into pits of fire, how they force the youth to
carry out their bloody acts. We must never forget the bloody inci-

dents caused by the Kuomintang reactionaries. We not only must not forget, but we must pay them back for what they have done. But we must realize and know clearly that it is we who have some of these faults, it is we who have done wrong things. Comrade Ho Tsiang-suei, I hope you will think over your past carefully and then criticize yourself thoroughly. From now on, you must build up your determination to become a new man and cast away your sins.

CHOW. Leader, fellow students! I want to tell everybody that from now on you have my own guarantee that I will definitely destroy the imperialistic and reactionary views and attitudes existing in my thoughts. The imperialists hope that we will have what they call democratic self-centerism and individualism, but don't be fooled. From today on, our entire self will be dedicated to the revolution, dedicated to discipline and organization. We will obey the call of the school!

MISS TSAO. Good, Comrade Chow Cheng-hua. (Shakes his hand.) We celebrate your improvement and progress. Fellow students, Chow Cheng-hua's improvement and progress have given us all a great lesson. We should accept his experiences and lesson to help us thoroughly rid our thoughts of the remaining unclear and muddy views and attitudes. The painful path which Cheng-hua took to change his thoughts, and the constant mental conflicts he went through, should teach us the lesson that we should solve what remaining problems there are in our thoughts much quicker, so that we can throw away our heavy burdens and go onto the path of the revolution!

(Voices, music and drums, gongs.)

MISS TSAO. Oh, fellow students! A group of students is going on the path of the revolution today. They have all answered the call of the authorities for men and women to go and work in the hard and rugged Northwest.* They are just about to leave. . . .

EVERYBODY. Good, good! Let us go and give them a send-off!

(The music becomes louder. A group of students carrying bags and sacks walk onto the stage under a send-off banner. On it is written: "Go where the revolution needs you most!" Following

* China's Northwest refers to Kansu, Shensi, and Ningsha provinces.

behind are those sending them off. Some of them are beating drums and gongs, some are doing the *yang ko*. Everybody in the cast comes onto the stage to give them a rousing send-off. Everybody sings: "Young Chinese Communist Party, yours is the perfect heart, you are the direction." Hands rise, all waving in fervor and enthusiasm. The curtain drops slowly.)

Some of these young men probably went all the way to Korea.

FAITH

THERE CAN BE NO CONVERSION, EVEN WHEN IT CONCERNS only dialectical materialism, without faith—unquestioning and complete. We might not expect to find such faith set forth, in plain words, as a requirement in an ordinary Communist political document, but in a play such as *The Question of Thought*, produced by the Party, it is a different matter.

Here the Party can be franker. The play was not intended, in the first place, for foreign eyes and ears. The translation I had made of the original text is the only one available in English at this writing. The play, indeed, may be ranked as a political passion play.

"We should have faith," pleads the Communist nun, Miss Tsao, speaking "in a tender and friendly manner" to pacify a despondent fellow worker named Chen, who is suffering from hurry-sickness—a serious affliction in the Communist medical dictionary. This happens in the first act, when the students seem so set in their old beliefs, so immune to the blessings of the new political faith, that Chen despairingly wants to give up. "I'm afraid I'm neither fit nor able to bring my duties to a successful conclusion."

"The students have been in this school for more than a month, and during this period," Miss Tsao tells him, "they have gone through the better-the-way-of-life-and-learning-attitude period, they have been through several criticism and self-criticism meetings to examine their thoughts and faults, and have had the opportunity of hearing lectures on the new outlook in life and on the evolution of society. Don't you think that these students have shown some marked improvement? We should have faith and believe and trust that they will change over in the long run."

Later she tells another doubter that they have all "reaped a harvest," which should have "increased our faith in reality, and this reality tells us that youth all travel on the road to progress and improvement and can all be changed over." Even the most backward "need only be willing to change over and repent their sins," she goes on. "We shall welcome them to our fold, because, basically, youth is not sinful. . . . Their sins should be charged to the account of the reactionaries." She turns to the group chief, who has been having a hard time of it, and says, "Everybody criticized you because they love you and hope to see you improve all the more so that you may guide and lead the students even better."

She turns to another comrade, who in the interval has been cheered by the enthusiasm with which the university students went out to sweep streets, refusing to return until they had swept more streets than had been their quota. "Spectators on the street were very much moved by what they saw, and declared that they had never seen such a fine school and such fine students," he exclaims ecstatically. This dialogue ensues:

MISS TSAO. Comrade Chen, didn't you just now, or a little while ago, express the thought that you had lost hope in the students?
CHEN. Well, that was . . .
MISS TSAO. I'm not joking with you, Comrade; you should have faith, and then we'll be right.

Faith in the correctness of the Party line is apparently the last chance given the political sinner who doesn't otherwise seem able to be convinced. Miss Tsao herself makes this plain. "The reactionaries," she says, "have been defeated.

Now the sick people"—and by this she means all those whose thoughts are still poisoned with opposing ideas—"are getting treatment; and if they still do not own up, and if they still are not frank about their past during this period of treatment, if they still do not want to save themselves, and to repent their wrongs, then they cannot blame anyone else."

Here is the fundamental difference between democratic discussion as the term is interpreted in Red China and its traditional meaning outside of totalitarian ranks. The free nations assume that democratic discussion implies a conference intended to reach the best possible decision that the minds of all who participate can devise, through a give-and-take process that makes the most of original thinking. The version of such discussion that the Communist apologists have assiduously spread to outsiders through their double-talk technique is wholly different; the term simply does not mean to Communists what it does to us. The play makes this plain.

A discussion meeting to them is an opportunity to understand what has already been decided upon, so that the participants do not find themselves in the unhappy position of being found wrong on policy. It provides a chance to decide how this policy can most efficiently be put into effect, and, perhaps most important, provides a means of putting Party loyalty on record. Those who attend a democratic group discussion have the job of criticizing themselves in order to find out whether they have done their level best in implementing the Party line—never in criticizing Party policy. Inside such a framework, discussion is allowed to become heated, and speakers may even pound the table. The problem in an indoctrination class is to prepare oneself for this. "If I don't learn seriously now, and don't absorb these new terminologies and new thoughts into my brain pockets, how am I to go into society in the future, and work for the people?" asks Yu Tse-niang, the pathetic clerk.

All this, one might think, should be obvious now to any observer of totalitarian tactics, but their approach and purpose are so completely different from ours that we are eternally being surprised when we see them put into practice.

It was shown by the failure of the American public to understand the performance put on by the Chinese Communist delegation to the United Nations and the way in which Jakob A. Malik, the Soviet Russian delegate, presided over Security Council sessions in the winter of 1950. Americans who stared uncomprehendingly into their television sets during those sessions may not have known it, but they were spectators at the same time of innumerable democratic discussion and self-criticism meetings in Red China, Albania, North Korea—in all the Soviet subject countries, and in Russia as well.

They were sitting in at the Revolutionary University in Peiping. They were watching *The Question of Thought* being performed in Shanghai. There was only one difference: non-Communist players in the United Nations performance did not obey the rules of such discussion meetings.

What actually took place at Lake Success, therefore, was that two basically contrary parliamentary systems tried to operate together simultaneously, each with its own set of rules. No agreement is possible under such circumstances, no matter how anyone tries, any more than it is possible to chalk up a single score for a combined game of baseball and football played at the same time on the same field, each according to its own rules. This isn't an exaggerated picture. Both are games, and both are parliamentary systems—only each has its own set of regulations.

The misunderstanding by Americans and by Westerners generally was in thinking that Gen. Wu Hsiu-chuan and Malik were merely defying or making game of the United Nations parliament. This was not so. They were only giving the West the opportunity to witness the Communists' version of what they consider to be an organized, disciplined meeting.

What the United Nations hadn't been told by Wu and

Malik was that under Communist procedure, such parliamentary sessions are intended to provide a forum in which
everyone may go on record as agreeing—not disagreeing—with
the required conclusions, where everyone must go on record
as persuaded.

Poor Wu and Malik were handicapped in the United Nations. There was a time limit to how long they could drag
out a meeting and how long they could reiterate the same
point, again and again, until the recalcitrant member would
wearily admit his error. There were more serious obstacles,
too. Wu and Malik could call recalcitrant members reactionaries and running dogs of imperialism, but that was as far
as they could go. They could take no further action against
them. Bourgeois limitations made it impossible for them to
throw the sinners into the hoosegow. They couldn't even
send any member of the Council to a thought reform institution. How could they be expected to succeed in their mission?
The odds were against them. They had no secret police, no
thought-seduction workers, no mind reform institutions, as
described in *The Question of Thought*. Perhaps it might have
helped if the Soviet bloc had put on a performance of this
play for the other delegations. While watching it, the United
Nations audience would have heard this warning: "Today,
whether we are in our country or in the rest of the world,
there is no third road, no middle of the way. On one side are
the imperialists and their lackeys, and on the other side are
the Communist Party and the people."

Wu and Malik had no other alternatives available to them
except to be as intractable as they were or to make a complete
break with their Communist masters. They had no third
road.

Exactly as the play gave a glamorous veneer to scorn of
parents and to the subordination of affection for political
ends, making these seem like acts of patriotism, so did it
make snooping on one's best friends and kinfolk seem the
right thing to do in order to save them from sin. The play
teaches that people should live in glass houses and they

should throw stones, and that each man and woman is his neighbor's and his parent's keeper.

In one of the early dramatic scenes the youthful Wang informs the group that he had been snooping on Miss Yuan in the bathroom, where he saw her using cosmetics. Wang, who is presented as a commendable character, then produces Miss Yuan's diary, which he has filched, and reads several romantic sentences. That such teachings, so contrary to the whole basis of both Eastern and Western civilizations, can be seriously put forward and so accepted, seems inconceivable.

MISS YUAN (excitedly). Where do I have cosmetics? Where do I have cosmetics?

WANG. When you were in the bathroom, you were like a little thief. In your hand was a small pocket mirror, and you were in a hurry wiping your face here and there. You think I didn't see you?

MISS YUAN (more excitedly). You dead devil, you dead devil! You're rumor-mongering, you're rumor-mongering. I'm quitting, I'm quitting! (Pulls a long face and dashes out amidst laughter.)

WANG. Hey, don't run away; there's even better yet!

MISS YUAN (turning around). What?

WANG (bringing out Miss Yuan's notebook). Look, everybody, this is what Miss Yuan wrote in her notebook: "Love, love, you have conquered my roomy heart. . . ."

MISS YUAN (dashing back). Aiya! Dead devil! Give it back to me! You don't care about your own loss of face! Give my notebook back to me. Give it back to me!

WANG. It'll cost you one package of peanuts; one package of peanuts! (Dashes out.)

MISS YUAN. Dead devil! Dead devil! (Gives chase, but runs into Ho Tsiang-suei and falls smack into his arms. Ho lifts her up; she pushes him away and dashes out. Everybody laughs.)

There can be no privacy, no secrets, in such an environment. The students room together, and their responsibility is to watch each other. A pillow placed in an unusual position, a bed moved to the side, all these are noticed, arouse suspicions, and their significance is discussed. The students refer to anything out of the ordinary in the speech or action of any of their comrades. The lesson taught by the play is that such spying on others is commendable and necessary by the simple artifice of showing it succeed. A suspect obligingly has hidden a pistol, and another has hatched a sorry plot. The play has the one voluntarily give up his weapon, and the other voluntarily disclose his conspiracy, as encouragement to Communist effort along these lines in real life. A nation-wide campaign in Red China for frankness and confession on such matters was accompanied by the same fulsome promises of forgiveness as made in this play.

Ironically, while newspapers in Red China were printing thrilling accounts of how many persons had come forward in exactly this way, and how everyone rejoiced with them over their reformation, a nation-wide purge was begun, and untold tens of thousands of persons were summarily executed. How many of these died because of the evidence they were lured into giving against themselves in self-criticism meetings or by seeing *The Question of Thought* will never be known. Untold numbers trustingly signed their own death warrants. Even to desire something that is contrary to Party wishes is considered an act against the wishes of the people, a sin. Only in religion can anything comparable be found. Chow suggests that politics and teaching be separated, and is informed by an enthusiastic element that this desire in itself is a wrongful act. All desires, and all deeds, however, do not fit into the category of frankness and confession. Unless it is a political error, something against the Party's wishes, the Party simply isn't interested. This is made plain in a good-natured episode when Yu admits in self-criticism that he falsified his age when he applied for entrance into the indoctrination school. He was so anxious to join!

"This business of being thirty years old was a lie, and am I not confessing it today in this thought conclusion?" he asks self-righteously.

Oh no, he is informed. "What you have been hiding is not

political in nature. What you should do is not hide what your political nature was and is, but to come out with that frankly. For instance, did you join the San Min Chu-I Youth Corps [Nationalist youth group], did you join the Kuomintang, or did you do anything bad in that way? You should examine your thoughts regarding those things."

He promises voluntarily, and everyone is happy, for in Red China, as the enthusiastic Liu Ging says, "We're not afraid of contradictions, of arguments, because as soon as our contradictions have become unified, we will all be able to progress and improve."

If anyone held any doubts as to whether "unified contradictions" wasn't a contradictory term in itself, he had the highest political authority to tell him nay. Mao Tse-tung has described Red China's form of government as a democratic dictatorship.

HATE

A teacher was taking her children through the exhibits in the Workmen's Cultural Palace in Shanghai. She stopped in front of a large picture of Uncle Sam. A Chinese newspaperman who happened to be passing stopped to hear what the children were being told.

The teacher pointed to the lanky, Yankee figure in the poster and said: "See that picture of Uncle Sam; this is the portrait of a cruel imperialist who is trying to enslave all the free peoples of the world. Remember this picture all your lives. Always remember he is a hateful individual."

This lesson, adjusted to various age levels, was being repeated to every class of students who were taken on these tours. They were part of what the Chinese people referred to as Hate Week. The official name for the week was National Campaign Week against United States Aggression in Taiwan and Korea. Children were given the day off to attend city-wide hate demonstrations. Similar scenes took place all through China. The festive air made these youngsters especially susceptible to the appeal.

The Chinese who told me about it—one of many—remarked, "Many of these young men and girls will constitute the guerrillas who will infiltrate behind American lines some day. Americans will wonder how that hatred was planted."

A description of the Cultural Palace, published in a Shanghai magazine, was especially interesting because it was attributed to the "collective writing" of three men—evidence of the political care put into the short composition. Here it is:

The six-storied Workmen's Cultural Palace is situated in the central part of Shanghai municipality. The ground floor has a stage and theater. The first floor has a social room, bookstore, chess room, music room, hospital, and gymnasium. The second floor has a library, reading room, arts room, sewing room, ballroom, etc. Every day, more than 10,000 workers pass their leisure time there. These workmen-comrades "change sides" not only politically but also culturally. All such welfare activity is due to the blood which the martyrs have shed for us. Such blood forms the foundation of our present-day happiness and our future victory.

Hate Week was the climax of a nation-wide campaign for signatures to the Stockholm peace petition. In case anyone misunderstood the intent of the peace petition, the final week of the official drive was arranged to coincide with Hate Week. Then, to make doubly sure that the idea was not misunderstood, both the peace petition drive and Hate Week were arranged to end on China's Red Army Day. Goebbels never fit anything together more neatly or more brazenly. Fervor was thus brought to a crescendo, and the drive for peace signatures was given a pointed connection with warfare. By merging the peace drive and Hate Week, and ending both with a military display, the Chinese Reds saw to it that the only persons who missed the point were the foreign apologists for Red China.

A Red Army parade featured the official conclusion of both the peace and hate drives on Red Army Day. Shanghai's parade started at the odd hour of one in the morning, in spite of rain, and continued until ten-thirty in the morning, because it was not supposed to interfere with defense production. Similar scenes were duplicated throughout China. In all cities and towns, peace signature booths were set up on roads, in theaters and bookshops, while song-and-dance teams went through the streets publicizing the drive. Peace doves became the required voluntary decoration for households, shop windows, and public places.

Loudspeakers installed the night before at all important points started Hate Week off by blaring forth anti-American propaganda. The message was that American imperialism had come out into the open, and that an American imperialist plot for world domination was now clear. Under orders, all entertainment houses, parks, shops, and department stores had their windows and central positions plastered with anti-American slogans. Huge, red-colored banners emphasizing hatred were hung across the main thoroughfares. The *Ta Kung Pao*, an influential Chinese newspaper that was still being referred to as independent by its liberal friends abroad, had a display of photographs of alleged executions of Korean patriots by Americans. Such exhibits filled the Cultural Palace.

Along with these spectacular displays were more subdued mass indoctrination procedures that depended on daily reiteration. In all parades, anywhere in the country, a common figure was Uncle Sam. He invariably was shown the same way, with a rope tied around his neck. He was led by a Chinese worker, with a Chinese Red Army soldier standing guard over him with a rifle. This Uncle Sam looked a very subdued individual indeed. The first few times an ordinary Chinese saw Uncle Sam in this abject pose, he was inclined to shrug his shoulders, scoffing at the ridiculousness of so misrepresenting his powerful neighbor across the seas. But after he had seen the same act a dozen or more times, the picture that came to his mind's eye was apt to be the same, beaten figure to which he had become accustomed.

This was the theory behind the entire campaign. As good a description as any was given to me by Henry Chao, a young office manager from a Shanghai textile firm. I met him in Macao, where he had come to meet his brother, who worked in Hong Kong. We gathered in the home of a Chinese professor who had recently escaped from Peiping, and who was a common friend of all of us. This was how I had the opportunity of spending Chinese New Year's in their company, and hearing Henry talk about his life in Communist China.

He was full of personal-experience anecdotes, such as the time the textile guild had sent a messenger to his boss to inform him that a "spontaneous" parade had been "voluntarily" set for the next morning. The parade had been called to support a campaign "to buy bullets" for the Chinese "volunteers" in Korea. There were only six employees in Henry's firm, and they all stood about and listened as the messenger listed them and said, "At least two of you will have to volunteer to march." They had the "democratic right" to decide among themselves who would volunteer.

"The boss asked me if I would please volunteer, and I agreed," Henry said. "We had to show up at four in the morning and we began marching an hour later. I managed to get away at eight, when I pretended to faint, and was sent home."

Henry also told about the time he passed a red traffic light by mistake while driving his employer's truck. He was given a traffic summons, and when he appeared at the police station, he was fined and given a two-hour lecture that went something like this:

"Chiang Kai-shek is no good; it is very bad to pass a red light; America is an imperialist aggressor nation; you should always watch out for red lights; Chiang Kai-shek is a bad bandit; and America is an aggressive, imperialist nation; next time, watch out for the red light; Chiang Kai-shek is a bad. . . ."

The lecture went on like this the entire time, until he became dizzy from the monotonous refrain, but Henry said he he had to keep awake and show alertness. It was a form of brain-washing.

One of Henry's co-workers found a watch one day and, being an honest soul, went over to the policeman on the corner to turn it in. This wasn't so easy. The cop refused to take it, but insisted that the finder himself go to the police station, where he was questioned about his political antecedents. They seemed to suspect there was bourgeois sentimentalism in his makeup. He was given a lecture for an hour and a half:

"Chiang Kai-shek is no good; all property belongs to the people in New China. America is an imperialist aggressor nation; individuals are custodians of the people's property; Chiang Kai-shek is a bad bandit, and America is an imperialist aggressor nation; honesty is an attitude toward the state; Chiang Kai-shek is a bad. . . ."

This dizzy refrain crept into every form of official or semi-official interview. Songs are popular on the Chinese radio, and, as in America, there is often a plug between songs. The disc jockey remarks:

"Chiang Kai-shek is no good; our next song will be a popular new tune everybody is humming; America is an imperialist aggressor nation; we are now about to play *Springtime in Soochow*; Chiang Kai-shek is a bad bandit, and America is an aggressive, imperialist nation; *Springtime in Soochow* is by a well-known people's composer, and is about the liberation feeling; Chiang Kai-shek is a bad. . . ."

"Can the constant dinning of this single theme into a person's ears really influence him? I should think that it would have the opposite effect," I remarked.

Henry thoughtfully shook his head. "You may not believe it," he said, "but while everyone you talk to will tell you that all this propaganda is nothing but a pack of lies, just the same a lot of these same people are themselves influenced by it."

The professor nodded gravely. "You're right," he said. "Anyone you pin down will say of course it's Communist propaganda and can't be believed. Even the Communist Party people will say it's propaganda, with the inference that they themselves are above it. Yet, and this is the peculiar fact about it, it is making tremendous inroads into the Chinese mind."

We stayed on that subject for quite some time. Our dinner had evolved into a little discussion meeting, with one basic difference from those in Red China. We did not have to reach a foregone conclusion by voluntary agreement. The three Chinese agreed that the Communist hierarchy was not so uninformed or naïve as to believe that its whole propaganda was being widely absorbed. The Party well knew that the Chinese people had been reared in a hard school that taught them to read between the lines and to suspect a selfish, biased motive in what they are told. But the Party knew, too, that through constant reiteration, even those expressing skepticism would absorb part of the propaganda, and through additional repetition this part would be constantly increased.

The Communist hierarchy knows, as did Lincoln, that you can fool all the people only some of the time. But in the calculations of power politics, if people can be fooled just long enough for the Party to put its objective across, that is sufficient. No more is necessary.

ALONG THE TRAIL

THE PHRASE "TO TURN OVER" APPEARS FREQUENTLY IN Chinese Communist literature. Originally, it was a colloquialism based on an old Chinese proverb that reads, "Some day, even the tiles on the roofs of the houses will have a chance to turn themselves over." The old meaning was that no matter how difficult one's life, there was always the chance to prosper in the future.

The Communists took over the phrase and adapted it to their uses. The hopeful allusion to future prosperity gave the Communist propagandist the opportunity to convey the impression that material prosperity would follow a political "turning over"—to their side. The Communists were gloating over the number of Chinese who were turning over.

I was curious about the procedure and made some inquiries. I found out that there was quite a technique to it. Take the case of Bob Ching, a pilot in the Nationalist Air Force who voluntarily went over to the Communists.

The Communist radio boasted about his turning over. He was sent out to attack his former colleagues, which they expected him to do, just as voluntarily. Perhaps he later went into Manchuria and Korea to tackle the American pilots who taught him to fly and were once his buddies.

Anyway, how did this fundamental change in his point of view come about? Bob was raised in an American environment. He seemed to get along well with Americans. How could he have switched to a cause which was proclaiming that the United States government was the enemy of progressive peoples everywhere, and that the masses everywhere in Asia would rise up and smite it to earth?

There are many Bob Chings in China, in many walks of life, and many of them have probably already met the American forces on the ground or in the air. Bob has many counterparts elsewhere in Asia. He was a soldier for whom the war was already hot while we were still considering it cold. Therefore, an understanding of him is important.

I found out about him on a journey in Taiwan, where I was visiting the Kan Shan training center in the south of that island. Here the instructors, who have plenty of World War II combat experience, speak an American English, and here it was that I met John Lu, Bob's former buddy, who told me the details.

"Yes, Bob's action was voluntary," Lu said. "That is, the Communists never put any direct pressure on him. They sent him no propaganda, wrote him no letters. His mother used to write him regularly, and her mail to him was never censored."

The mother lived in Hopei Province, in which Peiping is situated. Lu remembered the puzzled look with which Bob showed him a letter from her about a year before. Some Red official in her village had visited her. He had been very friendly and had asked her how her son was getting on in the Nationalist Air Force. This was her first information that the Reds had learned his whereabouts.

"Why don't you write him and suggest that he come home?" the Communist official remarked sociably. "We would gladly welcome him into the people's fighting forces."

Another letter soon afterwards told of another sociable visit from the same official. He had inquired about Bob again and had mentioned that everyone was contributing to the people's government according to his means and according to his indebtedness to it. With a son making the task of the people's government heavier, the old mother would want to contribute 120 catties of rice, wouldn't she? Each catty is one and a third pounds. The family had to borrow money to pay the levy.

There were other visits, each just as sociable, and each duly reported by the mother without comment. A younger brother had been recruited into the Red Army.

"Surely he would want to compensate for his brother's anti-progressive activities," the family had been told. The father, an illiterate but hard-working peasant, was taken to jail on a charge which Lu forgot, but which he remembered was trivial.

Bob had known of other men in a similar plight. He had known of cases where such reactionary stubbornness as his own had led to the recruitment of a sister, and he knew what this meant. He knew that gradually the entire family would be scattered and its possessions confiscated. There was never any direct pressure on the man involved, just the casual remark that the return of the wayward one would bring a halt to all of the family's woes.

Bob's mother had abstained in her early letters from making any suggestions to her son. Later letters clearly indicated the hopelessness of her plight, unless he would return. Finally, she urged him to return. The Communists promised that he would be given such preferred treatment! His patriotism would be so highly regarded!

Lu did not sound resentful when he told of the morning that Bob disappeared, taking his airplane along to "prove his sincerity." Lu was not resentful because he thought of his own family in Chekiang Province, and if the Communists found out its whereabouts, he would be put under the same pressure.

Lu was realistic. "We have heard from colleagues who went over," he told me. "The fancy Communist promises are as false as the lack of pressure. Those who go over aren't trusted, but are regarded almost as enemy prisoners, only without the customary obligations toward prisoners of war."

Many of the Nationalist fliers, while still on the mainland, had received direct appeals to turn over. These were usually form letters in which the patriotism theme was stressed. A similar letter would be sent to an entire group, obviously for the morale-disintegrating effect it had on the individuals. Who was disclosing their identities? Was it someone among them? These questions helped arouse a jittery feeling, which the Communists exploited.

In my visit to the Kan Shan training grounds, I could tell the aviators who had relatives on the mainland from those whose kinfolk were with them on Taiwan or were in Hong Kong, Southeast Asia—anywhere except under the Reds. The fliers who did not want to mention their names, who showed terror of their identities being disclosed, were those with loved ones where the people's government could lay a hand on them. It was torture by remote control. Or was it merely indoctrination by remote control? Actually, the Communists had achieved a strategy which combined, and still does, both.

"Why are you staying here at all?" I asked one aviator, who had a scar on his forehead from a Japanese bullet. "Life is tough here," I added. "The Russians have given the Communists jet planes. What makes you stay?"

Although this airman spoke English quite well, he was hesitant in his reply, much as almost any American would be if asked a question with such emotional overtones. He lapsed into Chinese-English, betraying his depth of feeling. "I like free," he said, repeating, "I like free. I not want Communist control. Communist control no good."

Then, on surer ground, he added, "I am a soldier. I am patriotic Chinese. I like China be free."

I had no time to ask him if he had a family on the mainland.

I came across personal evidence of this sort of pressure on

numerous occasions, particularly in Hong Kong, which I was using as a headquarters because of its excellent communications facilities with the rest of the world. A stocky, well-built Chinese named Fred Wang was working for one of the shipping firms, and I made his acquaintance. Fred had been with the Chinese Air Force during World War II. His father had died, but his mother was still alive. He no longer had any connections with the Chinese Air Force, and the firm for which he worked shipped merchandise into Red China, so there was no question of his being involved in anything contrary to the interests of the Communists. Indeed, he was at first quite sympathetic to the Communists.

We had tea one afternoon in a small Chinese restaurant on the side street where he worked. I happened to mention the case of Bob Ching. Had he known him?

No, he hadn't known him.

Had he known, from his personal experience, any similar cases?

Well, yes, he had heard of such things happening. As a matter of fact . . .

That was how he began to confide in me regarding his mother. Nothing serious had happened yet. The Communist authorities had only visited her, in Hankow, and suggested that her son might want to come back to China. They asked her to tell him that there was a good job waiting for him in the Chinese People's Air Force.

"My mother suggested that they get in touch with me directly," Wang said. "They told her they preferred she do it. She couldn't understand why."

"What are you going to do?"

"I've got a job here, why should I return?"

He indicated then that, although he was not opposing the Communists (he hoped they could bring the full rice bowl and contentment that they had promised to the masses), he was no Communist himself. He didn't want to become one unless he was convinced that theirs was the best way for his country. His demands were simple. All he wanted was that the constant warfare that plagued China since 1911 cease, and that his country be independent.

In the months that followed, he became more and more worried over his mother, more and more despondent over conditions in China generally, more and more disillusioned with the Reds. His mother had been supporting herself on a little property she owned. One day the sociable Communist visitor had informed her that her tax rate had been raised— raised so much that she had to sell half her property just to pay it.

"If your son had come home, this probably could have been avoided," he told her sympathetically. "Why don't you write and ask him to come? He can be a real protection to you." The Communist agent was oh so sorry for her.

Fred by now knew enough not to come home. His mother, explaining her plight plainly, never asked him to return. She was in a stronger position than Bob Ching's mother because she was the only one in the family still under Red jurisdiction.

"Our property will be able to pay the increased taxes and support my mother for only a short time more," Fred told me some months ago. "I shudder to think what will happen if they raise the rates again." If he could only get her out, he said he would not care about the property. But she wasn't being given an exit permit.

The last time I saw him he was undergoing a real mental struggle. The Communists were losing patience. They were not giving people so much time any more to wash their brains. Time was running short. They were having recourse more and more to the swifter purge method.

The scale of executions was becoming larger and larger since the promulgation of a draconian measure called "penalties for the counterrevolutionaries." Charges against counter-revolutionaries were becoming vaguer and vaguer. The Communists were no longer wasting time thinking up de-tailed charges against people with unwashed brains, or telling them much about their crimes, except that they were counterrevolutionary, before handing them over to the execution squads.

More and more, the Communists were concentrating on the school population—those not yet filled with imperialist poisons, whose brains could be washed with the correct ideology while still comparatively fresh.

There was evidence that the Communists, in the spring of 1951, had become convinced that there was no hope of effectively converting pronounced anti-Communists by lectures to reform their minds. There was every indication that the Communists had by then decided that the exigencies of war made it more convenient simply to cut off all heads still needing reform.

Brain-washing was for youths and the innocent; brain-changing was a secret police function, unnecessary in the present stage, and requiring techniques that the Chinese Communists had not yet learned from their Soviet Russian masters.

The madness was turning to rage.

HALLELUJAH!

The principal reason I went to Portuguese Macao for ten days in the fall of 1950 was to relax, to get away from cold wars and hot wars, political intrigues, and the struggle of minds. I was confident that there, of all places in Asia, I could assume the role of tourist. This little sixteenth century colony, very Catholic and very Confucian, across the wide Pearl River mouth from Hong Kong, fascinated and dazzled me. It has somber, Old World chaperones; gold shops and Filipino orchestras; refugee schools and a tolerance for non-Catholics; tinsel sing-song girls and sordid gaming halls; a quiet, wide Bund and the world's cleanest market, together with opium dens and smugglers; a composer-racketeer-philanthropist public enemy and public benefactor; a gold-braided, handsome governor; priests and nuns; and somehow or other, belonging in this list, postage stamps without mucilage. Tying all this together is the spirit of laissez faire as it existed before the monopolists got hold of it.

My schedule sent me to Macao for the last week in September and the first few days in October. The first anniversary of the establishment of the Chinese Communist capital at Peiping was October 1, but I couldn't see why this should interfere with my wandering through the twisting, cobbled streets of the hilly town, or my reading up on the early history of the West's relations with the East, when opium was just a commodity and American clipper ships outraced those of all other nations on the surface of the water instead of in the air.

I felt that Portugal, with its rightist regime, would see through any propaganda artifices that the Communists might try to put across. I didn't expect that it would adopt such a laissez-faire attitude toward them that the Reds could make this place a loophole as big as a cathedral window nor to find myself, for a day, transported in environment into Red China itself. Yet this is what the Chinese Communists maneuvered, not merely for myself, but for the whole Macao population.

Some days before October 1, I noticed construction gangs carting tremendous piles of bamboo poles and carved wooden beams to the most centrally located square in town, alongside the bombastic statue of the tragic, heroic Vincent Nicolau de Mesquita. The beams were extravagantly and minutely carved and richly painted in the traditional Chinese classical manner, with multitudinous red dragons intertwining their massive jaws and claws in every direction.

Scores of workmen immediately assumed the roles of monkeys and began climbing up the high bamboo poles even before they had finished tying them together, until a framework was built as high as a seven-story building. The beams were hoisted into place, and multicolored electric lights were strung all over the dazzling pailou. At the very top was strung a row of Chinese Communist red flags.

Arches of similar gaudy character, only smaller, were erected at important intersections in other parts of the city, and red flags hung on top of these. Shops on every street seemed to compete in the display of enormous portraits of the effeminate-cheeked Mao Tse-tung, the Prussian-trained Gen. Chu Teh, and the entire Chinese Communist hierarchy. Giant, illuminated portraits of the Red leaders were fastened above store fronts, and paper red flags and souvenir newspapers printed in red ink were free for the taking everywhere.

I went to the city officials and asked what was taking place. They had a good laugh. "The Chinese Chamber of Commerce asked to be allowed to observe the anniversary," they explained. "They said they were dependent on Red China for their business, and couldn't very well ignore the day. They said they'd like permission to have a little outdoor celebration, nothing much, no speeches or demonstrations or anything of that sort. That enormous pailou you saw goes up on the same spot every Chinese holiday season. You'll see, it'll probably be left standing there until October 10, the Double Tenth anniversary that the Chinese Nationalists celebrate."

This sudden appreciation of Communism by the Chinese merchants of Macao, as capitalist a coterie of businessmen as ever sold a chunk of gold bullion or a crate of penicillin, appeared out of character. Had the merchants, the whole population, in fact, gone Communist? A look at the streets, decorated for a festival season, certainly indicated so. A three-day holiday had been proclaimed by the Chinese, who numbered all except a few thousand of the city's quarter million population.

I first inquired about the role of the Chinese Chamber of Commerce. No, nobody I could learn about there had any affection for anything Communist except the good American dollars that Red China paid for what it wanted. The whole idea of their sponsoring the anniversary celebrations was one member's—a rather important member, because everybody knew he was the unofficial ambassador of the Chinese Communist government in Macao. He made frequent trips to Canton and Peiping and always returned with some new slick trick up his sleeve. Anybody in Macao who did business in Red China depended on his good favor and a couple of others ranking with him. This meant the entire commercial community, and it meant, too, the schools, for they were dependent on Red China's recognition of the graduation certificates given the Chinese in Macao.

There was no difficulty, therefore, in persuading the Chamber of Commerce to agree officially to sponsor the observances and to persuade its members to contribute a little of their profits to cover the expenses. So far as the plain people were concerned, a day off was a day off. The usual able Party members were on hand, very willing to take the troublesome details off the hands of the businessmen and to handle the programming and decorations. There was uninterrupted intercourse between Macao and Red China, separated only by a small arch called the Barrier Gate, and any additional guidance needed was easily obtainable. Only the white man needed a passport to enter or leave Macao.

Early on the morning of October 1, the cacaphony of firecrackers lured me toward Leal Senado, where the main pailou stood. Tons of firecrackers were blossoming forth in the form of dragons, lanterns, and bells. Macao has an efficient bus system, which covers all of the main arteries. Each bus was decorated with a couple of red flags in front, and on the back was hung a five-foot-square poster. There was a whole series of different caricatures on these. One set had for its theme the great industrial and agricultural advances that were being attributed to the new China, and another set glorified the Herculean strength of the Chinese Red Army, which was shown thrusting fiery swords into the snarling, swollen heads of snakes and demons, which represented unspecified but well understood domestic and foreign enemies of the regime. The two sides of a big auto truck that circulated in all sections of the city were plastered with posters advertising the Communist peace petition, showing soldiers and sailors and chubby-cheeked factory and farm workers signing together. The usual martial tone was given these crude sketches. As everywhere, through well-understood clichés and double-talk, the Communists were not allowing anyone to forget for a moment whom they regarded as the true enemy—the United States.

The radio was blaring forth from windows and shops, bringing to the people of Macao the intonations and words spoken in Peiping and Canton and wherever Red China was holding similar observances. No words were minced in these speeches. Except where families sat in the open to watch the festivities, all store fronts were boarded up. Everybody was out on the streets.

A young man whose name I had been given as a pro-Nationalist was dressed up in his holiday best, enjoying the glamour and relaxation from bookkeeping. He wasn't going to miss the fun, and anyway, why should he make a burden out of something he couldn't avoid? The orders for the celebration had been passed down by the Chamber of Commerce to its members, and each employer had passed the word to his workers that they were being given three days to celebrate, and by God, they better celebrate! Nobody wanted his company to get a bad name with the Reds.

Communist flags were flying high on schools. Able Party members had visited each school, and had informed it of its role in the festivities. Each school was given a quota of teachers and students which it was expected to send voluntarily to a mass meeting at the Apollo Theater. The principals passed the word to their faculty-student committees, telling them that voluntary participation was required, and requested the students and faculty, in the usual democratic discussion manner, to determine for themselves who would represent them. The only demand which the principal made was, for heaven's sake, to make sure that the able Party members at the theater checked off the school's name as participating.

Auto caravans raced through the streets, with lanterns and red flags hanging from their windows, tooting their horns and shrieking their sirens. Only the third or fourth time around did I notice that they weren't auto caravans but a single string of cars that kept along the same route all the time, giving the impression that every automobile in the town was participating.

The intermittent firecrackers, the festival crowds, the blaring automobiles and gaudily-postered buses, and the wonderful weather combined to give the affair a rare prestige. People couldn't help feeling that they were participating in something memorable and wonderful, which made them want to have a share in it.

Outside the Apollo were loudspeakers, and loudspeakers were strung up and down the block and onto the enormous pailou across the way. I joined the crowd entering the wide Apollo lobby, and by dint of long, patient squeezing and twisting, finally found myself inside the densely packed movie house.

I was enjoying this. I was enjoying the glamour and the color and the sound and the happy faces. I thought of what Harry Chang had told me, and I was able to appreciate a little more of what this frustrated young man had gone through.

I pressed myself against the side wall down front, took out my little notebook and, as inconspicuously as possible, recorded what I saw and felt. I was the only foreigner present. All the rest were Chinese.

My first reaction was that I was attending a church service. After all, it was Sunday morning. And here, on the stage, was very much what I had been accustomed to see in almost any Protestant church back in America. A youth choir was singing, the girls wearing long, white gowns, and the boys dressed in light slacks and white shirts. A young man with a soulful tenor sang solos. Except for two enormous portraits of Mao Tse-tung in color and Stalin in black and white, and Communist slogans on white streamers strung across the hallway, there was nothing in the environment that would seem unnatural to any bourgeois merchant or paunchy capitalist. Respectability simply oozed.

The audience was predominantly young, in their teens, twenties, and early thirties, with a fair sprinkling of real youngsters, and quite a few of their elders. There were about as many women as men, and some parents carried babies. The kids milled in and out, squeezing between legs and hips. The audience stood up to join in some of the songs, as in any congregation. The soloist was brought back to sing again by the fervor of the applause. He invited the audience to join the chorus, which it did; in this environment it would have seemed distinctly crude not to do so.

Fireworks, exploding outside, created a closer bond between those in the theater and the throngs gathered around the loudspeakers. The smell of gunpowder teased the nostrils of those within. A master of ceremonies—I was almost going to call him minister—was forced to interrupt what he was saying when a particularly long display of fireworks reached a crescendo outside. The walls cut off much of the usual cacaphony and harshness of fireworks, leaving only a distantly tantalizing sound and the pleasant smell. The theater was hushed except for this, and then loud applause broke out. The crowds outside and the audience inside were brought together in a mystic experience which seemed to join them to the peoples of Red China and to the entire Soviet bloc. While the applause was still heard, the tenor sang out a triumphant, martial song.

How could anyone, even if he had come because he knew that he had to, and not because he wanted to, have failed to be impressed by the curious sense of being caught, of participation in a momentous event? Would the young people in this audience ever forget it, and would it not color their future attitude sympathetically toward that which gave them this experience of personal elevation? This, after all, is what a church service tries to accomplish. And would they not resent and close their eyes to anybody or any philosophy that disillusioned them, and so cheapened the beauty of this morning in their spiritual lives? That this could be the medium by which dialectical materialism was being popularized seemed inconceivable. Surely there was a faith attached to it. Only in *The Question of Thought* did I find that faith proclaimed and interpreted in Communist language.

Brass cymbals heralded the entry of a modern ballet. A male dancer wearing a high white hat, a bright cassock with a red star on it, and high red boots strode onto the stage with leaping, defiant steps, and was joined by a second and a third in similar imaginative costume. Their modern dancing portrayed boatmen, soldiers, farmers—evidently the evolution of a people's revolution. Two girls, wearing purple skirts and red slashes, joined the ballet, and their Slavic steps were evidently borrowed from Soviet folk dances. The cymbals maintained an off-stage effect that brought me back many years to the Broadway performance of Eugene O'Neill's *The Emperor Jones,* with its backstage tom-tom that never ceased. The faces of the dancers were heavily made up, with their eyes darkened, which made them look like masks.

The audience was led in the singing of stirring songs during intermission. The shrill voices of the youngsters showed how much they enjoyed it all. A brassy saxophone and a big drum helped the singing. Every moment was occupied; something to stir the emotions took place every second. The theater was so packed that people were too uncomfortable not to pay attention. A Western type of orchestra, with violin, guitar, and flutes, was followed by a trio—a regular barber-shop trio—which gave the audience a chance to relax and laugh. The crowd joined with the tenor, and then, for the grand climax, the choir returned to sing *Onward Christian Soldiers* —only, as in the rest of the program, the words were insurrectionary and Communistic.

The program was skillfully arranged in order that the audience could leave at twelve-thirty, on the dot. They slowly filed out, with the same sense of bourgeois security that had permeated the meeting, to find the fireworks still going on and to join the festive street crowds. Many strolled down the avenue to the tallest building in the city, the Central Hotel, where half of the floors are gambling halls, one is reserved for private dining rooms, and the rest are allotted to ordinary hotel rooms. Even this establishment had an enormous floral display over its entrance, with blossoms forming the flag of Red China, a big star and four smaller stars, all in flowers.

On the afternoon of October 2, the construction crews came back and began hoisting down the beams and untying the bamboo scaffolding of the big pailou. The Double Tenth, with its connotation of resistance against subservience to any foreign country, passed almost unnoticed. This, too, was part of the program.

MALAYAN JOURNEY

When I went into the Malayan interior to find out how the civil war was going on in this country, I thought I had left the Chinese scene pretty well behind and I surely didn't expect to run into democratic discussion groups and brainwashing. There, on the field of battle, so far off the beaten track, I assumed that whatever indoctrination had been deemed necessary had already been completed. Anyway, I assumed that the Malayans did things differently. How wrong I was on all scores!

Right off, it became evident that the fighting had nothing to do with Malaya except as one flank in a Chinese Communist, All-Asia war. Right off, too, it became evident that there were comparatively few persons of Malayan blood in the insurrection—almost all of them were of Chinese blood and Chinese-speaking. A large fraction had been born in China, and most of the others were first generation Malayans of Chinese extraction. They did not consider themselves Malayans, but Chinese—racially, nationally, and in every way. I gained a healthy respect right then and there for the enormous task facing the British; the more alert among the Malayans; and the very, very few persons of Chinese or Indian blood on that peninsula who were trying to forge a Malayan nation, either wholly independent or as part of the British Commonwealth.

What had appeared as a civil war was actually an invasion, every bit as much of an aggression as the Chinese Communist participation in the fighting in Korea. Indeed, many of the leaders of the guerrilla warfare in Malaya had been imported into that country from China by the British and the Americans during World War II. Those thus brought in were practically all adherents of Mao Tse-tung. The idea was that these Chinese would help the guerrilla warfare against the Japanese. Once in, they busily underwent whatever training they could get from the West, took whatever supplies were given them by the British or Americans, and exerted their main energies to democratic group discussions in the jungles and to fighting other Chinese who refused to join up with them under the Red flag, promptly dubbing them bandits.

Here was my chance to investigate brain-washing from a different slant—the extent to which it operates on the battlefield, and the degree to which it wasn't just a phenomenon of the Chinese mainland, but part of the Chinese Communist pattern wherever it was able to extend its influence.

The Chinese add up to more than half the population of Malaya, including Singapore, and constitute an immensely important segment of the population of all Southeast Asian countries and Indonesia. Where these population figures include persons born in those countries of Chinese parents, or where the culture is Chinese, as in northern Indochina, these totals become even more significant. They put the phrase "China's national racial revolution," which I frequently came across in Red China's indoctrination textbooks, into a new perspective.

The role of Red China in such distant areas as Malaya, separated from China by other countries, was of extraordinary importance in determining the extent to which a political ideology was being utilized for what was essentially Chinese Communist imperialism. The suspicion with which the peoples of these other Asiatic countries look upon Communism in general, and Chinese Communism in particular, becomes understandable. Even their low standard of living and their inadequate education, which normally would have softened up these masses for the Red ideology, have had little effect. Even in the Philippines, the role occupied by Chinese in the Huk insurrectionary movement is of decisive importance.

In order to reach Malaya's guerrilla areas, I decided to take a train rather than go by the swifter but less informative airplane. My first destination, after arriving at Singapore, was Kuala Lumpur, the very neat capital of the Malayan Federation. A description of my train trip might be enlightening from the viewpoint of giving a feeling of the country.

I visited Col. Colin Tod, the British army PRO (that means Public Relations Officer; the American Army calls it PIO—Public Information Officer—because soldiers too frequently mistook the premises for prophylactic stations) to make arrangements for my travels. He told me that most correspondents went by air, but that there also was a train, the day train.

"Oh, so the guerrillas have stopped the night train," I remarked.

"Well, not entirely," he said. "We do run a train each night, but civilians aren't allowed on it. Only the military."

"What about newspapermen?" I asked. "They're neither fish nor fowl."

"All right, if you insist," he answered. "You might find it interesting."

So that was how I got on the night train. The British army's top public relations man phoned the RTO (Railway Transportation Officer), and in due course I was given a little note on Malayan Railway stationery. "The holder, Mr. Hunter, has, by arrangement with the Military Authorities, permission to travel by Train No. 100 Up, with 1st Class civilian ticket."

The note arrived while I was in my hotel, going over the

local newspapers of the past few days. Several items caught my eye.

Kuala Lumpur—a derailment in Kluang yesterday forced cancellation of the through day mail from here to Singapore today.

Today's train ran as far as Gemas and returned while the train from Singapore went up to Kluang. There were no trains between Gemas and Singapore today.

The second item read:

A train guard was found unconscious when the down goods train from Kuala Lumpur arrived at Gemas, in Jahore, yesterday evening. He had been shot in the knee.

Bullet holes were found in the guard's van. The crew did not hear any firing.

There was also a third item—they read like local social notes—which follows:

Johore Bahru—Three British Other Ranks [this meant enlisted men] in the Kuala Lumpur-bound mail train from Singapore were wounded, one of them seriously, as a result of shooting by bandits tonight.

The train, which carried a full complement of army personnel, faced bandit action at the 49th mile between Yulai and Sedenak. It left with mail for Kuala Lumpur at 8:31 P.M. from Johore Bahru. The wounded B.O.R.'s have been taken to Kluang Hospital.

No wonder, when I asked for my bill at the hotel desk, eyebrows were raised when I said I was going "by train—tonight."

Even the military, I noticed, when I appeared at the ticket office to purchase my seat, have to get permission to take the night train. The third-class compartments—just seats, like an ordinary American coach, minus the upholstery—were filled by native troops. These included some of the Malays, wearing new black shoes and "RAF Regiment" patches on their shoulders, who had come down from Hong Kong with me on the RAF's *Dakota*—the drayhorse of the Asian skies—in an all-day flight.

White troops occupied the second-class coaches, which had cots lengthwise down both sides. My first-class car had compartments and upholstered seats that could be converted into berths. I put my musette bag and bundle of food on one of the two teakwood beds in my compartment and felt the mattress. Hard, the way physical-culture experts say it should be. Very English.

A couple of white soldiers sweated under the load of boxes of Gurkha rations, which they deposited in a first-class compartment adjoining mine. The English love the Gurkhas, and the Gurkhas love jungle fighting. They are of Mongoloid stock—squat, husky chaps from Nepal, who seem to think that a rifle is something to make a noise with before you get down to the real business of fighting with a curved, clean, white, razor-sharp blade. "We make sure the Gurkhas get their rations," one English soldier explained. There apparently had been some looting on previous trips. I noticed that signs on the train were in four languages—English, Chinese, Malayan and Indian—a clue to complications in this part of the world.

Beside the food boxes, the compartment was occupied by Capt. Stanley William Frederick Francis of the Royal Artillery—Stan for short. His job, besides protecting the Gurkha rations, was to bring the train safely to its destination. He got such duty about once each month. He was a lean, athletic man, amiable and modest. I had to question him persistently to discover that he had been captured in Singapore by the Japanese and transferred to a prison camp on Taiwan, where he was put in charge of a few hundred British and an equal number of American POWs. He was released in time to be parachuted into Greece for the postwar guerrilla fighting there, and was now attached to a training camp for guerrilla fighting at a place with the fantastic name of Nee Soon, deep in the jungle. This was where advance detachments of new British forces were given a brief spell of training in jungle mountain warfare in order that they could, on arrival of the remainder of the regiments from England, show them what they would be up against from Chinese underground forces.

I had with me a couple of bottles of beer, two bottles of pop, an egg sandwich, four small, green yet ripe bananas, and had added two bars of chocolate and an orange that I had bought at the station. The buffet car had been dispensed with along with the civilian passengers.

I stood on the platform chatting with Stan before the train left at seven in the evening. The first five cars were crash cars, closed freight coaches supposed to take the brunt of shooting and wrecking.

"Don't the guerrillas have enough sense to hold their fire until the passenger coaches come up?" I asked, not wholly without self-interest, for the passenger coaches were all made of wood, and I remembered the newspaper items I had read a few hours before.

"No," he replied. "They don't use their heads. They just hit and run. They run as soon as they hear a shot by us. If they used their heads, or stuck for a fight, there wouldn't be one of us alive. After all, the jungle is perfect cover. You can't tell where anyone is hiding unless you see where he's shooting from or stumble over him."

A flatcar with an armored car tied on top brought up the end of the train. Our locomotive was preceded by a small pilot train that kept about five minutes ahead. Its job was to feel out the road, so that if there were any explosives attached to the rails, or if the track had been torn up, it and not the regular train would take the punishment.

An English police officer strolled up. "He's in charge of the radio," I was informed, evidence of a coordination between the military and civilian services that was more visible in the field than in the cities. United States naval radio equipment had been installed in the boxcar, near the end. The radio enabled the train to keep in constant touch with the situation all along the line from Singapore to Kuala Lumpur. There were military guards, too, stationed on the pilot car ahead and at the front and end cars of our train. They were equipped with walkie-talkies.

"Often," I was told, "a bullet will smack against one end of the train, and no one at the other end will hear it." (Yes, I knew that; one of the newspaper items had mentioned it.) Our train crawled in the dusk across the fifteen-mile Singapore Island and then over the wide causeway bridge to the Malay Federation, which is a curious set-up of nine Malay states and two British settlements, Penang and Malacca. The British scrupulously retained a civilian, peacetime administration over all of it in spite of the war. They weren't recognizing any war—it was officially an "emergency"—and they were then still insisting on recognizing Red China, although Red China assiduously paid no heed to the proferred hand of friendship. The military, in accordance with British tradition, was subordinate to the civilian regime.

When we stopped at Johore Bahru, on the Federation side of the causeway, Stan excused himself. "I have to see about loading the dogs," he said. "What dogs?" I asked. "If the train is shot at," he replied, "we stop just long enough to unload the dogs and a detachment of Gurkhas, and off the train goes. The orders are for us now not to stop any longer than that. It's a new tactic."

Sure enough, I heard barking, and a pack of hounds climbed into a coach reserved for them.

Plaintive tunes of Malayan opera floated across the evening air from a nearby pagoda where the townsfolk had gathered to imagine themselves in another, better world. During our twenty-minute stop, the stationmaster, an Indian, made his routine report to the captain. This conversation was discussed by Stan and the radio operator in my compartment a few minutes later, when we pulled out.

"We won't get in until noon now, instead of at dawn," said Stan. The locomotive operator was going to crawl all the way and not proceed past any point until sure of it. "The stationmaster told us to expect trouble at Sendai, about an hour away," Stan added.

"What trouble?" asked the radio man.

"That's all he told me. Maybe an ambush."

"Why didn't he tell you any more, and why didn't he tell the engineer himself?" I asked.

"He didn't want to be seen saying any more than a few words to me, and if he had spoken to the engineer, he might have been noticed, reported, and shot. He's easy game, he and his wife and children, for a guerrilla in the tall bush around the station."

Stan alerted the guards, Gurkhas, the "RAF Regiment," and the British troops. "Everyone, instead of relaxing or sleeping, will now have to be alert until about an hour out of Sendai at least," he said.

The train ordinarily is blacked out, except for a small light concealed behind the black curtains. I turned out my light and looked out of the window. The sight was eerie. A moon thrust glistening streaks here and there through a dense wall of foliage. The day before, I had looked down upon this land from an airplane. It was as if I were an ant, held a few inches aloft over a big head of broccoli. The jungle growth was as thick as that. Now I stared at it from a wee trail cut through it for the rail line. I could understand how a few thousand desperadoes could keep the entire country in a state of emergency.

The guerrillas had machine guns, and, when they ambushed a train, fired a line of shots across a coach. I noted that the sleeping compartments would be just about in a line with a Bren gun held by a man outside. I struck the wall of my compartment with my knuckles. Yes, thicker at least than a match box. Had I been wise in making this trip?

I picked up my portable typewriter and stood it on my cot between the window and my chest. I picked up my musette bag, thick with camera and extra clothing, and laid it between the window and my head. The typewriter and camera were expendable; I, a little less so. Thus, reinforced as much as possible, I went to sleep. It doesn't take long for a situation that you can't possibly change to create a fatalistic attitude. I woke up at eight in the morning wonderfully refreshed by the miracle of sleep.

The native train attendant with the skullcap, evidently a Moslem—I had also noticed an item in the paper that said they didn't like to be called Mohammedans—brought me a mug of strong tea that he had made himself. The civilian was getting special service. I shaved, then looked out of the window.

Jungle, rubber plantations, tapioca, native villages, jungle, rubber plantations, tapioca, native villages, jungle . . . jungle . . . jungle. . . . Sometimes the mountains seemed quite near. Sometimes our train was set deep in the embankment. Always it was a sitting duck.

The houses were all on stilts—low, bungalow-style structures with thatched roofs of *attap*, a palm stuff. The children were invariably dressed in light clothing, invariably clean. The grown-ups were in pajamas, sarongs, or slacks, the accepted outdoor attire in Malaya. The contrast with China, and with everywhere else I had been in Asia, was startling. The houses in these villages were spaced airily apart, and the standard of living, while low by American standards, was much higher than what I had seen in Asia generally.

We arrived at Kuala Lumpur a little before one in the afternoon. I bought a copy of the *Malay Mail*, the only English-language paper published in the town. An item on page seven attracted my attention. The headline read: "Train Derailed in Selangor." Kuala Lumpur is in the state of Selangor. Here is what it said:

The pilot train preceding the night mail from Kuala Lumpur to Penang last night was derailed due to terrorist action in the Tanjong Malim area in north Selangor. Normal running is expected to be resumed today.

There had been trouble, but it was on the 250-mile stretch north of Kuala Lumpur, not south of it.

YOUNG MAN IN MANACLES

The young man had iron manacles around his wrists. He was lean and wiry and wore a tattered shirt and ragged, khaki shorts. His two jungle companions had been slain, and he had been captured when surprised by a small British patrol that had torn a leaf out of the guerrillas' book of tactics. The three of them had been ambushed on a trail leading to their jungle base, not far from the camp where I was now staying.

There was no question about what was going to happen to this young man. He was going to hang. There would be a trial, of course, under due process of law as amended by the emergency regulations, and then he would die. Emergency, as already noted, was the tactful parlor word used by the British when they meant the war being waged against them in Malaya, a particularly dirty war.

The young man had already been some years in the jungle, and reports on him had previously been brought to British intelligence. He looked like such a nice fellow; looking at him, a person's initial reaction was to sympathize and to help. He sat quietly, his thoughts buried behind dark eyes, like a schoolboy caught playing with forbidden toys.

I would have known what those toys were, even if I hadn't just read about a chap who looked the same in the newspaper that I had brought with me from Penang. This comrade had taken a bus ride through the outskirts of that luscious island. He had occupied the seat directly behind the driver. After the bus had proceeded a few hundred yards, he had whipped out a pistol and fired point-blank at the nape of the driver's neck. That it had to be this particular driver was just too bad; the orders were to disrupt bus service.

The chap in front of me looked very much, too, like the young man who had given me the interview about the course he had taken at the North China People's Revolutionary University. I imagined him, too, fitting well into a role in *The Question of Thought*.

He was twenty-four years old and already a veteran of jungle warfare. He had joined the guerrillas in 1947, when he was twenty. He must have had a lot of experience in those last three years. Of Chinese extraction, born in a Chinese village in Malaya, where he had spent all his life, he said that he was being used in liaison work between his camp and nearby villages.

He covered a regular beat, collecting "taxes" that were arbitrarily set by the guerrillas under the pretense of operating as a government, and receiving "contributions" of foodstuffs and other supplies needed by the insurgents. He might have been a salesman under normal conditions.

There was an item in the same paper about a mission fulfilled by still another comrade. This had taken place near Ipoh, in the world's most extensive tin-mining area, where I had spent a recent week. An American movie, *The Adventures of Marco Polo,* was being shown at a town called Sungei Siput. A black object was rolled through a wooden railing in the theater, and when the dust cleared, fourteen men, women, and children were sprawled in blood. Four of the children died within the next few hours. One was a Chinese girl of seven, another was a Chinese boy of thirteen, and there were two Indian boys, twelve and sixteen. No Europeans were among the injured. The terrorist who threw the hand grenade was chased into a Chinese squatter area, where he escaped.

This wasn't an unusual day's score. There wasn't much that editors back home considered news in it—a few killed yesterday, a few killed today, some to be killed tomorrow undoubtedly, but never enough to warrant more than a couple of paragraphs every once in a while when filler was needed. This was all in the day's work for that clean-cut chap sitting in front of me and for his fellow students not far from me, in the mountains, screened by thick forest and a morass of twisted bush and mangrove.

How did they get that way? Surely a youth like this, who was stealing a glance at me from the side of his deep, black eyes, did not go out and kill people he never knew without feeling that this was the right thing to do. Who had told him so? Surely he could not be a "bad boy" intrinsically; he must have been taught.

Leaders of guerrilla groups keep diaries and fill notebooks of what they are taught and what they teach, and the British often find them, either on the bodies of the guerrillas they kill or on captives such as this fellow. I asked if I could see some of the diaries that had been taken in this area, up in the north, where the Malayan Federation approaches Thailand (Siam).

I was shown a heap of worn, scribbled notebooks and torn pages over which Chinese translators were working. These were crammed with notes on lectures, wayside killings, and democratic group discussions. The summaries and remarks scribbled in them had one feature in common; they all spoke of these operations as part of an All-Asia war, not just a Malayan fight.

What was apparent, too, was that it was being taken for granted by the jungle forces that this was how the rest of the world regarded it. That these other countries could be so nearsighted as not to understand the scope of the fighting simply didn't penetrate. Yet the British officers and officials with whom I had been chatting during my travels in Singapore and Malaya were all talking as if this were purely a local, Malayan issue—a domestic affair wholly separate from what was taking place in the Philippines, in Indochina, in Korea, and elsewhere in Asia. This wasn't a mistake peculiar to them. The Americans were talking of the "Korea war," and the French were talking of the "Indochina war." This local conception of it just didn't exist among the Communists, which gave them an incalculable strategic advantage right from the start. The Reds were able to plan and operate on the basis of one war, shifting men, equipment, and pressure for reasons of strategy.

The second outstanding fact brought out by my inspection of these diaries was that, while the guerrilla forces were actually fighting the British, and while the United States government was assuming that it was successfully keeping its hands out of the Malayan conflict, Communist teachers never allowed their men to forget that the United States was their main enemy, even though there were no American soldiers in Malaya.

The morale of the Malayan Communist forces was being stimulated by the information given them that they were not a small, isolated group fighting a lonely battle, but part of a powerful, all-Asia army, with a great ally behind them in Soviet Russia, which would not let them down. This was heady wine and was responsible for keeping numerous jungle groups in the fight under the most galling and discouraging conditions.

One notebook told about a discussion in a jungle discussion meeting on the subject, "Controversy and unity among the imperialist countries of the world." Here was how the lecture was summarized:

The imperialist countries, under the guidance of the American imperialists, are endeavoring to escape from their doom by following, together, an imperialist, anti-peoples, and anti-democracy policy. They hope to start another anti-mankind, aggressive war. They are standing firm in their policy against the Soviet Russian-peoples' democracy-communism-national independence movement. They are cruelly oppressing and exploiting the laboring class in their own countries. They are trying ruthlessly to destroy the People's National Liberation Movement of the colonies and semi-colonies. They are unified in this respect, and their basic principle is the same.

This is how it read as translated for me by the Chinese, with the addition of some prepositions and articles, a little grammatical revision, and lots of spelling corrections. The temptation always faces a writer to make such passages read more smoothly by changing the wording to fit our manner of thought. Unfortunately, while doing so improves the English, it often gives a false impression of the thought processes that go into the original writing. The phrase, "the Soviet-Russian-peoples' democracy-Communism-national independence movement" sounds awkward, of course, in English, We would say "war of aggression against mankind," too, rather than "anti-mankind, aggressive war." But the Chinese language is succinct and forcible in this manner, while lending itself to generalities that sound like a scientific approach—like the terminology of dialectical materialism.

On another page in this typical jungle notebook was this: "The imperialist countries, under the leadership of the American imperialists, have been engaged for the past nine years in carrying out activities under the anti-peoples, anti-democracy policy."

One would think that persons so far in the jungle, so far off the beaten track, would not be concerned with world affairs. The whole strategy of their command was based on making them world-minded, as evidenced by the way the world situation was simplified in another jungle notebook, in these words:

Owing to the reactionary, capitalist policy of the imperialists, the world has been divided into two opposing blocs since World War II. One, headed by Soviet Russia, is the democratic and anti-imperialist bloc. The other, headed by the United States, is the imperialist and anti-democratic bloc. These two blocs are carrying on contrary policies. Similar conflict exists on all the major problems of the world, and at present this antithesis is becoming worse. Examples of two such opposing policies are the world peace movement and aggression. This is the most important controversy between Soviet Russia and America, between America and the people's democracies, between American imperialism and the colonial people.

The young man wearing manacles said yes, he had been a Communist Party member. He had been introduced to communism by a fellow student while in his Chinese-language school. There was no effort on his part to conceal the Communist direction of the guerrillas. All units had a political director. When they referred to him, they used a vague term that recalled the able Party members of the North China Peoples Revolutionary University. Here, on the field, they were called headquarters members, because they were sent out by headquarters, and hence possessed special qualifications and authority.

The "headquarters member" (also referred to as headquarters comrade) set the line on the basis of directives received from higher up, whose orders were law, he said. This line was taught in the discussion groups off jungle paths in thickly wooded mountain recesses.

I resumed my study of the diaries and notebooks.

1. Jungle Days and Nights

Crumpled sheets of notepaper and tattered diaries enabled me to penetrate life in guerrilla camps under every conceivable circumstance, took me with the guerrillas on their assault missions, into their most secret Party discussions, and, more than any of this, into their minds and hearts. These captured papers gave me an unprecedented opportunity to accompany not one group, but many, from day to day, through bamboo forests and tapioca plantations, and into concealed crevasses between dense forest in the most impenetrable recesses of the jungle; and to know what they thought, for they wrote much of it down.

A few nights before, in comfort, I had looked out of the window of the massive, comfortable Runnymede Hotel on Penang Island, across the Strait of Malacca from Sumatra. A great storm had burst upon the city. The hotel shook, the wind riotously tore at the window frames. Everything seemed in motion from the storm except one thing—an enormous hardwood tree. I could hardly believe my eyes, for the very branches held rigid; the wood had grown so protectively hard that the storm was unable to budge them. I expected the storm to tear the leaves from the limbs. They barely trembled.

This was a jungle tree, a giant hardwood tree such as the Malayan jungle rears in nature's cataclysmic struggle for survival. Richard Wagner's fabled warfare between the forces that seek light and the forces that thrive in the dark could have been set in the Malayan jungle. The trees thrust far, far up toward the sky in one straight, noble grasp for sunlight, and only then, when they have gone beyond all else that lives on sap or blood, break forth into tremendous balls and tables of foliage and blossom.

Beneath these seekers of light thrive the parasitic growth that fights for darkness, entwining and twisting onto, into, and around everything else that grows, forcing the trees to climb higher, always higher. This is what the Redwood forests of California would be if opposed by a myriad of giant undergrowth. This is the jungle where a curious war was now being fought between human beings.

The diaries that came from the jungle were pathetic, cruel, and at the same time child-like and cunning. One, taken from the body of a guerrilla leader, had this self-criticism, dated only three days before he was fatally shot.

23/1/51: Morning. Held a self-criticism meeting. One of the comrades in my section gave a short self-criticism talk that aroused my feelings very much. I have lots of defects in me, but I have not made any attempt to overcome them. I am therefore unfit to be a warrior. I now determine to overcome my defects.

Among the torn sheets was the draft of a letter that could have been inserted without change into the dialogue of some such propaganda play as *The Question of Thought*. The letter was intended to congratulate guerrilla troops for an apparently successful ambush, which it said was in accord with the tactic of "exterminating the enemy to protect ourselves, and robbing the enemy to reinforce ourselves." This was achieved, the letter pointed out, only by "confidence and unyielding purpose," and in words that Miss Tsao, the diligent Party nun in the play, might well have spoken, declared:

Blessings follow upon confession and reform. The victory you have won is closely related to thought reform. . . .

Some of these blessings so piously expressed were related in a green-covered notebook I picked up next.

17th, 2:30 P.M.: Started the journey. At 5 P.M. stopped for rest in Kampong. At 6 P.M. started to gather information. At 7:55 P.M. we returned to Cheok Choo. Results: killed two running dogs and collected six identity cards. Ah Jin was most scared during the operation, and Khee Seong the best behaved.

Running dogs does not mean Englishmen; running dogs means their own people and is the term the Chinese Communists use in referring to Asians who work in harmony with any foreigners except Soviet Russians. The seizure of identity cards was part of a Communist drive then under way. Their own Asian people again were the sufferers; they had to lose both time and money and go through much inconvenience to obtain new identification papers from the authorities. The Communists sought in this way to upset the administration and to obtain official documents which they could use for their own agents.

This particular diary had much in it of an informative and amusing nature:

July 18: While preparing curry, a row started up between Ah Loong, Feng Kong, and Ah Lip.
25th: Planes were droning above where we rested. At 9:55 P.M. bombs were dropped and light machine guns started firing. This went on until 12:45 A.M. Passed the night in a dilapidated house.
26th: Woke up at 6 A.M. and returned to the jungle.
30th: Distributed 20 pamphlets printed in Malayan. Arrived at kongsi* and asked the workers to buy things for us. The workers invited us to eat with them. After we ate, we crossed the river.
Aug. 15: In the morning there was not enough food to go around.

---

* Kongsi: a Malay meeting place, from the Chinese word for company. "In kongsi" means, colloquially, to be in cahoots.

We ate rice with two spoonfuls of curry water. At 7 P.M. we set out. At 8 P.M. crossed a river while going through a tapioca plantation. Comrade Geok Hwa fell and was hurt. Arrived at 36th milestone at 2 A.M. and had rice broth before we returned at 4:30 A.M.

16th: In the morning the people sent us cooked food which included pork and salted vegetables. At 2 A.M. they again sent rice broth.

19th: Morning. Brought buns for breakfast. Each person got a share of three buns. In the afternoon, brought six watermelons. Comrade Ah San had a bowel movement at the sentry post.

Night, Comrades Teik Heng and Goh Ban returned with $3 in subscriptions.

This reference to subscriptions is a tactful way of referring either to the taxes the Communists impose on the villages, or the contributions collected under pressure.

20th: Took breakfast at 10 A.M. In the afternoon we had rice left over from the morning. We asked the Political Committee comrade if he cared to have some, and he said yes. We were afraid to eat, but he said if you are all hungry, you can prepare coffee. The two comrades, Teik Heng and Goh Ban, acted very annoyingly during the discussions. They were repeatedly warned but without avail. Finally the Political Committee comrade told them that if they did not stop, they would be shot. Only then did they stop.

I would have liked to know what questions they brought up at the discussion meeting.

25th: 5 A.M. A monkey had a movement on the head of the Political Committee comrade. We passed the night in the bamboo jungle.

28th: Breakfast at 6 A.M. At 8:15 the Political comrade, Teck Lan, and Ah Kok went out to gather information, leaving five comrades waiting in the jungle. The Political comrade then left us.

That mental struggle was a part of the learning procedures in the jungle was shown in frequent diary notes, such as this one, found in a hand-bound, pink notebook.

Nov. 28: I was able to get nothing from the main camp. From the very beginning I was in this hopeless position. What have I done for the sake of the revolution? Why do I not overcome my defects? I hope I can overcome all my weak points and serve the revolution as much as I am able.

The diaries cleared up the point of who was more important in the Communist fighting force on the field, the military or the headquarters comrade. This problem came up even in regard to regulations on military etiquette in the jungle. Here are some references I found to it, and to learning—political learning—in a diary with a pink cover.

14th, morning: Our headquarters comrade gave a lecture. "The enemy is very fierce at present." He then talked about our military etiquette, that we have to salute the headquarters comrade during the parade. When the headquarters comrade is not there, we should salute our platoon commander. If the commander is not there, we have to salute the section leader. The commander was accused of not taking the roll call and not hoisting the Red flag during each parade.

15th, morning: Platoon commander and Political Committee comrade gave speeches, reminding us of the parade. We mustn't salute during the fall-in.

16th, morning: The headquarters comrade gave speeches again. Last night we held a general meeting to commemorate victory. A member from the masses participated in the meeting. Another conference will be held in due course.

17th, morning: Lectures were given by headquarters comrade advising us to intensify our training, so that we can be heroic warriors.

18th, morning: As above. Apart from military affairs, we were advised to study politics as well as culture. We must depend on our own will power.

19th, morning: Lectures as usual. We must plan our work for learning. Without planning, one can never be able to get a good result.

20th: As above. We decided to hold a second self-criticism meeting on the 22nd, to give every comrade a chance for self-criticism, and to improve our thoughts.

23rd: Lectures as usual. Those who have no self-criticism may remain silent. False self-criticism is not permitted.

24th: Lecture as usual. Happiness is not a material that can be obtained by our hands . . .

With this curious final comment, the diary terminated. Did a bullet end it here, or was it a summons to action that proved to be the diarist's last call?

A single slip of paper had some notes scribbled on it, probably material jotted down by a leader for use in talks he was about to give or possibly a resumé of talks he had heard.

15/1/51: First. A meeting will be held in the afternoon, and a concert at night to celebrate the recent victory.

Gist of talk: During the morning parade every day, it is necessary to salute only the supreme commander. It isn't necessary to salute all the commanders. If during a parade, both the commander and headquarters commander are present, then it is necessary to salute only the headquarters commander. The platoon commander has no right then to receive the salute of the comrades. In a word, we must salute the highest ranking commander only.

Second. Will the daily lecture become mere prattle only? Do all the comrades keep in mind what is told them? There seems to be great doubt. If my daily talks to you were considered by you as the daily prayer that monks recite, then they would be meaningless. That is why, in future, all comrades should pay greater attention, and the section leaders and political warriors should make a record of the speeches, and then urge the comrades to study them. In this way, they would do much good to the comrades.

A black-covered notebook gave an enlightening description of how fighting and indoctrination went on together.

27/12/50: Meeting tonight. The next day we were scheduled to go out on an operation. Six men of the 4th section. We promised to achieve our objectives.

28th: 9 A.M. Nineteen men set out. We rested in the bamboo jungle at 4 P.M.

30th: I went out scouting with four other comrades. Commencing 8 A.M. until 1 P.M.

31st: We ambushed six enemies who were traveling on foot. Three of them were killed and three wounded. We captured six firearms, consisting of 1 Sten gun, 3 American rifles, 2 British rifles, and a quantity of ammunition. Three of our comrades were killed. The battle started at 11:30 A.M. On the morning of Jan. 1, a number of enemies came to the vicinity of our ambush positions and had a rest for about half an hour near our sentry post. After that, when they passed our prearranged ambush position, all of a sudden a signal shot was fired by our section commander. I then immediately followed up with a burst of fire from my gun and rushed up to the enemy in the estate. While I was chasing after him, I saw some more enemies hiding along the roadside firing back at us. After a short time the enemies were surrounded by us, and they surrendered themselves. I rushed on to him and took over his rifle, as he was out of ammunition.

This little bit of individual heroism, this exhibition of individualism left in a man, did not go unnoticed—nor was it to go unrebuked.

7th Morning. Held a criticism meeting about the battle at Naka Rd.

Evening. Received information that enemies are approaching.

Night. Continued with the criticism meeting, and adjourned at 9 P.M.

8th: Morning. Continued with criticism meeting. The following comrades are being picked up as cowards: Din Kuat, Teik Bong, and—the worst of all—Kim Swee and Bok Siang.

Night. Information was received that enemy soldiers entered Sungei Galong and that more than 10 British soldiers have been firing into the jungle with their Bren guns and light machine guns. More than 100 soldiers and more than 20 military vehicles were seen at the 36th milestone. Section No. 2 immediately moved off to another place of ambush. One of the 11 men in my section was sick. He was Kin Keow. Balance, 10 men in my section.

9th: We hid ourselves in ambush positions on the hill.

Noon: While I was checking the financial accounts of all the comrades in my section, I found that the amount of cash in Lai Swee's possession was in excess. I asked him for an explanation, but he refused to give any. I then referred the matter to the Political Committee comrade, who called him up and asked him if he had reported the matter to his section commander. He was instructed to report to the section commander in future and obtain permission before doing anything.

10th: Held a criticism meeting about the assault on the enemy at the 39th milestone. Our fighting tactics must be strictly observed to avoid the loss of lives among our comrades.

Night. I called for a section meeting and explained to the comrades about military etiquette and our daily lives, and advised them that smoking and using torches at night should be prohibited. Comrades Lai Swee and Ah Yong were found to have violated this rule.

11th: Morning. Continued with the criticism meeting. I was penalized a demerit for trying to fight the battle of my own account, without taking instructions from the superiors. I was also criticized for not instructing the comrades to carry their necessary equipment; in fact, I was also criticized for not keeping secrets. The reason was that I had revealed the arrival of a headquarters member to another comrade.

12th: Morning. Attended class to study a book, entitled *The Iron Force*, about determination in carrying a battle forward to final victory. We must obey our superiors at all times.

13th: Morning. A general meeting was held. I was given a demerit for not directing the comrades in my section to surround the enemy. I cornered and chased after the enemy myself, and hence, the commander's order was ignored. I was also criticized for capturing a watch from a wounded enemy.

16th. Morning: Class as usual, but I did not attend because I was busy with the closing accounts of the food supply committee. Lai

Swee was accused of smoking cigarettes at night. He was warned not to do so again in view of the present situation.

17th: Held a criticism meeting about our plan of work, the summing up of reports, etc.

18th: Morning. Continued with the discussion and adjourned at 9 A.M. I explained to the comrades about Party discipline.

19th: Morning. Continued with the meeting and discussed the four new Party reservists who were introduced and recommended to me.

Night. While I was taking my bath, I received a report that Comrade Ah Bek had stolen some milk and sugar.

20th: Morning. I asked Lai Swee if he had stolen some sugar and milk, to which he replied in the negative. I then requested Comrade Ah Pheow to ask him if he would admit the facts. He finally admitted that he had done it. Held a discussion meeting on the Wright Incident.* 7:30 P.M. Had a meeting at which we criticized Comrade Lai Swee.

21st: Continued discussion of the Wright Incident. Then at night there was another meeting, the Second Non-Party Members Assembly, which was presided over by the Political Committee comrade. Two comrades were given verbal warnings. Six comrades of Section 2 gave speeches. During the morning parade, the Political Committee comrade announced that Comrade Lai Swee would be prohibited from putting on our uniform for a period of three months, effective today.

22nd: Morning. We held a criticism meeting on the "half yearly working week." * * A letter of commendation from headquarters for Section X was read out to all comrades.

---

* The Wright Incident: The case of a Malayan Communist political agent who operated underground, posing as a business man before the war, and who reappeared afterwards, then evaporated. He was apparently a trusted agent who was accused of acting too much on his own authority. He was widely believed to be a foreigner, possibly an Armenian, but I was informed in some British circles that his foreign name was only a cover for his Chinese identity.
* * "Half yearly working week" possibly meant some form of "contributed labor" for the Party.

Night. A second meeting was held to encourage our comrades to correct their errors. Comrade Ah Liak had a bowel movement beside the camp. The Political Committee comrade asked all the comrades who did it, but none came forward to admit it. In the self-criticism meeting tonight, Comrade Ah Liak came forward and admitted that he had eased himself beside the camp on the previous night. The meeting was then adjourned until the next day due to the rain.

2. Jungle Days and Nights

The diaries and notes showed the close watch which was kept on the behavior and thoughts of all comrades. Superiors kept reports on each man's habits and character. A pink notebook, signed Hoe Heong, contained these minutes of various section meetings.

AGENDA

I. Discussions.

A. *Daily Life.*

B. *Mutual Criticism.*

II. Other Matters.

A. *Defects.* 1. Some comrades are not so friendly to each other. (No mutual understanding with regard to resting and sleeping places.) 2. A few comrades failed to observe or abide by the rules which in fact should be kept by all the comrades in the camp. (Equipment was not kept neatly.) 3. A few comrades did not properly give the necessary salutes. 4. A few comrades are careless regarding their situation. (Sometimes talk too loudly.) Good points. 1. Much attention was paid to cleaning weapons and sunning ammunition. 2. Strong craving for knowledge. The learning plan resolved during the previous meeting was successfully carried out. A few comrades have accomplished more than required by the plan. The supply of articles to the wall newspaper is praiseworthy.

B. *Mutual criticism.* Comrade Ah Piow. Defects. 1. Bad temper and bad manners. (Started to grumble with the commander when he misled the way while acting as guide). 2. Individualism. When he misled the way, he refused to listen to the opinion of other comrades. Worst of all, he refused to base his judgment on aid given by the compass. 3. Reckless in speech. 4. Pays no attention to situation of camp. (Often talked very loudly, no matter whether on the move or in the camp). 5. When on the move, not vigilant enough. (In observing surrounding areas.) Good points. 1. Sense of comradeship. 2. Strong liking for learning. 3. Successfully completed work asked by the commander. 4. Can stand hardship.

There were several pages of such thumbnail sketches. This constituted powerful material that could be used as a weapon to break any man if at any time it was found advisable to do so by the headquarters comrade, by other superiors, or by anyone with a grudge who had access to the record of defects. Much of the material was gathered in discussion meetings.

The attitude of the guerrilla soldiers toward learning was one of the principal measuring sticks used in judging a man. A blue-covered notebook kept by one minor leader had these minute appraisals of his men:

Comrade Ah Geok: Defects. 1. Taking afternoon nap without making a report. Good points. 1. Sense of duty (to cover up the track and cut telephone wires). 2. Liking for learning. 3. Comradeship. 4. Can stand hardships.
Comrade Seng Huat: Defects. 1. Dirty. 2. Did not have courage to criticize other comrades. 3. Did not care for the well-being of comrades in his section. Good points. 1. Good manners. 2. Liked learning. 3. As rear guard, he was thorough in covering up the tracks. 4. He was greatly concerned over sick comrades. 4. Willingness to do orderly work.
Comrade Si Hock: Defects. 1. Unwillingness to carry out military etiquette. 2. Hot temper. Good points. 1. Comradeship. 2. A liking for learning. 3. Very careful regarding handling of weapons.
Comrade Ah Liek: Defects: 1. Took afternoon nap without making a report. 2. Equipment not well taken care of. 3. When on

sentry duty always tried to occupy the nearest sentry post, and very particular about the time. 4. Likes to speak rude words. 5. Lazy regarding learning. 6. Unwillingness to obey the commander. 7. In spite of the section leader's refusal to let him take afternoon nap, he went to sleep as usual. Good points. 1. Voluntarily assisted the other comrades in covering up the tracks. 2. Voluntarily assisted the other comrades in learning.

Comrade Si Bong: Defects. 1. Taking afternoon nap without making a report. 2. Lack of unity and spirit of comradeship. 3. Could not stand hardships. (Besides not taking up sentry duty, he did not make a report to the section leader). 4. Not candid enough when talking to the comrades. 5. Unwilling to carry out the necessary salutations (salutes, etc.). 6. Unwillingness to accept words of advice from other comrades. 7. Does not have the attitude of a soldier. 8. Does not have the will to overcome defects. 9. Mentally, he is suffering from negative views about the revolution. (After being criticized by the comrades, he told them that in future, when he encountered the enemies, he would stand up and let them kill him.)

Comrade Ah Soon: Defects. 1. Lack of unity and comradeship. (Quarrels over sleeping place. Despises comrades who have defects. "If I had so many defects as Comrade X, I would long ago have tried to kill myself.") 2. When we were on the move he fell sick, and the comrades stopped him from taking bamboo shoots. Later, he said that if he fell sick in future, he would refuse to move a step farther. If forced, then the other comrades must carry his haversack for him. Comrade X advised him to be good and reasonable, but he said he wanted to stay bad. As regards learning, he said that if it were not required by comrades during the meeting that each comrade write 200 words, he certainly would not write them.

Comrade Chooi Lai: Defects. 1. Sometimes loses his temper without cause. 2. Fell sick when the unit was on the move. Without making a report, he did not go to the sentry post to do his duty. 3. Lack of comradeship. 4. Unwilling to carry out military etiquette. Good points. 1. Willingness to learn. 2. Willingness to accept other comrades' criticism.

The admission of new Party members in a solemn jungle ceremony was referred to in another diary. When the Communist guerrilla forces weren't working or fighting, they were kept busy with discussion meetings until they were allowed to go to sleep, drunk with fatigue. Here are some of this man's typical notes:

Oct. 6: 6 A.M. Helped the members of the precautionary corps. 8 A.M. The commander gave orders to start review work and the compilation of reports. There are two persons, one a robber and the other a traitor. These two persons must be liquidated. Otherwise it will be a grave error. 9.30 A.M. Took rice. 10 A.M. I went on sentry duty. In the night a meeting was called, with Comrade Lin in the chair.

The next day, his diary records a meeting to study a booklet on "telling the entire Party." A couple of days later, he mentions a meeting "to discuss the dismissal of four comrades." That evening, a meeting was held "to study questions of Party affairs, how to increase Party membership, and problems of contacts and daily livelihood for Party units."

Oct. 10: After breakfast, attended a meeting to discuss lessons. The headquarters comrade presided. At 12 we adjourned and had rice broth. The meeting resumed at 1 P.M. Last night the comrades discussed my demand to give up my rank as a section commander. I admitted all the criticisms about myself.
Oct. 11: In the course of the discussions, the question of Chinese people joining the Special Constable Corps being set up was discussed. The majority of those people are bad elements. They should be annihilated.

The Special Constable Corps was a police force then being organized to work in cooperation with the military to defend Chinese villagers against the taxes and collections which were being arbitrarily imposed by the guerrilla forces; to give the Chinese populace the protection they needed if they agreed to defy Communist demands for intelligence data; and to give it instead to the anti-Communist forces. Protection was the crux of the matter so far as these Chinese peasants and small villagers were concerned.

Oct. 12: At 7 A.M. a meeting was called to admit four new Party members. Comrade Chin Lim presided. The meeting was rather solemn. Following this we had a social party. Eng Khuan was the master of ceremonies. The party was very enjoyable because everyone did an act. The party ended at 11 P.M.

Oct. 17: Morning. Sent out two comrades to collect tapioca. Got a wild goat and an anteater, which were brought back and slaughtered. 5 P.M. Troops on the move; it rained on the way. 10 P.M. Rested while some comrades went out to gather information. They returned at midnight.

Oct. 19: Woke up at 3 A.M. to eat rice. 4:20 A.M. set off for the ambush. Two comrades from the section were sent out to distribute propaganda material. 10 A.M. The battle started. We captured two new-type rifles, 45 rounds of cartridges, a bayonet, and two ammunition pouches, and at 7:24 P.M. we withdrew. We captured a total of 10 guns. 5:20 P.M. Rested and prepared cocoa milk. 11 P.M. Rested; two comrades went to collect information.

Oct. 20: Felt sick in the morning, so rested in the old house. Some people came to give information. In the night some comrades went out to reconnoiter.

Oct. 28: In the night I went to the village with six comrades from the command section. After taking our meal in the village, I accompanied two comrades to transport rations. At 11 P.M. we returned to camp.

This obviously referred to the collection of foodstuffs and other supplies from one of the lonely, helpless villages.

Oct. 29: 7 P.M. Went down for dinner. 7:30 P.M. set off for investigation work on XX road, returning to camp at 2 A.M. Heard three reports of the enemy from a nearby rubber plantation.

Oct. 30: During breakfast Comrade Kok Heng lost his pack. He started yelling. He made a very bad impression on the Self-Protection Corps. When Seng Huat and myself pointed this out to him, he became very angry. When the headquarters comrade and myself gave cigarettes to Teoh Cheng, who was going out, he was not satisfied. He said that everyone should be given them. But when he was asked to get the opinion of the headquarters comrade on this, he was silent.

There, deep in the jungles, the self-criticism often took on a frenzied character, in which penitents competed with each other in confessing their sins. A group leader had this in his notebook:

Jan. 22, 1951: All comrades are present in the field. They are ready to attend the criticism meeting, scheduled for 7. P.M.
What a good sign it is to see the majority of comrades do their work without hesitation. The self-criticism made by the comrades at the meeting was all frank. Some even told us how they came to know the real taste of masturbation, how they felt when they first joined the army, how they missed their families, how they thought of killing the headquarters comrade, how they feel now. A heavy downpour came during the meeting, and on this account, the headquarters comrade ordered that the meeting be dismissed. The meeting will resume at the same time tomorrow.
23rd: The meeting started about 10 A.M. There was nothing different from what took place yesterday. As a matter of fact, masturbation is quite ordinary, only comrades must bear these points in mind:
1. Masturbation will ruin your lives and will affect your revolutionary work.
2. We must always try "to part from the evil and follow the good."

There was other evidence in these diaries, too, that Party demands for the sacrifice of one's whole being for the cause did not work out as well as it sounded in *The Question of Thought*, even with the Party resorting to learning meetings to fill every waking hour that wasn't consumed with work and violence. This is what a yellow-covered pocket notebook contained:

Sept. 25, 1950: At 6 P.M. comrade commander came to sentence Comrades Lok and Fong. They were sentenced because of love-making. The behavior of Comrade Lok was incorrect. He was blemishing the prestige of the Party.

Oct. 2: At 7 A.M. the commander asked us to write out a report about what Comrade Lok had done, so as to forward it to headquarters. In the night, three of us commemorated the first anniversary of New China. After breakfast a criticism meeting was called to discuss what Comrade Lok had done. The meeting lasted to noon. At 2 P.M. the meeting was resumed, to discuss the war policy up to the present. The meeting lasted to 5:30 P.M. when we had our dinner and rest. At 7 P.M. we started the discussion meeting. At 10:30 P.M. we retired.

Oct. 4: At 7 A.M. called for a meeting to discuss defects and means of correcting them. At 8:30 the rain stopped, we had breakfast, and at 10 A.M. continued with the meeting until 1 P.M., when we had a rest. At 2:30 we reviewed past activities. Traitors must be annihilated and they should not be given any mercy. The meeting lasted until 5 P.M., when we started a review of the identity card policy. Many identity cards have been collected from the people, and the numbers are being taken down. The people should be encouraged to report missing identity cards. In this way the British imperialists will not be able to handle the registration, which will be very beneficial to us.

Oct. 5: Called a meeting to review past activities, and this meeting ended at 9 A.M. This was presided over by Kok Heng. At 11:30 A.M., while having our rest, information was received that troops had come into the village and had also reached the 8½ mile point. We packed all our things. At noon it started to rain very heavily, and we found out that the information given us was false. One small unit was sent out to intercept the enemies: it was thoroughly drenched and returned after discovering that everything was well.

A slip of paper contained this curious example of self-inflation in self-criticism:

1. Drank milk without permission. 2. Avaricious. 3. Masturbation. 4. Favoritism. 5. Individual-heroism; self-assertion; self-esteem.

6. Slept during sentry guard duty. 7. Am wrongly motivated toward the army.

Another slip of paper contained the proud boast, "I am a member of the Racial Liberation Army."

Then I came upon a self-criticism paper signed Tiong Wei, section commander, dated January 21. Reading his confession I realized that this was the same man who had succumbed to the sin of "heroic individualism" while engaged in an ambush. Here is how he described his defects:

1. Belief in heroism. One day three members of the masses came up to our camp, a female and two males, so in order to show them that I was the leader there, I ordered that the bugle be sounded at 8:30 P.M. [signal for dinner] instead of at 9 as usual. On another occasion, some comrades of the Min Yuen* came up to our camp. They came in two groups [units]. As soon as the sentry reported their arrival to me, I immediately instructed the sentry to let them in, without obtaining the consent of the Political Committee comrade. On one occasion, while we were with the Self-Protection Corps, I ordered our comrades to do the cooking without instruction from the platoon commander. I did not pay particular attention and due respect to the order given by the platoon commander during the battle at the 39th milestone. I did not hear his order to surround the enemy; when he repeated this order the second time I did not lead the comrades of my section to surround the enemy but instead I chased after an enemy myself, thus showing my heroic spirit and behavior. During the self-criticism meeting I did not give the true report of my daily life and the true facts of events.

2. Self-interest thoughts. During the battle at the 39th milestone, I captured a watch from a wounded enemy. I had been longing to possess a watch. When the opportunity occurred, I decided to capture a number of watches to hand to the commander, after which I figured that I could recommend that one be given to every section leader, and so get one for my personal use.

* Min Yuen: Undercover civilian section of the guerrilla warfare.

Some of the self-criticisms were entitled "thought conclusion," and among them, in one badly torn exercise book, were listed four kinds of error. The desire for equality was included. Some sinners had to go far back to find material for their confession; the jungle warrior who wrote the following went back more than two and a half years:

1. Disobeyed a higher ranking officer. (In 1948, some time around October, I disagreed with my higher ranking officer on the erection of temporary camps. The higher ranking officer chose a spot with which I disagreed, and so I went out to do something else when called to help by some comrades.)
2. Self-indulgence. (When I was leading comrades, as a jungle route courier, from Pachik District to Goo District the other day, I reported to my officer that I was not feeling well, and suggested it would be better to choose another comrade to act as jungle route courier in place of me.)
3. Gossip. (When Commanding Headquarters Comrade Kuen and some of his mates went to the village from the communications post in Bukit Selembau the other day, I told comrades that it was not fair to leave us at the post not fully armed.)
4. Equalism. (I used to feel indignant over the way uniforms were distributed.)

A theoretical study of self-criticism, with the best definition of it that I had yet found, was in another jungle notebook:

What is the right attitude toward self-criticism? Self-criticism is a positive method of ideological struggle inside the Party, to overcome erroneous thoughts, to correct various ideological errors, to elevate the Party consciousness of the Party members, and to assist the comrades. That is why the purpose of criticism is to protect, not to assault, to have good-will discussion, not evil and wicked assaults.

What should be the main principle of self-criticism? The main principle of self-criticism is that it should bring out political and ideological viewpoints. If ideological viewpoints and other important, basic problems have gone astray, then the work will go astray too. If they are right, the work carrying them out will be right, too. The right or wrong of these problems is of great importance to the revolution and to the people.

What is meant by backbiting, or criticizing behind one's back? Since the motive of criticism is to assist the progress of the comrades and the Party, then in order to achieve the desired result and aim, all criticism should be done openly. Some comrades have something to say about other comrades, but they never speak out openly. They always talk behind one's back. Those comrades who are criticized by them gain no benefit from this criticism; this criticism even will bring bad results. If criticizing behind a person's back is not stopped, there would be much chaos inside the Party. If there were no unity among the comrades, then the enemy could take the opportunity to infiltrate into our Party and try to break up our Party organizations.

If one's motive is good, in order to obtain the best results from criticism and to determine whether one's viewpoint is correct or not, one can discuss his points of view before a meeting with the comrades in his same group, or with superiors. This way of going about it cannot be called criticizing behind one's back, and the Party has no objection to it, because its purpose is only to ascertain whether such criticism is to be brought up at all, and the best way to bring it up. If, after such an exchange of views, the criticism has not been brought up in a meeting, then this can be called criticizing behind one's back, which is prohibited by the Party. To exchange such views with comrades who are not in the same setup is definitely to criticize behind one's back.

The next paragraphs were on how to differentiate between "good-will criticism" and "assaulting criticism," but I feared that if I copied too much of this, I would not have the time to take down other more significant items.

Songs of violence and ambush, under the anachronistic title of *Chinese Folk Songs*, were found in some of the notebooks kept by unit leaders. Among them I found this, signed Tiong Wei:

How nice to sing a folk song. On June the 19th we went up to the battlefield and lay in ambush at the 36th milestone. For a total of seven hours. And there came up a military truck.

There came up a military truck. The comrade in command then gave the order. Then we aimed at the front part of the truck.

The driver fell off immediately.

The driver fell off immediately, and the truck of a sudden came to a stop. Comrades were all so anxious, and with a single blow, we killed six and wounded four of the enemy.

We killed six and wounded four of the enemy. Of the four wounded two were serious. And then the order for hand-to-hand fighting was given. We immediately rushed to the car. And it was there that we captured a light machine gun.

There that we captured a light machine gun. With three useful carbines. At the same time with one Sten gun. And two of the rifles. Making a total of nine big and small guns.

Making a total of nine big and small guns. With more than 200 rounds of ammunition. Suddenly there came another truck. On hearing the sound of gunfire they turned away and tried to escape.

They turned away and tried to escape. The comrades pursued from behind, with Stens and carbines took away their dog lives. And we dragged out the corpses from the car.

And we dragged out the corpses from the car. The commander gave the order to burn the car. For the whole half an hour the skies were red. The masses nearby laughed for joy. For at least they were being liberated for half an hour.

For at least they were being liberated for half an hour. The commander then ordered the retreat. We were safe all the way. Finally we arrived back at camp. And this is the end of my song.

ACTION UNITS

The phrase "a band of terrorists" sounded theatrical. When does an "enthusiastic element" become a "terrorist?" Is a band of terrorists a figure of speech or a loose description of ordinary disorders? Is it just a guerrilla group? Is there actually

such a job description as terrorist or such a vocation as terrorism? If so, where do they learn the tricks of their trade?

Such questions seem so exaggerated, so out of touch with
anything in real life, that Americans and other Westerners
can hardly be expected to take them seriously. Yet, when I arrived in the Indochinese capital at Saigon, I found that two
editors had been slain only two weeks before. A third editor
was slain while I was there. This was just in my own profession. An Englishman from Hong Kong, passing through, had
been murdered, without any apparent reason. The restaurant
where I ate had a steel webbing in front, putting the diners
in a sort of cage. The restaurant had been hand-grenaded a
short time previously.

I found both the native and French presses running routine items about violence, with curious references to prisoners saying they belonged to such and such an action committee. What did all this mean? How did it happen in
practice? People just don't pick up hand grenades and rifles
and go hunting in cities. Yet it seemed that this was just
what was happening.

Inquiry soon revealed that the impression of reckless violence that these incidents gave me was wholly superficial. I
found that there was nothing hit or miss about modern terrorism except by design. In Indochina, at a time when the
United States was still talking about a cold war, terrorism
was merely another arm of politics, practiced alongside the
formalities of international diplomacy.

There were numerous recent cases of restaurants bombed,
with perhaps a woman diner killed and a couple of patrons
injured. I investigated these first.

The Moscow-trained Viet Minh leader, Ho Chi-minh, had
devised a regular tax program. He made believe that he was
in actual control of all Indochina, setting up a tax system on
that basis. Then he sent out his collectors. The hand grenades that were being tossed into restaurants were usually
just forcible reminders that the proprietors had missed a pay-
ment.

The Communists, in their realistic manner, recognized that they could not expect to put their thought control program into operation in areas where they were not in power, and so they did the next best thing. They devised a tactic to achieve their objectives in another way by adapting their program to put the populace in non-Communist areas in a position where they would have to act as if Indochina were already a Communist country. Those entrusted with enforcing this make-believe were the action units, which outsiders referred to more appropriately as terrorist units.

The beauty of this system, from the police-state viewpoint, was that it made no difference whether the man was anti-Communist, pro-Communist, or a political atheist, any more than an American's being a Republican or a Democrat has anything to do with whether he will send in his income tax form. Under the system, every foreign firm that does business in the interior must pay a toll, directly or indirectly, to support the Communist regime. Many larger firms thus paid two big tax bills. Sometimes the taxes were collected, en route, from shipments. A food truck might be taken over, or a supply wagon. The basis of such collections was not at all the actual physical power exercised by the Communist forces. It usually was the desire of native people, and many foreigners, to continue as nearly normal operations as possible. The Chinese communities, primarily middle-class merchants, conspicuously avoided antagonizing the Communists.

Their explanations to me were to the point. They had heard that Red China would shortly be admitted to the United Nations. Even Britain had recognized Red China. If the Western world set this example, they asked me, how could they be expected to hit their heads against a stone wall? Fantastic as it sounded, they were not sure which side we were on, in practice. They were too wise to be taken in by protestations of neutrality because they knew there could be no neutrality in dealing with Communism. You either gave in to it, fought it, or bought time from it at the price the Communists set.

They had to live here, these Chinese pointed out. They were not sure what compromises or negotiations abroad might take the floor out from under the anti-Communist campaign in Indochina, nor could they be sure of the extent to which Red China would be allowed to strengthen the Communist regime that both Peiping and Moscow had recognized in Indochina. This was the theme that I had heard in Malaya, and which I heard everywhere I went in Asia.

The hand grenades thrown into a home, the bullet fired into a father's stomach, were forms of warning of what happens to those who don't go along with Party requirements. I found the native press running bitterly anti-French stories, intensely anti-American news, but nothing to which Moscow might take serious exception.

Were all these reporters and editors Communists? I asked a number of them, and they seemed stunned at my naïveté. Of course they weren't Communists. They were against Communism. But they just wanted to stay alive, they and their families. They showed me this Reuter item:

Saigon—A Vietnamese gunman today assassinated Lu Khe, editor of *Anh San,* Saigon's biggest vernacular newspaper, the third killing of a Vietnamese newspaperman in two months. The gunman, riding a bicycle, fired three shots at Lu Khe as he was leaving his home for his office.

And:

Saigon—Agents of the Communist Viet Minh movement today sent letters to most of Saigon's principal journalists, "sentencing" them to death unless they cease the publication of their newspapers.

What the Reds actually wanted was not that these newspapers cease publishing, but that they compromise, agreeing to handle news the way the Viet Minh demanded, in return for being allowed to stay in business. Most reporters had their own experiences to relate of letters and phone calls threatening them and their loved ones with death unless they, too, made believe that this was a Communistic country, and so they ran their news columns accordingly.

The Viet Minh radio had attacked the editors just before they were killed, accusing one in particular of being pro-American. That was the arch-heresy. The accusation wasn't that these editors were *supporting* America; it meant they were not *attacking* America. Here again, while there were no American soldiers anywhere the Communists were not allowing the people to forget that America was the main enemy. This, of course, could only be the consequence of central direction.

So, as with the tax system, whether a man was pro-Moscow or anti-Moscow had nothing to do with power politics as exercised in the kind of warfare that was being fought by the Reds. He had to act pro-Moscow, otherwise a terrorist would be called into action. Alongside this form of editorial pressure, I found that pro-Communists or fellow travelers had vociferously insisted on their democratic rights "to print any news they wished." Following a recent wave of terrorist killings a drastic censorship had been imposed on the press by the authorities. This, like the desolation of Indochina's villages, was all grist for the Communist mill.

The best English translator a foreign legation had on its staff while I was in Saigon resigned. The pressure on him for "aiding the imperialist enemy" had become too forceful.

Who were these terrorists? Were they any Tom, Dick, or Jane, given a hand grenade and a rifle and a blacklist of names, and sent out? Not at all. They had to undergo careful training before they were allowed to go out on a mission. They had to study terrorism, which was being taught as a branch of modern political science. That this was being taught in a matter-of-fact way was in accordance with the viewpoint so much stressed by the Communists—dialectical materialism.

The authorities frequently captured young terrorists of both sexes, and the stories they told of their training agreed too minutely to permit of any doubt, even if I had not come across the same thing so often in other countries of Asia. The details they gave, too, of the location of their training grounds coincided in essential details. Many inhabitants of the areas where the training schools have been set up had managed to escape, and their eye-witness accounts confirmed what the arrested terrorists confessed.

These terrorists were alike in their comparative youth. Many were in their teens, often in their early teens. They were the ones who were most likely to escape suspicion and to engage in rash enterprises. All were alike in that their practical training had included Marxism and Stalinism to make them dependable. For many, this had been their first schooling. Virtually none had had any higher education. They were all similarly situated economically—nothing to lose, but everything to gain in Party rewards, Party prestige, and in more tangible ways once the Party came into power. What was the difference between this situation and that obtaining in racketeering gangs in the United States? Except in degree, none.

The members of the action units ranged from disillusioned intellectuals to illiterate criminals and from unhappy wives to ordinary Stalinists. Prisoners who had been freed from their cells by the Communist troops when entering a town, and refugees from justice—those who had a price on their heads and a motive for staying out of the clutches of the regular authorities—were particularly numerous in the terrorist groups.

The training groups were in the mountains and the forests and, in some instances, inside Red China. The instructors themselves were often products of these schools, although the heads, as was true with Party posts generally in Indochina, had usually been to China or Moscow for thorough training.

The training given to the action units included specialized instruction in the simple manufacture of bombs, in throwing hand grenades, in the use and improvisation of explosives, in incendiarism and general sabotage, and in evasion in cities and crowded areas. Espionage was part of the schooling. Assault propaganda was an important part of the training, in a special section, for agents who arranged the propaganda setting for demonstrations and other activities that the Communists desired, either under their own name or under the cover of a liberal or even an anti-Communist outfit. Learning, in its political sense, went along with all of this as a matter of course.

The students, as often as practicable, were sent back into their home areas to operate. Thus, they could be expected to get about easily, for they had known the terrain from childhood—often the difference between capture and success. Those who were captured in Saigon were frequently young men and girls who had been raised there, and only sent north for special schooling.

I glanced over the Saigon newspapers for the preceding week. An article told of the sentencing of a grenade thrower named Lien Trong Dat, twenty-three, to twenty years of forced labor. He told the court that he belonged to Action Committee No. 7. He said he had thrown a grenade into a restaurant, wounding two soldiers, and that he had also participated in the bombing of another restaurant and a film theater, causing twelve more injuries. He made a detailed report to headquarters after each such attack.

"What was your reason for picking these restaurants?" the judge asked.

"They hadn't paid their taxes."

"What was your mission in Saigon; you weren't sent to buy peanuts?" the court pressed.

"I was charged with the collection of taxes," the young man replied, as if this were a legal procedure.

Another news item was headlined, "Young Viet Minh Agents in Aprons." It told of a girl of eighteen, Le Thi Mai, and another of seventeen, Tran Thi Luong, who were couriers with special areas to cover, operating between terrorist groups and their headquarters. Another item told of a restaurant grenaded the night before. And still another of an ambush. And so on.

A MUFFLED SOUND

Indochina is a good example of an ideological front where democratic group discussions have developed into action units and where the phrase "a band of terrorists" is in daily use.

I took a trip along the road that leads from Haiphong toward the mountains where Indochina becomes China. There was a big hole in the highway ahead, and patient villagers were working under the pitiless sun, under anti-Communist orders, filling it up. Some were particularly sleepy, and should have been; they had helped blow up the road the night before under Communist orders. Only their fellow villagers knew who they were, but wouldn't tell.

The village was a typical one. Every foreign type of building (all were, except the thatched huts) had been blown up a month or so before when the Communist forces retreated as part of their scorched-earth policy. Thatch, bamboo, and brick had made corners of the buildings habitable again. The villagers, starting at scratch, worked hard to resume a normal existence.

"Who blew up the village?" I asked an inhabitant.

He smiled at so naïve a question. "We did."

"You mean the people now rebuilding it?"

"Yes."

"Why?" I persisted.

He looked at me as if I had come from another world. "We were ordered to."

"Whose orders?"

"The Communists."

I wondered, but didn't ask—he wouldn't have known—

whether the emissaries who gave the orders were called able Party members or just headquarters comrades.

"Who ordered you to rebuild?" I inquired instead.

"The anti-Communists."

"How did you feel about blowing up your village?"

"We suffered in our hearts as we set the fuses."

Do Tien Tuy came up; he had taught school for the Communists, in this Red River Delta region, until a couple of weeks before. He had been a schoolteacher in the village, too, before and after the Communists had taken it. They were to take it again, a few months after I left, and then to lose it once more.

"Did you teach any differently for Ho Chi-minh's Reds?" I asked Do Tien Tuy.

"What I was supposed to teach was to read and write a bit, and to be faithful to Ho Chi-minh."

"Why did you return?"

"I heard American aid was coming, so I fled in the night."

There was a steady stream of refugees coming in from the high places where the Reds were in control. They, too, had heard that American aid was on the way.

He pointed to the unkempt, soaken fields. "All we want is to sow and work our rice paddies. As you can see, most of the fields are untilled. We have begun a little." He pointed to a plot delicately green with rice seedlings. "If they would only leave us alone. . . ." He left the sentence unfinished.

This region is one of the richest, most thickly populated rice areas in the world. The favorite Communist agrarian reform appeal makes no sense to its inhabitants. Almost every family has its own farm. The rich farmers are just other farmers who have more land. There are few worker-farmers who are not also farm owners.

I turned to a police officer. "Why can't you find out who blows up the roads and does all this other violence?"

"The villagers don't dare tell," he explained. "Revenge would be swift. So they do just as they are ordered, by no matter whom, if he has the power. Meanwhile, they try to grow enough to feed themselves."

An elderly man came up, with—as he believed—prettily blackened teeth. He explained that many of the villagers had sons, husbands, and daughters in the hills with the Communists, many of whom were forcibly recruited. Desertion is dangerous; the Communists had sentries along the escape routes, with orders to shoot to kill. Appeals were sent down for food and clothing, for life was difficult for the Reds in the mountains. A father or mother then took a river path or a hill road at night to deliver food or a tattered pair of pants. Life was hard in the village, too, and a business deal was a business deal. So the villagers made a bundle of some scarce possession and went to sell it to the Communist forces.

"Their money isn't much good any more, so we demand something in exchange," another villager said.

"What?" I asked.

"Oh, a water buffalo, perhaps."

"Where did the Reds get it to give to you?"

"Oh, I suppose they stole it from some other village."

"Didn't they sometimes steal from your village to pay another village?"

"Of course."

"Why did the villagers accept such treatment? Why didn't they resist?"

Several voices replied at once, all in agreement. How could you resist when you didn't know what tomorrow would bring? All minds were on Korea. Red China was only a few miles away. This had been Chinese soil not too many years before; the culture was still Chinese. The Red radio was daily threatening death to those who compromised with the enemy, and this meant the United States and its ideas.

The embankment at the side looked familiarly like a railway line, but the tracks were gone. Their removal was part of the Communist scorched-earth policy. Farther on were the scattered rails, and here and there a gutted freight car. An iron bar from a coach hung in front of one village, serving as the warning gong in case of attack.

I joined a convoy taking some American officials on a tour of some of the region. The villagers gathered about, talked freely, and pleaded for simple assistance. They said they needed farm credit, farm implements (not the fancy gadgets Americans use), and simple clothes to cover their bodies and those of their children. A glance readily showed that they were speaking the truth. If only they had farm credit, they would be able to accomplish all the rest themselves. If . . .

"If what?" I pressed.

"If the Communists could be prevented from raiding the villages and continuing their policy of terrorism."

The villagers cheered and waved as we departed. First to leave were the cars containing the American and Viet Nam officials, then those with the newspapermen. I was in the last car, just in front of the armored car, in the turret of which French soldiers sat, triggers ready, watching the paddies. Such preparation hardly seemed necessary on a road so peaceful.

So peaceful, I thought, when I heard a muffled sound. My attention was immediately distracted by the sight of a string of villagers running from the crossroads in the distance, where we had left them, to their little village half a mile away.

"They seem anxious to get home," I remarked.

A little farther down there was a big pouf. The chauffeur heard it and stopped, for a tire had evidently blown. My companion, Graham Jenkins, the enterprising Australian representative of Reuters who has had years of war experience in the Pacific islands, heard it too. We all got out for repairs. The tires were intact. We were puzzled until we heard the zing of the sniper's bullet.

The armored car bringing up our rear heard the shots too, and replied with the ra-tat-tat of its machine gun. Aimless shooting just for morale purposes. The paddies stretched on both sides of us as far as the eye could see; any effort to locate a concealed sniper was like hunting the proverbial needle in the haystack. The last thing to do when a sniper is aiming at your car is to get out and stand in front of it. We all three thought of this at once, and it took less time to get back into that station wagon and drive off than it does to type it.

Did the villagers know the sniper? Of course. Did they disapprove? I believe yes. Would they tell on him? Of course not. Their own lives would be the penalty.

In the next village we stopped to eat in the only intact structure in town that could accommodate more than a single family. It was a corner of one of the wrecked Confucian temples, over which a roof had been hastily constructed of bamboo and straw matting.

We ate some pork dumplings, a half dozen different soups, sugared lotus seeds, and the ever-present soft drinks manufactured by the Chinese. All was plainly prepared, but served in ceremonial style by tattered hosts. Matting had been placed on the mud floor. The disease-bearing flies were kept on the move by soldiers standing at our backs, each soldier with a fan which he kept gently waving over us. The remnant of ancient splendor seemed out of place until one of the soldiers stopped fanning for a moment and an avalanche of flies descended.

What was the noise I had heard when we left the last village? I found out later. It wasn't anything unusual. The Communists had disapproved of the show of attention shown the Americans, and were expressing their disfavor in the usual manner. As soon as the Americans had left, an enthusiastic element had flipped a hand grenade among the villagers. The crowd had muffled most of the sound. Among the injured was a boy of thirteen; his leg was badly torn.

PUBLICATIONS

CAUSE AND EFFECT

DURING KUOMINTANG RULE, CHINA HAD MAGAZINES SPE-cializing in current affairs, movies, fiction, and comics. A few Chinese artists drew cartoons and humorous sketches, but their market was very limited because few editors would accept their work. One would have thought that with the low literacy rate in China more space would have been given over to pictures, and that a cartoon magazine might even be put out on matters of topical interest. There was nothing of this sort. Occasionally, a few patches of space in the newspapers carried cartoons, but these never aroused much attention from the editors. Neither did the authorities, to the slightest degree, encourage artists in their work. Still less did anybody apparently think of employing this art as a medium for propaganda.

The Communists stepped in to fill the gap. In the usual Communist manner, once having decided to do so, they resorted to no half-way measures but went at it on a nationwide scale, with all stops out. They were particularly successful in exploiting the field because it was wide open and they could make the art of satirical drawings a sharp weapon in their propaganda. The seriousness with which they regarded it is fully shown by the extent to which they went in producing cartoon magazines and books and putting more and more such drawings into other kinds of publications. From the start, the Reds insisted that each cartoon or sketch do more than arouse a smile, provoke a laugh, or create shock; it had to convey a political message, and this message had to be the specific one that the Communists were anxious to put across.

Obviously, the artists and cartoonists, who before had had to accept outside menial jobs to make both ends meet or give up their art ambitions entirely, were terribly excited and enthusiastic over this new prospect of not only getting their rice bowl filled, but seeing their art work in print. That their sketches now had to convey a message was secondary; what they craved was an audience.

The Communists saw that they got this audience. So long as they ate and had a place to lay their heads, the financial part of it was secondary. There should be no misunderstanding over this aspect of it; what these artists wanted more than anything else in the world, like all artists good and bad, was an audience. The Communists provided not only the audience but masses of audience. Consequently, the Reds had no difficulty in capturing the artists of China for their cause, much as they had captured the bulk of the writers. Communist success in this, as in their military successes, was based not on their own merits, but primarily on taking advantage of the stupidities and blindness of their enemies.

The political price the Communists asked for providing an audience was not given a second thought by the average Chinese artist because he considered politics a very secondary matter anyway. And by the time he had been taught to give it importance, he had gone through a brain-washing and could be trusted to identify social significance with Communism. There were certain heroic exceptions who deserved extraordinary tribute because of the most discouraging environment in which they found themselves.

In the published cartoon magazines most of the sketches were extremely mediocre and superficial. They had only the one quality of conveying what the cartoonist was trying to say at first glance, enabling readers to grasp the idea immediately even if they had only the slightest education. This clarity in putting over a political message was the only demand made by the Communists. Ambitious cartoonists, who heretofore had had no hope of being printed and who would have been laughed out of any American editor's office, now had pages in public media open to them. If they couldn't qualify even for this, they always had wall papers which afforded prestige to their contributors. Under this impetus the number of artists and cartoonists in China multiplied manyfold. The quality of their work? Well, that's another matter. But that it has generally shown a steadily increasing proficiency cannot be denied.

In Kuomintang days, only gentlemen enjoyed cartoons. The magazine *West Wind Monthly* published a few cartoons in each issue, drawings which were not by native artists but were picked up from foreign publications such as *The New Yorker*. Anyway, *West Wind Monthly* was read only by real intellectuals.

In the present-day Chinese cartoon magazines in which sketches take up half or more of the contents, the drawings are presented in such a way that even primary school students have no difficulty in understanding them. The captions are usually in commonplace and vulgar language—and vulgar here means language which in our society is restricted to the barracks. The cartoon magazines quickly found popular favor. Students liked them because the cartoons expressed blatant lip service to their patriotic feelings. The Communist message was always carefully wrapped in patriotic tinfoil. Workers and other poorly educated people also liked the cartoon magazines because here at last was something they could understand. They had no trouble in easily grasping both meaning and the message. The pictures and the captions that accompanied them are forceful and expressive. Here, too, they found an outlet for feelings of frustration and dissatisfaction. What if the details differed from what actually upset them? Here was somebody slamming the table and letting go with a soul-calming string of curses.

They had vague misgivings from time to time over some of the international allusions, but by the time they were alert to foreign affairs, the reiterated theme of the cartoons had usually achieved its purpose in creating the attitudes desired.

These cartoon magazines are also most appealing to youths who do not have a chance of continuing their studies. Ambitious, they usually earn their living as apprentices and clerks in firms and shops. Observant of much that went on around them, they saw how their manager walked pompously in and out and sometimes rode in an automobile. Often they saw how unjustly money was earned and profits made. Dissatisfied because the education they had did not permit them to read more serious publications, they also found the new cartoon magazines appealing. They were ready to accept the accompanying propaganda contained in these publications, for the sketches attacked the old society in which they had suffered discrimination and injustice. They were told that their boss, or anyone else for whom they had a grudge, was a rotten capitalist and a damned imperialist. They liked Americans as a friendly and kindly people who helped others in distress, but the incessant Communist campaign to classify all non-Communists, and Americans in particular, as capitalists and imperialists, just like their bosses, confused them. In the environment which I have described, many—many more than we would like to believe—ended up by believing. This is how hate is built up. I feel that these antagonisms are not yet deep-seated and in many cases are very vague, but the Hate America drive has succeeded at least in creating grave doubts where none existed before.

The real intellectuals and persons with an education beyond that of high school are not attracted to these cartoon magazines; they prefer serious literature. Most of them, and the older generations, are repulsed by the filthy language used. The misrepresentation of fact is so apparent to them that it has slight effect, if any. The Communists, however, don't care. They have brain-washing and the execution squad to take care of the minority. They are satisfied in knowing that forceful vilification and fabricated history are most efficient in forming prejudices among the working class and the younger generation, thus serving their purpose of arousing class and racial hatreds.

1. Symbols and Themes

A small booklet caught my eye while I was glancing over recent magazines and newspapers. There were only sketches in it, and although I had never seen the booklet before, I was surprised how familiar I was with the contents. I recognized each of the pictures and had the impression that I had seen every sketch time and time again, although I had not seen those particular ones. Obviously, it was a guide for artists and cartoonists. As I went through the booklet more carefully, I understood that it was intended for propagandists. I took it for granted that it had been written for some special group charged with the dissemination of the official Chinese Communist point of view. Although I knew that it had been picked up with the other publications in an ordinary bookshop in Red China, I never suspected that it was intended for popular use. Only later did I discover that this was exactly its purpose, and this was how I found out about a new and daring venture by the Communist propagandists in the field of political indoctrination.

Propaganda directives in totalitarian countries have always been considered highly secret material. When one is discovered and published abroad, it makes a startling newspaper scoop. Every caution is exercised to prevent it from being seen by the native public or by foreigners. If their own people were to find out the way in which the information given to them had been twisted about and even manufactured, how could they be expected to fall for it? And if foreign countries were able to know what lines a nation wanted followed, and how it sought to manipulate information, they would obtain a very valuable insight into its real aims and would know what to expect from it in the future. Discovery of propaganda directives, in effect, would be like cracking a country's secret code. This little booklet I had picked up, and other material of this nature, indicated that Communist China would join the fighting in Korea. What it made absolutely certain was that it would enter the fighting if the North Korean forces were defeated. It gave itself no alternative.

The Chinese Communists threw ordinary precautions overboard, and the reason could only have been their race for time; they felt that the requirements of popular indoctrination as quickly and as extensively as possible were greater than the danger of exposing their hand. They must have trusted to past experience that any unprecedented, seemingly fantastic procedure would simply not be believed in normal, decent society in America and Europe, and that those who did see through the tactic would be overwhelmed by the dust storm that fellow travelers and Red agents abroad could be trusted to throw up over the issue to effectively counteract any adverse reaction in those lands.

As far as the Chinese people were concerned, no opposition organs existed in Red China in which this new technique could be exposed for what it was, the most brazen maneuver yet devised to deceive one's own people. For the crux of the whole idea was to make the public pull the wool over its own eyes and actually have fun doing it. The booklet was frankly entitled *Cartoon Propaganda Reference Book* and was put out by the Anti-United States and Aid Korea Committee of the Central Institute of Fine Arts,* a government institution under the Ministry of Cultural Affairs. The mission of all such government bureaus was succinctly explained by Lu Ting-yi, director of the Communist Party's Information Department, in an article in which he declared "art must serve politics" as "an important weapon in ideological education and ideological struggle." The purpose of the booklet was explained on its front inside cover.

* See Appendix B.

1. Volumes in this series contain basic material for propaganda sketches to be used by schools and other organizations in various places.

2. The compilers hope that all propaganda agencies will organize artists everywhere in the country to publicize current affairs with sketches. We also welcome criticism and suggestions from artists to help improve our working skill.

3. Volumes in this series will be published whenever sufficient material is gathered. They will not be printed at regular intervals.

How this material was to be arranged and the captions that were to be used, in accordance with the usual interpretation given democratic discussion in Red China, were left to the free will of the artists and writers so long as they conveyed the idea desired by the officials. The purpose was to reach the innumerable amateur cartoonists and writers and designers who contributed to the thousands and thousands of minor publications throughout China, the wall newspapers, shop papers, and technical sheets put out in almost every school, church, factory, organization, and village. Make-up men and designers for amateur play groups and designers of floats for parades could all be reached by such publications. Population levels could be reached that otherwise were only brought into a campaign by circuitous, involved roads, with the danger that by the time it got to those levels the Communist program would be interpreted differently than intended. Professional artists and writers could also be reached, and the entire procedure of putting across a propaganda line was immeasurably simplified by cutting across the crippling limitations imposed by the usual secrecy in such matters.

The reaction that ordinarily would accompany such a tactic, one of complete popular skepticism and even disbelief in the propaganda line, was greatly reduced and in many cases eliminated by the technique itself. Instead of appearing as a propaganda line imposed in some sinister manner from above, the impression was given that this whole outlook was developed by the people themselves. This is where the most sinister aspect of the entire technique lay. The propaganda directions did not emanate as such from the Communist Party or even from the Peiping government, which actually was the case, but from a front, in this case the Anti-United States and Aid Korea Committee.

Source material is difficult to obtain, particularly for amateurs, and here was a plentiful supply of it for amateur cartoonists and artists, showing the way every important personality should be drawn, in simplified fashion, and showing how every important political issue of the day should be represented pictorially. The Party, with its usual skill in exploiting the indomitable, finer qualities in any people, assumed correctly that once a cartoonist or artist had followed the models shown in the propaganda sketch book, he would be inclined to believe that they were true, and even to argue that they were, for weren't his own creations and honor at stake?

The result was a complete unity achieved in all of Red China's media for the communication of thought, from the daily press in a big city to an amateur play troupe in a distant middle school. That was why, no matter what the publication or organ and no matter where it came from inside Red China, there was always a faithful similarity in expression. Sketches always showed General MacArthur with the same lank, rapacious look; President Truman with the same countrified, silly stare; Dean Acheson as the anglicized lowbrow; Winston Churchill as a Goering type; and every other important figure in public life represented in a similar stereotyped manner. Issues of the day were also given a theme that never varied, unless and until the political line changed.

Even in pro-Communist publications abroad, these symbols and themes were copied. When I returned to America, I found them reproduced with exactitude in the literature being put out by the Communist fronts concerned with Asian affairs.

The contents of the propaganda sketchbooks could be

classified under four headings: personalities, themes, tags, and how to draw ordinary objects that frequently appear in connection with these. The first booklet put out in the series contained simple sketches of rifles, tommy guns, cartridge belts, and bayonets. There was also a page of tags to label or identify sketches. This page of tags revealed the purpose and theme of the whole booklet, the drumming up of distrust and hatred of America as part of preparation for war with the United States. Here is a full list of the tags sketched in that first issue: a bomb with the letters U.S.A. on it; a coin and a money bag with the dollar sign; an atom bomb; a pear-shaped capsule marked "rat plague germs"; three shoulder patches, with respectively, the letters United States, a dollar sign, and a skull and crossbones; Uncle Sam's high hat with stripes and stars; and a swastika flag and a helmet marked United States. If there was any doubt of the meaning, the page was entitled "American symbols seen in cartoons."

Of immense significance was the way in which the booklet showed artists how to draw different nationalities and races. Red Chinese and Red Korean soldiers, and Chinese and Korean peasants were sketched in different simple postures. The soldiers were shown well equipped and neat, well shaven and clean-cut, curiously Western in appearance, erect and husky; and the Chinese a little more erect and better uniformed than the North Koreans. The American soldiers were depicted as smaller, craven individuals with gangster faces and Semitic noses, slouchy, paunchy, snarling, and often in need of a shave. In case the amateur artist or the professional didn't get the point, the sketches were entitled "Ugly gestures of American troops in their war of aggression in Korea." The American soldiers were portrayed in every conceivable cowardly or nasty position and captioned as "blaming each other," "praying to God," "robbing wherever they go," and "competing in fleeing for life."

The pages given over to Chinese and Korean peasants were equally informative. A sturdy peasant was shown with a rifle slung over his back and a cartridge belt around his waist. I couldn't tell from the picture whether a man or woman was intended. The connotation was given that Communist workers and peasants just naturally consider themselves as guerrilla soldiers, ever ready to infiltrate behind the lines of the enemy or to shoot a passing anti-Communist soldier from behind.

Two sets of Chinese civilians were shown—the kindly, intelligent faces of a young man and a girl, and an old couple.

A full page was given to President Truman, who was referred to as "chief of the war criminals." A hangman's noose was the frame for six representations of him in various poses as a wizened, frantic, ridiculous figure with paunch and skinny legs, and in a leaping tantrum in which he is knocked off his feet by bad news in the paper.

The next page concerned "War Criminal MacArthur," always shown either with a dollar sign or a skull and crossbones as his insignia; "Warmonger Dean Acheson" in various buck-toothed, highly frantic poses; and "Warmonger Churchill" as an incendiary, smoking a bomb and looking like a pig-headed Prussian officer. There were "three ugly faces of Chiang Kai-shek," symbols of "a fleeing Syngman Rhee," and empty-faced Japanese notables.

The themes outlined in the propaganda sketchbook were the few, universal ones I came across consistently in all Chinese Communist propaganda. The main theme was directed to all the peoples of Asia, and was that the United States was actually following the pattern laid down by the Japanese ultranationalists of World War II, which aimed at military conquest of all Asia. Here, once more, if further evidence were needed, was proof that the Communists never hesitate to tackle a propaganda theme simply because it is ridiculous and untrue on the face of it; the more inconceivable, the more their propagandists appear to prefer it for its shock effect, and probably because a denial of what is wholly untrue usually becomes so involved in detail that in the confusion sight of the intrinsic lie is lost.

Acheson was shown in the map room with Truman and MacArthur, pointing for guidance to a condensed quotation from the notorious Tanaka Memorial,* reading: "In order to conquer the world, we must first conquer Asia; to conquer Asia we must conquer China; to conquer China, we must conquer Manchuria and Mongolia."

This is not so difficult a line to put across as it appears on the surface to the well-informed Westerner. The young student or ordinary intellectual in Asia doesn't know about this background of more than twenty years ago. He has been brought up with the conviction that the enemy strategy menacing China, and Asia generally, is as outlined in that quotation. All that the Chinese Communists have to do, therefore, is to switch nationality symbols by first confusing United States aims with those of Japan in the minds of the Asian peoples, and then making them think of the United States where they formerly thought of Japan.

This was the theme of a page entitled "American imperialists taking the old trail of the Japanese bandits." A bandaged figure of MacArthur was shown marching down the road with a dead Japanese soldier striding beside him, his face a skull and a swastika insignia on his arm. This was the message, too, of the cover illustration, which shows a Japanese skeleton rising from his grave to wave to an approaching, vicious-looking American soldier with a death's head insignia. This cartoon was entitled "Spirit of Japanese bandits beckoning to the United States imperialists." The United States was also shown releasing Japanese war criminals, who smilingly saluted the United States commander as they left their prison cells.

On the inside back cover was another theme of the greatest possible significance, which was that the great and powerful military might of Soviet Russia will be behind Red China if it gets into difficulty. This was shown in a series of

* Tanaka Memorial: Alleged report by Premier Baron Giichi Tanaka on July 27, 1927, to Emperor Hirohito, on a program for world conquest by Japan.

three sketches entitled "The Combined Force of China and Soviet Russia is Unbeatable in Defence of World Peace." The first sketch, dated 1918–1920, showed a giant Soviet soldier repulsing a puerile, silly-looking Uncle Sam, John Bull, France, and Poland. The next sketch, dated 1945, showed a giant Soviet Russian soldier crushing the Nazis with his right fist while he held up Japan by the neck with his other hand so that the Chinese Red Army could thrust a bayonet through him. Comparative sizes of such sketches are always significant. In this set of three, the Chinese Red soldier was shown much smaller than the Russian Communist but much larger than the Americans or other Westerners.

The third, and most ominous of the sketches, was dated the present. Again the giant Soviet soldier embraced the slightly smaller Chinese Communist soldier, with great Red armies behind each of them, while a puny American-led enemy stood helplessly in front.

2. Symbols and Themes

Other issues of the *Cartoon Propaganda Reference Book* were all equally packed with material serving as directives for the amateur and professional artists and cartoonists of Red China. The later ones contained even more glaring examples of the brazen confidence with which Red China was exposing its intentions. The Communists assumed that they had their foes in a trance, during which they had to achieve as much of their program as possible in the short time remaining before the awakening. How else, for instance, could I explain the all-Asia war program plainly outlined in these other propaganda sketchbooks?

A muscular, tall Malayan guerrilla in a native sarong was shown bashing in the head of a puny English soldier who wears the traditional British military tropical uniform of shorts, tropical shirt, and sun helmet. His rifle has fallen from his hands, and the enormous club with which he is being hit over the head is labelled, "Malayan People's Army."

My astonishment was even greater when I was able to find these booklets on sale in Hong Kong. I had not expected to, but there they were on the book counters. Here, in this British colony, guidance books were sold glamorizing and teaching the killing of other Englishmen in the British colony of Singapore and in Malaya generally. This wasn't a matter of freedom of speech, for I can't imagine even the most extreme proponent of unlimited freedoms suggesting that it included the right to sell lesson sheets on murdering one's neighbors, in so many words, without any beating around the bush. Such tolerance was self-defeating and inexplicable. The population of Hong Kong, nearly 2,000,-000, was all Chinese except for about 10,000 to 15,000 Europeans, principally Englishmen, including troops. With a few exceptions, all the Chinese-language bookshops, including most of the big ones, were either entirely or overwhelmingly pro-Communist. These bookshops refused to accept literature which the Communists disapproved of. Indeed, a number of the bookshops and publishing houses were actually registered with the Chinese propaganda bureau in Canton, across the border in Red China. Exactly as in Malaya and Indochina, the Communists were making believe that they already held Hong Kong, and they included it in the jurisdiction given Canton officials. The Hong Kong bookshops registered in Canton followed the instructions given bookshops and publishing houses anywhere in Red China, even to the extent of sending to Canton copies of anything they published, for censorship. The Hong Kong authorities seemed to prefer the delusion that as long as the few English language bookshops, patronized only by the English themselves or by the relatively few Chinese who could speak English, were not Communist, the situation was well in hand. This was the sort of make-believe being indulged in generally by the Westerner in Asia.

The Chinese populace of Hong Kong was thus restricted

in effect to Communist literature, virtually all of which followed an intensely anti-American war line, with the anti-British war line only differing in degree, not in sentiment. The Communist bookshops were operated exactly the same as bookshops anywhere in Red China. Sales were secondary; what was considered of primary importance was that the propaganda be read, especially by the youth. These shops could be more accurately described as public reading rooms. Day after day the scene inside them was the same. Clientele lined up in front of the counters, reading the inflammatory pamphlets and books from cover to cover. Youngsters of six and seven crowded about the children's counters where there were stacks of picture books with Uncle Sam, instead of the wolf, portrayed as the villain in virtually all stories; the British were depicted only a little less unfavorably. Middle school students swarmed about counters which had propaganda more suitable for their age. The salesmen had strict orders not to interfere with anybody's reading. The only rule was, if you didn't buy, you had to read.

This gave the Communists a virtual monopoly of reading material for the Chinese, as the city authorities had unearthed a curious health ordnance forbidding newsdealers generally from selling magazines, many of which were anti-Communist, except in the few established kiosks in the city. The magazines could, however, be sold in the bookshops. Since the bookshops generally refused to accept any except pro-Communist publications, the Communists, with their usual faculty for playing both ends against the middle, intimidated the few main kiosks so that they usually refused either to sell anti-Communist magazines at all, or kept them hidden in a drawer, bringing them out only when specifically requested. This blanket restriction even kept English-language publications off the streets, including *Time, Newsweek,* and local magazines such as *Newsdom* and *Orient,* whose sales were immediately hurt to such an extent that *Newsdom* had to change from a weekly to a semimonthly.

The scandal extended to all Chinese-language media,

even to the movie-production lots in and near Kowloon, the mainland city in Hong Kong colony. That the Chinese Communist authorities from Peiping and Canton had their own censors attached to most of these movie-production firms in the British colony, who went over all script and reels before distribution, was an open secret. Since the Chinese-language films for most of the Chinese communities outside of China itself were produced here, control of their content was of the utmost importance in determining what a Chinese anywhere in the world saw when he went to a Chinese-language movie.

So perhaps I was a little naive when I was surprised to find copies of the *Cartoon Propaganda Reference Book* in the bookshops of Hong Kong.

The all-Asia war theme was enunciated in the *Reference Book* in an alluring manner. There were several pages given over to the guerrillas and native peoples who inhabit Malaya, showing them in Indian, Eurasian, Malayan, and Chinese costumes, mostly barefooted, but all with rifles or bayonets. They were sketched in various working postures—shoveling, driving an ox cart, carrying a bundle, and sowing. Wholly aside from the propaganda content, these booklets comprised about the best set of sketches of native costumes that I saw in any such simple, cheap edition anywhere in Asia.

Half of one such booklet reproduced sketches of typical native couples in the clothes they usually wear in Japan, India, Burma, Thailand, Indonesia, and even in the Middle East. The page on Indochina was just as flattering to the population, and just as helpful in inciting armed violence. An Indochinese was shown working as a coolie, with a bamboo pole on his shoulder, and the same figure was shown with the bamboo pole replaced by a pistol. Another sketch, in case the artist missed the point, showed a robust Indochinese, in coolie straw hat, thrusting a bayonet into the back of a scared little French poilu. There are two sketches of peasant Indochinese women, one holding a rifle.

There wasn't much imagination or creativeness in these sketchbooks. They weren't intended as art for art's sake, but they were simple and well done, with the desired themes told over and over again, and with the slight changes required by such differences as locale.

Almost any student could be attracted to the page of flags of the various countries in the Soviet bloc. The impression of great power that Peiping wished to convey was shown by a symbol I came across frequently—a row of these flags on a commanding part of the sketch or page. In this instance, the flags were flying clear over the upper half of the globe.

All that an amateur had to do in order to draw an acceptable cartoon that looked professional was to arrange the symbols or themes he wished from these booklets and trace them. This was also a shortcut for the professional artists of Red China, confronted with the ever-increasing tempo of campaigns for greater production and the additional prestige and privileges such increased production gave.

In these later issues, I found more pages of Chinese and Koreans in working and fighting postures which conveyed the desired impression that each Asian is a guerrilla warrior fighting on behalf of the Communists. A sketch of a girl in cap, long, bobbed hair, and cartridge belt and rifle presents a romantic figure that makes guerrilla warfare look like a pleasanter life for a girl than classroom or clerical work, and immeasurably preferable to being a shopgirl or working on a farm.

Along with the glamorizing of life under Communism and the presentation of symbols of how attractive and natural it is for any boy or girl to be a Red soldier or a Communist guerrilla were pages symbolizing life in the United States as a nightmare of poverty and crime. The Asian, looking at these, might be convinced that no matter how hard his lot, it was better than being a downtrodden, exploited, hungry American.

What is even more convincing to youth than the economic angle is the appeal to ideals. Life in America was represented as morally distasteful and degenerating. The usual clichés were presented in simple sketches easy for reproduction in whatever arrangement the artist may have preferred. There was the fat gangster, a cigarette in the corner of his mouth, drawing an ugly pistol from his coat. There were a couple of hooded men staring up at a tree from which only the dangling feet of a lynched man could be seen. Shackled Negroes, in striped prison garb, were doing road work. There was the usual stereotype of a completely hooded man with a club, and in the corner of a page was a poverty-stricken American family—husband, wife and baby, and grandmother and two children—put out on the street to starve because they hadn't paid their rent. Children in knee pants were sticking a pistol into the stomach of a passer-by, robbing him of his clothes. The only heroic character shown was the American Communist.

Animal symbols are always attractive and effective, so these were not neglected in the propaganda sketchbooks. The British lion hobbled on crutches, with his ribs literally showing and his claws bandaged. The United States was a long viper, dollar-marked, and was being strangled by a strong fist. Other symbols showed friends or enemies variously interpreted as dogs, rats, crocodiles, horses, wolves, monkeys, cats, and eagles. Sometimes a public figure was given an animal head, as the delegates around an international conference table. The Voice of America was symbolized as a drawling wolf in tuxedo, with a dollar sign on his lapel.

A reiterated theme conveyed the impression that the United States was leading all non-Communist countries by the nose: Turkey with bloodstained hand, a bloody axe at the side, bowing like a beggar in front of another symbol, Uncle Sam's hand holding out a hangman's noose; a fat soldier, his insignia unmistakably marked U.S., leading a frightened Turk by a big nose; and the Pope piously blessing an atom bomb and a skull and crossbones.

Nationality symbols understandable to most people were sketched so that the artist could apply his drawing to any country he wished. A Japanese torii gate, the Eiffel Tower, Big Ben, the Arc de Triomphe, a row of skyscrapers, the

Great Wall, and a Peiping gate were all conveniently sketched.

The field of calculated manipulation of minds is as broad as the world. Brain-washing and brain-changing, as we have seen, are special techniques for particular purposes of a limited nature. Learning is the broad term used for political indoctrination in general. The medium for this learning is propaganda, and propaganda is applied to everyone. Everyone in Red China, illiterate or literate, old or young, male or female, must submit to this learning. Even the word, used this way, is a propaganda term.

WARMONGERING

After my return to America, I showed a few friends of mine some of the typical Chinese Communist publications that I had brought with me. I was surprised by their reaction. They went over them in shocked surprise, and then turned to me and exclaimed, "I never imagined anything like that!" Even a leading New York newspaperman, who has handled some of the biggest stories to pass the foreign desk of his news agency, was perplexed. "I've never seen anything like it," he declared. Frankly, he said that he had no idea what the words warmongering and hate campaign actually meant until he had looked over this material.

Such incomprehension has been America's greatest vulnerability. One of the favorite words used by Communists is warmonger. Only by reading the Communist publications such as *Cartoon Monthly* can people understand what warmongering really means.

Cartoon Monthly is a Shanghai publication with a nationwide circulation in China and in such communities as Hong Kong. Alongside the issue of December 1950, Soviet Russia's notorious *Crocodile* appeared tame in comparison. What the Chinese publication lacked in the quality of its art it made up in virulence.

Several main themes were repeated time and time again, each time in a slightly different setting. They were so ridiculous and so patently false that an American would be inclined to laugh them off. Unfortunately, they do not sound so illogical and impossible inside the Soviet bloc, where no contrary information is permitted. These themes, unbelievable as they sound to us, are that the United States is actually weak while Red China is unbeatable; that there is no alternative to victory by Red China because Soviet Russia can be depended on to back it up with all its power in case of need; that Soviet Russia is the most powerful country on earth; that the United States is hateful and Soviet Russia is a true friend of China—all this in such a way as to portray America as the principal enemy, which will have to be conquered by revolution or by war. The caption over an almost full-page cartoon on the inside back cover read:

The Pipe and the Tie. According to Reuters, Truman likes beautiful ties while MacArthur prefers ugly pipes. These two butchers have been massacring the innocent women and children of the world. When the time comes, they will be judged by the righteous people of the world. Two beautiful presents which they like will be prepared for them—a scaffold in the shape of a pipe, and a tie very appropriate to their conduct. These gifts will certainly prove to be suited to taste.

A small retouched photo at the bottom of the page showed President Truman with a flowing tie and General MacArthur smoking a big corncob pipe. Beneath a gallows and noose the two dignitaries crouched, bloodstained and drawn as though in the *Cartoon Propaganda Reference Book.*

The cover and back page were in brilliant yellow, red, green, and brown. On the cover was a sketch of the Statue of Liberty with her robe blown open, disclosing the Nazi insignia concealed beneath; and three platforms on which Americans crouched, as usually portrayed by the Reds—gangsters, priests with dollar signs on their cassocks, Ku Klux Klanners and prostitutes amid moneybags, and an evil fig ure clutching an atom bomb. A tattered balloon, marked "Hydrogen bomb—U.S.," was clutched by a scared officer. The back cover was an equally vitriolic representation of the Voice of America. The attention given the Voice of America should encourage it, for unless its broadcasts were deemed dangerous it would not warrant such publicizing. It was portrayed as "the deadly beauty", a sinister siren with the body of a long, sinuous snake, designed to represent the American flag. Its tail passed through the eyes of a big skull. The siren was wearing a doughboy cap marked U.S., and her microphone rested on a pile of silver dollars, which in turn were stacked on an atom bomb, as designed in the propaganda guidebook.

The callous contempt in which the Communists hold their public was demonstrated in the treatment of the atom bomb. One of the main propaganda themes in Red China is that people need not be afraid of the atom bomb. One page of cartoons in this magazine was entitled, "Why the Atom Bomb Cannot Win a War." The first reason: "An atom bomb is only as powerful as an ordinary 3,000-lb. bomb." The average reader of *Cartoon Monthly* would probably not dispute this and would go on his way confident that, after all, the atom bomb wasn't so powerful. After all, it's not as large as a two-ton bomb! That a political organization can be so ruthless toward its own people as to mislead them on such a matter would be unbelievable, if it weren't here in black and white. No typographical error can be responsible, as I first suspected. An elaborate chart showed the increase in the size of bombs since 1940. The artist who drew this pseudo-statistical job in the quack scientific manner of dialectical materialism, and the able Party members who passed it must have known the enormity of their falsehood.

The cartoon alongside showed frantic Americans stopping an American flier from dropping the atom bomb, and the comforting caption read: "The atom bomb is too expensive for large-scale production."

Significantly, as always whenever Chinese Communists

endeavor to dispel public doubt over the consequences of some particularly dangerous move, the boast was made that, if necessary, Soviet Russia would support Red China with its armed might, always presented as invincible. "The Soviet Russian army, and not the atom bomb, smashed the Germans and the Japanese," read the caption over a cartoon showing a giant Red soldier sweeping up Hitler with one hand and Hirohito with the other. Another cartoon showed terrified America staring at an atom bomb in the outstretched arm of Soviet Russia. The caption: "The U.S. is not the only country which has the atom bomb; Russia also has it."

The theme is repeated in another form where a sturdy figure was shown pounding the table with his fist and pointing to a frightened little group of men clinging to an atom bomb. "Vishinsky roars, warmongers tremble. To safeguard peace, Soviet Russia isn't the least afraid of war. . . . At those who throw bombs, bombs will be thrown."

While Red China was minimizing the power of the atom bomb, at the same time the so-called Stockholm peace petition was being signed throughout the country. A front organization, set up with the overwhelming title of Chinese People's Committee in Defense of World Peace and Against American Aggression, announced in October of 1950 that 200,000,000 Chinese adults had already signed up—almost all the adult population of China. Millions of signatures more were announced thereafter. Sometimes the number of signatures for a certain city was well over its adult population. The Party wasn't fooled into believing that all these signatures actually had been obtained. Everyone knew that people were signing their names or any name that came into their mind as many times a day as they were asked. Signature booths were set up everywhere anybody went, indoors and outdoors. The petition wasn't the objective; the objective was the publicity effect, which we should not underestimate. The Stockholm peace petition was a glorious success from the Communist viewpoint.

Moscow and Peiping know well enough that the atom

bomb is a weapon immensely more potent than other weapons but still a weapon. If anyone doubts that Communist Russia can and will use it first if they believe it will be to its advantage, they are dangerously naïve. The whole purpose of the Chinese Communist drive was to put the United States, which has the weapon, in a position where it would feel that it could not use it, and to achieve this objective by sheer propaganda.

The intent was to create a state of mind around the world which would regard American use of the bomb so adversely that the psychological damage would offset any military benefit we might obtain from it in a theater of war. In late 1950 in Asia this objective was achieved. If the military situation had been such in the Korea-Manchuria theater that use of the bomb was required to save an otherwise irreparable situation, we were not in a position to drop it without alienating all the rest of Asia as well as the Chinese people and our European allies. This is psychological warfare in its most striking form.

Not only was the atom bomb described as something not to be feared, but the United States itself was interpreted as not to be feared in a page entitled "The American Paper Tiger Dissected." The United States is constantly referred to in the Chinese Red press as a paper tiger. A paper tiger is a Chinese colloquialism for anyone or any organization that pretends to great strength while actually weak. In this full-page cartoon the paper tiger was divided into sections with a different sketch in each. A devil was shown at a microphone representing the Voice of America while a ranting figure stood alongside with a swastika over him. The caption: "Plotting to start the war." A skeleton with a scythe was entitled "Lurking economic crisis." A Wall Street magnate tugged at a scared figure, and this sketch was labelled "The slaves are unwilling to die for them." Workmen waved banners reading "People's opposition to war; difficulty in raising soldiers." Generals were shown frantically telephoning "The back line is too far, the front line is too long." A bandaged German soldier is shown in a sickbed reading "*Mein Kampf,* continued by Truman." Drowning soldiers underneath raised a banner proclaiming "We want to go home."

This United States-is-weak theme was repeated in still a different form on another page entitled "Imperialist America is Lacking in Armed Forces." One sketch showed emaciated figures of the United States, Britain, and France raising an inflated balloon looking like a soldier in front of a Russian soldier double its size. The caption: "To invade such a young nation as Korea, imperialist America had to throw all its military forces into the Far East. It drew all its reserves from the country, eight divisions, as well as the armies of its satellites, and still lacks manpower." Another sketch said: "According to estimate, the highest possible limit for mobilization by imperialist America and all its satellites is 40,000,000, while that of Soviet Russia, China, and the democratic nations totals 80,000,000."

Typical humor is of the sort provided by a set of two panels. Acheson, embracing a skeleton, was shown acting as barker for recruitment in front of a curtain with a poster depicting a couple kissing. The poster read "Join the army, and you can travel all over the world." The second panel showed the wind blowing open the curtain, disclosing rows of crosses in a military graveyard. The caption: "Join the army, and you will travel to another world."

The Communist editors knew that cartoons such as these would not be seen by Americans, and so they did not print them with the idea of influencing recruiting morale in the United States. They printed them to deflate American military prestige among the peoples of Asia, and to convey the idea that it wouldn't be difficult to defeat the Americans in a war.

My first inclination was to ignore a vile caricature. If this magazine or the cartoon were not so typical, its omission would have been warranted. But it was typical. It confronted me with the same sort of problem, the answer to which has contributed so much to our naïveté and misunderstanding of basic situations around the world, and which as much as any other factor has been responsible for the sudden shocks we have received in our foreign relations, from which we awaken only at great cost and sacrifice. We constantly shy away from distasteful facts when they run counter to our illusions as to how other people think and react. We wear tinted glasses in viewing foreign affairs. We insist that all other peoples speak and act as we would do in America, with the tolerance that is part of our heritage, but we fail to appreciate that environment and not birth are mainly responsible for a person's thoughts and actions.

If we had been told, for example, the unutterably filthy curse word—the worst that can be used in the Chinese language—that Mao Tse-tung applied to America in his *New Democracy,* in contrast with his expressions of deepest affections for Soviet Russia, we could not have been caught by surprise by the vicious extremes to which he went in his anti-American policies when he set up his government in Peiping.

Chinese Communist propagandists do not hesitate to refer to subjects which among us are taboo. In the caricature referred to, a man, unmistakably President Truman, was shown kneeling behind a microphone on top of a coffin draped with the Stars and Stripes. He was breaking wind—the caption uses the plain word—into the mike, and the message that comes out is labelled Voice of America. A fat "Wall Street boss" has handed him sheets of broadcast script on which are written "rumors, slander, anti-Communism," while Truman reads from one entitled "Plan for aggression in Korea."

The Communists know that such ribaldry, with an unexpected twist, passes for cleverness and creates amusement, and they also know that the Chinese people—like many others—really appreciate anything that amuses them in this way. The Reds do not hesitate to exploit this field and many another for propaganda purposes. They entered this one all the more eagerly because they have it exclusively to themselves. Their enemies are far too dignified to talk so crudely, in such vernacular. By using the language of the street, the Communist puts himself on the level with these people, who fail to realize that this is patronizing but instead are thankful over the feeling that they are being treated as equals. This, too, is a propaganda trick to which the Chinese Communists do not hesitate to descend. They go down to the gutter to talk to a man in gutter language—leaving him in the gutter. The man often feels that this, at least, is better than not being talked to at all. It pays off in revolutionary movements and with recruits who will become blind fanatics.

This magazine, like all others of its kind, contains a number of cartoons contributed by embryonic artists in factories, schools, and other institutions. These are the persons to whom the *Cartoon Propaganda Reference Book* is ostensibly directed. The Party knows of the prestige attached to acceptance of any contribution because its publication assures that it will be seen and envied by the creator's fellow workers and that the organ running it will gain in readership.

The Party also knows that the artist never will say, "My work is lousy; it was only accepted because I allowed myself to be used as a mouthpiece for propaganda." Oh no, he will rather defend the propaganda with which he had to wrap up his drawing. This is one of the tactics to which the Communists have resorted in order to give the impression that the Party line is spontaneous with the masses.

This and any other issue of *Cartoon Monthly* could not have passed a self-criticism meeting or a bombardment meeting of its staff if it had failed on the theme of alleged American atrocities against the Chinese people. So we have the required cartoons—one, of two American sailors riding a jeep, raising the thumbs-up victory insignia as they speed on after killing a passer-by; another, of a drunken American soldier with the usual long, long nose, beating a rickshawman to death; a third, of American naval motorboats allegedly knocking over Chinese vessels and leaving their victims to drown; and a fourth showing a gang of American soldiers in an alleged mass rape at a dance hall.

Again and again, I came across evidence of how worried the Communists were over the heritage of real affection left among children by the ordinary American soldier, sailor, and marine. His instinctive sharing of candies and titbits with kids and his reputation for being a pushover for any youngster who asks for something has left in the minds of these youngsters and their elders what the Communists sincerely regard as imperialist poisons, the sort that can only be cured by brain-washing. A more recent issue of the magazine ran two half-page cartoons by one of its best-known comic strip artists on this subject. They showed a little boy with three hairs—a well-known Chinese cartoon character—standing outside a bar with a can, waiting for alms. A grotesquely drunken American sailor was shown emerging, whacking the boy from behind with a beer bottle, then jeering at the bleeding child as he lay stricken on the ground. The other portrayed an unshaven, untidy gob passing two Chinese children, one with three hairs. The two lads asked for a coin, which the sailor smilingly took from his pocket. He pretended to toss it over their heads for them to run and pick up. They bumped into each other in the attempt and then, in the last of the four panels, while on the ground with big lumps on their heads, the sailor jeered at them—still clutching the cash.

There is no accusation vile enough to be concocted and hurled at the Americans in this Communist hate campaign which, because it was so extreme and so distasteful, we ignored. We pretended that such vicious accusations were naturally without effect, if only we closed our eyes to them. This holier-than-thou attitude was duck soup for the Communists.

In all such publications, the Communists exploit the craving for knowledge among all people. The magazine has a carefully written department called "The Cartoon Classroom." Here is a summary of its adroit propaganda. I summarize the article entitled "Humor and Satire," by Shen Tung-hung.

Cartoons are not careless, maladroit, and meaningless sketches. They are simple sketches full of meaning. They are like short, forceful essays. In Soviet Russia, cartoons are called satirical drawings. Cartoons, indeed, should deal merciless blows on enemies, be friendly to friends, and sincerely investigate oneself. Drawings without meaning, without satire, are actually not cartoons.

Moreover, cartoons should have humor. Only with humor can satirical sketches uncover the truth with one stroke. Only with humor can cartoons provide wholesome smiles and render useful education.

Russian artists are well versed in satirical drawings, and that is why the magazine *Crocodile* is welcomed by many Russian readers. Besides reading the magazine, readers also contribute their own ideas to it.

I hope that the readers of this magazine will pay heed to the humor and sarcasm in our cartoons. Especially today, when the whole nation is ringing with the slogan "Hate the American imperialists, despise the American imperialists, scorn the American imperialists," should we develop our talents in humor and sarcasm in creating the most piquant and the most humorous satire. Let us hate, despise, and scorn the American imperialists—the deadly enemies of the people of China!

Cartoons are essentially a one-man job, but individualism of this sort is always regarded as dangerous by the Communists. Only in a group, with the check that numbers provide against ideas that do not fit into the political groove, do the Communists feel that political heresy can be avoided and people's thoughts kept on an even keel politically. "An essay on the collective creation of cartoons" by Fang Ing in another issue of *Cartoon Monthly* brought this out with only slight concealment.

Collective creation is the advanced, efficient method of creation. We have an old proverb that says, "Three blockheads make one sage." This means that the thoughts and actions of the collective are forceful.

Promoting collective creation does not mean neglecting individual creation. It is intended to strengthen the collective creation on a foundation of individual creation, to use collective creation to give the individual what he lacks, and to enrich the contents of individual creations.

A successful collectively created cartoon must be collective not only in respect to the technique of creation, but also in respect to its contents. The thoughts of each member must be harmoniously welded together and expressed in suitable form.

In order that the thoughts of all the participants may be unified, their standpoints, viewpoints, and techniques should first be unified. That is to say, each of them should lead a normal and collective life.

I believe that with the progress of this epoch and the needs of society, more and more attention will be paid to collective creation. Collective strength expressed in collective creation will certainly produce great and rich results.

1. "Talk-Books"

Through the length and breadth of China, in small villages and big cities, the street-corner lending libraries have been landmarks for as many years as people can remember. No more than a few wooden shelves, the libraries are stocked with small, paper-covered books telling stories in pictures, one picture to a page, with a brief explanatory caption underneath each. The stories were usually fanciful folklore, mad adventure, fairy tales, and torrid romance, often against a classical, pseudo-historical background. The clientele comprised all kinds of plain people—workers, apprentices, rickshaw runners, housewives, coolies, peddlers, servants, housemaids, and school children. For only a few cents they could borrow a set of books which most of them had little or no difficulty in reading. Poorly printed, their pages usually dirty from long use, their contents lurid to the extreme, the books nevertheless offered the most popular reading matter for the general public.

The Nationalist government often tried to ban the street-corner libraries because their material was unsuitable for the young and was excessively sensational for anyone. Here and there the authorities succeeded for a while in closing them. Nothing was ever offered to take their place. The publications filled a real need, and where they were banned, a black-market distribution naturally developed. Suppression was never effective anywhere for any length of time.

Wherever they were in control, the Communist authorities also banned the circulation of the old, paper-bound books. Too clever to leave a vacuum, they placed orders with the printing companies that formerly put them out for even larger lots of a similar type, similar in every respect except one—the contents now contributed to propaganda and indoctrination. Going a step further, they assigned some of their best writers and cartoonists to provide the stories, the net result of which was that the Red regime easily succeeded in winning—by default, as usual—the tremendous mass market. The picture story books became sharp weapons of propaganda, possibly the most effective medium the Communists possessed among the mass of the people. They distributed them all through China, and in Nationalist territory as well, wherever they could take advantage of civil rights. Neither the Kuomintang nor the liberal Third Force elements entered this vast field until about a year after the entire mainland had been lost to the Communists.

Most of these readers had little or no education, and the picture books were the only ones they could enjoy without too much mental strain. Where the old style were banned, and in Communist areas, they found only the new, Communist ones available. To these people, picture books were all alike. The new ones were not quite to their taste in the beginning, but they soon got over it. The picture books had been the main pastime of many, and they weren't going to be stopped by a little propaganda. They absorbed it hook, line, and sinker—and gratefully.

One reason for the old books' great popularity was that

they provided recreation for a whole village or for all the workers of a big textile or power plant, most of whom were illiterate or nearly so. The wandering storytellers, a profession that goes back ages in China, used them to read from and to elaborate upon, basing their stories partly on the text, partly on the pictures, and partly on their imaginations. This was how the books came to be known as "talk-books." Workers paid a storyteller to come to their plant at lunchtime or during some recreation period to entertain them in this way. It became a regular practice in many factories and institutions. The wandering narrators, after asking the workmen what favorite story they wanted, sat on the stage in front of a table and recited the entire story dramatically, almost always by memory.

Here the Communists stepped in. They had no trouble assigning able Party members to request a publication put out under Red inspiration. Often they didn't have to conspire; the authors they had assigned to the job produced a far better story than the usual Chinese pulp writers. With a keen eye to coordination, a tactic muffed by their enemies, the Communists publicized the talk-books and exploited the idea by furnishing an especially interesting movie or novel in this form. When an exceptionally good talk-book was published, they saw to it that not only book critics praised it but also that it came out as a regular novel or even as an operetta.

I was surprised at first when friends of mine, who were graduates of Chinese colleges or universities and were opposed to the whole political philosophy of Communism, knew the talk-book stories from cover to cover.

"Some of them are good, really good," they said. "They're so good that you just don't pay any attention to the propaganda."

When I had them translated I agreed, and I understood how it came about that some of the Communist talk-books became classics universally known in China. Piles of the talk-books, of every conceivable plot, from the most virulently anti-American to the most calculatingly subtle, were heaped on the counters of most bookshops in Hong Kong, where they contributed largely to the indoctrination of the Chinese-speaking population of the colony.

The Communists resorted to talk-books to reach the minds of the plain people in support even of their bond drives. Even here the hate-America theme is amply evident. One talk-book was frankly entitled *Buy Victory Bonds; Bonds Are the Duty of All Citizens* was the subtitle. A couple of lines of text accompanied each full-page picture. The following text was worth reading by itself as an example of how cleverly the Communists pushed even so unpopular a measure as a bond drive.

1. A meeting, where representatives of all professions are buying bonds.
2. The pedicab driver, Hu Ming-hsiang, is applauded for his purchase of 100 units.
3. Children's delegates from the Pedicab Children's School deck Hu with flowers.
4. The delegate Hu Ne-ne was Hu Ming-hsiang's eldest daughter.
5. Hu was asked to give a speech.
6. He said, "In Shanghai, before liberation
7. "Our comrade Chang Dah-tse was killed by an American sailor.
8. "Once, I drove an American sailor to a dance hall.
9. "The drunken sailor didn't pay the fare.
10. "I argued and he kicked me.
11. "I hated not only foreigners, but also myself.
12. "Due to bad leadership of the reactionary government, I went astray, as did the others.
13. "I gambled with my friends.
14. "Sometimes I lost all my money.
15. "No rice at home, so my wife and children cried.
16. "When I won
17. "The others forced me to invite them.
18. "We ate up all our money—blood and sweat.

19. "My wife and children cried when I came home.
20. "I was ashamed, and determined to save.
21. "After liberation
22. "I admired the hard work by the People's Liberation Army, and I wanted to learn how to save money.
23. "I started a Parity Units savings account in the People's Bank.
24. "In five months I saved 200 units.
25. "Once I visited the Labor Union.
26. "I read the wall newspaper.
27. "Much was written about Parity Bonds.
28. "Here was a good chance to save.
29. "After all, there's so much profit to share, and the bonds will accelerate liberation.
30. "Bonds will enable the government to restore production.
31. "Bonds will enable the government to stabilize prices.
32. "They also will enable the government to promote public welfare.
33. "The nation will increase production, while the individual saves.
34. "The total bond issue is 200,000,000 units, to be paid up in five years.
35. "One unit equals 6 catties of rice, 1½ catties of flour, 4 feet of cloth and 16 catties of coal.
36. "Parity value is computed on the basis of the commodity prices in six big cities.
37. "Besides the guarantee of its original value, there is 5 per cent annual interest.
38. "I felt that this was stupendous, and that if I didn't buy, I was not worthy to be a Chinese.
39. "I converted all my parity savings into bonds.
40. "I now save one third of what I earn.
41. "This I also use to buy bonds.
42. "Even high officials know that I have bought 100 units of bonds. I am grateful over this."
43. After Hu had finished, a woman representative, Yuen Shih-fang, stood up to speak.

44. The manager of the Sun Sun textile firm also spoke.
45. The representatives of all the professions resolved to follow Hu's example.
46. Enthusiastically, the chairman concluded the meeting.

The sketch of an American sailor taking advantage of the poor pedicab driver was enough to arouse racial and anti-United States feelings; if the story had not made a bond purchaser out of the reader, at least he would have received a little indoctrination on the side.

There was another type of talk-book, the kind that beat the war drum. If any other element in China had put out such material, there would have been plenty of foreign observers to make sure that world attention was aroused to what immediately would have been branded as warmongering of the most flagrant sort. One of the best known of these talk-books, *The People's Daughter,* was based on World War II history. It is particularly interesting because it gives an account of partisan fighting behind the lines in Central Europe. Also, it is an inspirational story to inspire young Chinese men and women—the hero is a woman guerrilla—to emulate the heroes. The edition I have was published in January 1950; unfortunately, it is impossible to determine how many of the young people who later fought the Americans in Korea were inspired to become guerrillas by the book.

To the Chinese, the curious twist given the story was in making the heroine a Lithuanian girl fighting for "her country"—Soviet Russia! The average Chinese reader, particularly any who reads talk-books, cannot be expected to know that the Lithuanian people were decimated, and that untold numbers of them were forcibly deported by the Russians in as ruthless and unwarranted an occupation of another people's territory as has happened in Europe in the past half century. There were many Lithuanian guerrillas (the hitch is that they were in action before World War II) who sacrificed their lives in the same manner as the heroine in *The People's*

Daughter, but not on behalf of Moscow—but for freedom from it.

The simple drawings were designed to teach what is important to the Communists, who know that women and children can be very effective in war, particularly against an army with the bourgeois gallantry of the American. The heroine engaged in tasks "impossible for others, shunned by men." She organized propaganda teams, "hiding propaganda material inside the Bible" in churches; destroyed railway tracks; became a sniper; tossed hand grenades; transported wounded across a freezing river; recruited guerrillas; and fought alone to cover a retreat, until she was finally wounded and captured, after killing many of the enemy.

Communist literature always has its leading character indescribably tortured in an effort to extract information; and always, as with this heroine, the "cruelest tortures" are resisted, until "undaunted, she walked the road to martyrdom" and died before a firing squad.

On the last page was a girl in Joan of Arc posture, with rifle in one hand and waving comrades onward with the other as she pressed forward, Soviet flags to her right, Soviet flags to her left. The last sentence: "Do not forget this heroine who fought for the liberty of the people and the unity of her country's territory." A more callous distortion of history and patriotism can hardly be imagined, but that should not blind us to the fact that in *The People's Daughter* the Communists devised a thrilling and surely effective piece of war propaganda. In such propaganda stories the Chinese Communists always exploit an emotion that is much easier to arouse in youth than desire for personal comfort and financial reward; it is the spirit of sacrifice and willingness to face hardship and danger. Instead of shying away from tragedy in order to give the stories a happy ending, the Communist glamorize the sorrow and the pain, making their heroes and heroines suffer calmly and die fearlessly. Thus is created the impression that the Communists are doing their recruits a favor by letting them give up everything they have, even their thoughts and their loved ones, for a political cause.

2. "Talk-Books"

Knowledge of Chinese isn't necessary to understand the contents of a talk-book I picked up one day, supposedly a history of Sino-American relations. Its cover showed a lean, senile, hook-nosed old man, with an evil glint in his eye. Dressed as Uncle Sam, he wickedly pointed out the direction for a squat Japanese militarist accoutered with a cannon, cannon ball, bayonets, and a samurai sword.

The subject of Sino-American relations has annoyed the Chinese Communists ever since they came to power. The record of American relations with China over the years has been so fair, so open and above board that its underlying friendliness appears irrefutable. The totalitarian philosophy of the Communists, however, can't afford to admit a single good deed by the United States or a single act motivated by good will. I have never been entirely able to understand why such a simple admission could endanger the whole Communist structure, but that this is their approach has been evident time and time again. The extremes to which the Communists have gone to prove that there hasn't been a single action by the United States, at any time since 1776, that has been friendly to China, even by accident, demonstrates a state of mind, I think, which will prove the Achilles' heel of Communism even if it were to conquer the world. The facts of Sino-American relations are too self-evident for the Communists to refute by ordinary discussion. Their recourse has been to generalize, to paint black on white and white on black, with psychopathic consistency. The February 1 issue of the Peiping magazine, *People's China*, in a lead article entitled *American Imperialists Never Learn* blithely declared:

Certainly it would be hard today to find one person among the 475,000,000 Chinese who is so ignorant as not to realize that the basic policy of American imperialism, today just as fifty years ago, has been to turn China into an American colony by whatever means are at hand.

A long article was published in the same semi-official magazine by "a Marxist historian" in which each of the better-known historic American acts of friendship and cooperation with China was taken up and completely distorted, without the slightest documentation, by resorting to the "everyone knows" tactic—sheer fabrication of history. When no single specific example could be found to support the Communist charge that the United States had always been a military aggressor against China, the pseudo-history falls back on this logic:

Naturally enough, no aggressor likes to resort to war if he can obtain as much as he wants by other means. And since the American government found such other means at its disposal, it fell into the role of a treacherous but outwardly amiable "friend."

How, then, to explain the Burlingame Treaty of 1868, a treaty of equality and friendship that was unprecedented in China's history with the West? "We all know," the article airily declares, "that America's hands were so full of reconstruction after its Civil War that it had no time for foreign affairs, and anyway, reconstruction was 'more profitable than foreign adventures.'"

One might have thought that the open-door policy would have been difficult to twist. Not for the Communists.

The open-door policy is an imperialist policy by which China was relegated to a semicolonial status. It was with its own interests in mind, and not those of China, that the United States set forth this policy.

The talk-book I picked up presented the same line pictorially. The first page showed Uncle Sam, pistol out and foreclose-that-mortgage look on his face, forcing the empire of the Manchus to sign a treaty. In the next panel Uncle Sam stood by, pointing to China as the target while he passed shells to the British to fire. The following picture, identical with the cover, but in black and white, charged the United States with instigating Japan's first war with China, which certainly should be news both for Japan and China. Despite America's consistent record of opposition to Japanese aggression in China—an opposition that led directly to Pearl Harbor—the succeeding pages of the talk-book made Uncle Sam in some way or another responsible for each of the Japanese interventions in China. Also included was the page obligatory to all Chinese Communist publications of this kind, which showed unshaven, drunk American soldiers indiscriminately beating up Chinese men and raping their women. Our World War II record in China was falsified in such a manner that our aims defended the Japanese invader from defeat by the Chinese Communist army. Finally—with the United Nations Relief and Rehabilitation Administration record so recent—enormous American ships were shown loaded with loot from China and Uncle Sam as a potbelly supervising the vandalism. The Red propagandists, of course, passed over Soviet Russia's wholesale postwar looting of machinery and of complete factories in Manchuria—the industrial arsenal that China was banking upon to make reconstruction possible. The same fat, hook-nosed Uncle Sam was emptying Chinese shops of all their merchandise. The propagandists here glibly ignored the fact that, even while this talk-book was on public sale throughout Red China and Hong Kong, hordes of so-called Russian advisers were emptying Chinese shops in just such fashion. The intent obviously was to divert Chinese indignation over Soviet Russian excesses by making the United States the scapegoat. A blind and crippled Uncle Sam, a cannon strapped to his back, was ultimately shown stepping toward the edge of a precipice.

Don't Kill Him was a story that can only be compared to the most tear-jerking soap operas ever heard over the American daytime kitchen radio, and *The White-Haired Daughter* was a masterpiece in the field of collectively conceived picture-book literature.

When I first had it translated, *Don't Kill Him* sounded unbelievable even for the Chinese Communists. An old mother actually begged the Communists to spare the Red soldier who had killed her son. The story subtly discredited not merely the family system, but family affection and family attachments generally. The old mother, out of loyalty to the Red Army, said her son was only an opium smoker, so "why kill a good soldier for him?" The mother actually denounced her son, but in such a dramatic scene that the reader's attention was cleverly drawn elsewhere, not realizing that the lesson was the betrayal of one's nearest and dearest. Finally, when the killer's life was saved, mainly through the efforts of the old woman, who threw herself over him at the execution ground, crying, "Shoot me first," he marched off with the rest of the Red Army. Through her tears the old lady sobbed, "Comrade, you are too good! I shall miss only you, and not my son." The text, referring to sin and repentance in the usual quack evangelical manner, as always brings in the blame-America-hate-America theme. So passes dialectical materialism for the masses; it is also psychological warfare as well.

This literature was infiltrated into thousands of Chinese villages before the approach of the Red Army. Often it was the only reading matter available. In the cities similar literature was sold "under the counter," or thinly disguised in other stories by writers who posed as liberals until the arrival of the Red Army gave them the opportunity to safely reveal their past Communist ties.

Communist magazines and other publications now often allude, in a matter-of-fact manner, to how cleverly they outwitted the authorities in distributing such literature in non-Communist areas. Tsai Chu-sheng, film director and an official in the Ministry of Cultural Affairs, in an article on the Chinese movie industry, refers to "progressive film workers" in Nationalist areas of China, particularly Shanghai, who after Japan's defeat "still managed to produce what the reactionaries labeled 'seditious propaganda.' Despite severe restrictions, they set up or supported private companies with a core of talented artists and directors.'"

An article entitled *Publishing for the People*, which appeared at the same time, boasts how pro-Soviet and other revolutionary publications were published and sold secretly. Mao Tse-tung's *New Democracy* was disguised as *Analytical Studies of Classical History*.

Perhaps the best known of the talk-books, and the one on which the Communists exerted most of their skill, is *The White-Haired Daughter*, which has been converted into a novel, a ballad, a drama, a movie, and an operetta; and has been used as the basis of a number of popular songs and the subject of innumerable articles and essays. The story, a collective product, has been written in verse as well as prose, and with different illustrations.

Hsi-li, daughter of a poor farmer named Yang Pei-lao, walked home through the wind and the snow. She carried a small package of noodles, the gift of her aunt, who hoped to marry the girl to her son, Dah Tsun. Walking thus, she found her father dead in the snow. Yang had been trying to hide from his debtors because New Year's is settlement time. However, a heartless landlord, Hwang Shu-jen, sent his wicked retainer, Mo Shun-tsu, to press for his money. When Yang couldn't pay it, Mo brought him to his master's house, where he was forced to sign away his daughter to become the servant of the landlord's mother, a cruel Buddhist woman.

As Yang returned home to celebrate a sad New Year's party, he couldn't bear what had happened and committed suicide in the snow, clutching the tell-tale agreement to his chest. Here Mo found the weeping daughter and dragged her off her father's corpse and took her to Hwang's mother. Hsi-li's life was tragic. When Dah Tsun tried to visit her, he was refused admittance. In the ensuing fight, a servant, Dah Su, joined Dah Tsun in beating up the retainer. Dah Tsun escaped, but Dah Su was thrown into jail.

Hwang encouraged his mother to smoke opium to put her in a coma, for he was plotting to rape Hsi-li. In a heart-rending scene Hsi-li served lotus soup to the old woman, who, finding it either too sweet or too hot, beat her up. In anger, the crabbed old woman thrust an opium needle through the girl's tender lower lip.

One evening, while boiling soup, Hsi-li broke the kettle. She ran out of the house in fear, only to run into the arms of Hwang, who carried her into his apartment on the compound and there raped her. The next morning Chang Hsun, a kind-hearted woman servant who was searching for the unhappy girl, found her just in time to prevent her suicide by hanging.

Hsi-li was later convinced by a vicious retainer that the landlord would marry her. Indeed, arrangements were made for a marriage. However, just before Hsi-li gave birth, she learned that all the preparations were for another girl.

In her bitter grief she berated Hwang. He and his mother beat her and decided to sell her into prostitution. Chang Hsun, overhearing, helped Hsi-li escape in the moonlight. She was pursued into the woods by the landlord and retainer, but they gave her up for dead and abandoned the chase when they found one of her shoes in a swamp. Hsi-li tried to go to her aunt's home, but she was lost. Sleeping that night in a mountain cave, she gave birth to a boy.

Finally making her way to the village, and through the window of her aunt's house, she heard her uncle tell how bravely she had died in the swamp. Ashamed, she decided to kill herself and the baby, but her mother-love prevented her, and so she vowed to live on to revenge herself. She brought up the child in the cave, hiding from everyone, and only ventured into a nearby temple when it was empty in order to filch food offerings.

Two years later, war broke out with Japan, and the Kuomintang army fled from the neighborhood, letting the enemy march in. One day, the landlord and his retainer were caught in a heavy downpour and took refuge in the temple.

Hsi-li entered to seek food offerings. Her arduous life and sufferings had turned her hair, which had grown long, entirely white, and when the two men saw the apparition, they fled, thinking she was a demon. She recognized them and, infuriated, chased after and threw stones.

The two men dashed back to the village to tell everyone about the white-haired demon in the temple. The superstitious villagers believed them. News came that the Communist 8th Route Army had attacked the Japanese, driving them from the city. Dah Su left jail, and Dah Tsun returned, now an officer with the Red Army. Everyone was happy to find out how kind the Red Army was to the people. [This is one of the "must" scenes in every such talk-book.] The Communists immediately reduced all rents. In the meantime, the landlord and his retainer were still spreading superstitious rumors about the fearsome white-haired spirit in the temple.

Dah Tsun was appointed officer in control of his old village. He set to work on a program of breaking down old superstitions, driving away wicked retainers, and liquidating evil landlords. Dah Tsun and Dah Su decided to find out about the white-haired demon and, while hiding in the temple, saw her haggard form approach. Dah Tsun fired, wounding her in the arm. She rushed to her cave, from which her two pursuers were surprised to hear a baby's piteous call for its mother. Hsi-li fainted, and Dah Tsun, exploring the cave with his torch, recognized her.

There was a gloriously pathetic reunion, and the men led her back to the village to live once more in sunlight. A liquidation meeting was held, and all the villagers gathered to tell their grievances and accuse their old exploiters. Hsi-li was told not to be afraid, but to voice all of her complaints, which she did. Bowing to the verdict of the people, Hwang was taken into town. The villagers discussed his fate, and all the mistreated demanded his execution. He was accordingly done to death. The last caption read, "The day has arrived for revenge and for the poor to take over."

This melodrama was a virtual textbook for the peasants.

Smuggled into farming areas, it contributed much toward paving the way for the entry of the Red Army. Later, it became an incentive for public trials. Songs from the ballad version are sung at mass liquidation meetings. The Communist radio, as I write this, has only recently broadcast an account of how virtually the entire population of a big city, Mukden, came out to witness such a purge trial, and how they got into the spirit of the occasion by singing songs from *The White-Haired Daughter*.

Daughter has a double meaning—a farmer's daughter and, in this case, the people's daughter.

SCHOOL DAYS

EDUCATION

I OBTAINED A COMPLETE SET OF THE NEW CHINESE COMmunist textbooks for primary and high school. Some were available in bookshops in Red China, others on the black market, others through indignant teachers. These textbooks are now the basis for the education of China's young, from their first day in class when they are about six, to the time that they leave high school as young men and young women up to twenty-two years of age.

Out of these schools come a goodly share of the brains and brawn for China's Red Army and its guerrilla forces. What these tens and tens of thousands of young persons are being taught is therefore of the utmost consequence to us and to the free world. Are they being instructed in the ways of peace or of war? And, if war, is it war for defense or for aggression? What role is reserved for Soviet Russia in this?

The answers, I felt, better than any other available source would reveal the actual long-range policy of Communist China, and how it regards its ties with Soviet Russia. The answers, I was sure, would go a long ways toward telling us what the prospects are for achieving the type of world that was envisaged at San Francisco when the United Nations was born.

What diplomats can hide in their statements becomes evident in their country's textbooks. Is Peiping actually motivated by the desires to rebuild its war-torn country and to provide peace and happiness for its own people, as its friends would like us to believe? Is this the attitude that actually motivates its relations with the United States, Soviet Russia, and the rest of the world?

If the intent of the Chinese Reds is something different, this is vitally important for us to know. One way or the other, only knowledge of the true situation can save us and the world from incalculable disruption and catastrophe. I felt, too, that in China we would have a better opportunity of finding out the motivations inside the Soviet bloc as a whole than anywhere else in the world.

I expected that the Chinese Communists would use the schools to further their own political beliefs. That was only natural. But how far was this indoctrination to go? That was the crux of the matter. Were they presenting the world situation as a struggle to the death between the forces of good and the forces of evil? Were they teaching an inevitable war? How millions of minds are thus forged becomes a political factor of great military significance. Indeed, it can become a decisive military factor.

Educational reform has always been among the first tasks undertaken by the Communists, which has been the main boast of their friends. The attention which the Reds gave to education was second to none; they obviously considered it fundamental to their whole program. They were going on the assumption that the future would be determined by how far they, and fellow Soviet bloc countries, could indoctrinate young minds.

The importance of these new textbooks was enhanced by the fact that they were standard for all of China. The tot in Peiping who went to primary school studied from the same textbook as the little boy in faraway Canton or Chung·king. The teen-agers in Peiping, Kunming, and Shanghai all used the same texts. What was more, the Peiping regime made sure that these schoolbooks were used exactly the same way in all of these localities.

China for several generations has been following the six-three-three-four-year educational system. The child first goes to primary school for a six-year course. Next comes junior high school, with a three-year course, followed by senior high, also with a three-year schedule. The university comes last, with four more years.

The normal Chinese child who graduates from primary school does so when about 12, from junior high when about 15, from senior high when about 18. The age range of pupils in primary school is from 6 to 15, in junior high from 12 to 18, while university students are between 18 and 26.

High school provides young people in the age range which the Communists can tap at once, providing them with needed working and military personnel. High schools provide, too, the biggest continuing reservoir of educated men and women. They are then of the age which provides the sturdiest military material.

What was quickly evident from even a limited inspection of these textbooks was that Red China had a definite, continuing policy, based on certain specific, inflexible precepts, governing relations at home and abroad, as much an international as a national program. And . . . well, let my findings speak for themselves. They are too ominous merely to summarize.

Almost as soon as the Communists expelled the Nationalists from the mainland, they distributed a textbook, obviously prepared beforehand, entitled *The Present Situation in the World*. All high schools were instructed to use it as an adjunct to their lessons concerning politics. The language was modern Chinese, easy to follow by children between twelve and eighteen. The first page teaches that capitalism is near its end everywhere and that "this is the fundamental characteristic of the world today."

This "dying capitalism," the textbook says, exists today in the form of imperialism, and it then goes on to name as imperialist nations such countries as the United States, Britain, and France. In the very first few pages are the following quotations:

Before World War II, Germany, Japan, Italy, Britain, the United States, and France were spoken of as the six Big Powers. The war brought total collapse to half of them. France was weakened by the war and lost its qualifications as a Big Power. Britain has a hard nut to crack in trying to keep up the adornments of a Big Power. This leaves the U. S. alone to prop up the crumbling world mansion of capitalism. . . .

After the war, there were two camps left in the world. One is the anti-democratic camp, which is headed by imperialist America. But this camp has only a strong appearance, while its interior is exhausted of resources. This camp, in fact, is nearing its end. . . .

The other camp is the anti-imperialist, democratic camp, with Soviet Russia as its leader. The ranks in this camp are strong and powerful.

This is pamphleteering, not teaching. Ordinarily, such wild generalizations are best ignored. But when all the high-school children in a nation as enormously populated as China have this pumped into their impressionable 12-to-18-year-old heads, it becomes too hazardous to ignore. If these children had some unbiased information for comparison, there might be some excuse to disregard it and trust to the innate good sense of all human beings. But no other information is available for these young people. Parents don't dare cast doubt on what is taught in school. They would be liable to the fullest penalties of the law against counterrevolutionary activity—the most serious crime under Chinese Communism.

This was only the first chapter. The next chapter is entitled, "Number One in the Imperialist, Anti-Democratic Camp—Imperialist America." This is divided into several sections. The first is intended to break down the belief that the United States is rich and democratic by saying that only a few are rich and that there is no democracy. "Not only has the United States no democracy, but it is marching along the fascist road," it says. More important is the next section, which teaches these young students that the United States is menacing the world. This section is frankly headed, "The Expansion Policy of Imperialistic America—Its Aggressive Policy." This textbook, it must be understood, did not appear after the fighting started in Korea; it was distributed to all the high schools a year before. This section refers to America's "dream of ruling the whole world," a theme returned to again and again in Communist textbooks. Examples of America's expansionist policy are "the infamous Trumanism, the Marshall Plan, and the North Atlantic Charter."

The Chinese students who read this might deduce that a nation that can do these things might be quite powerful, so the next section is dedicated to destroying this fear.

The United States is strong in appearance, but exhausted inside; it is a paper tiger. Under such circumstances, the domestic market of the United States becomes smaller and smaller. At the same time, due to the great amount of waste during the war, and subsequent postwar economic difficulties in other countries, its foreign market has also greatly shrunk. In order to save themselves from the economic crisis, the American imperialists adopted two measures, "foreign aid" and "military expansion." But these two measures will not be able to solve the basic problem.

All this is just in the first two chapters, and this is a textbook of more than one hundred pages! The third chapter analyzes the rest of the "imperialistic, anti-democratic camp." Spain, Turkey, and Greece are lumped together and brushed aside as "fed by imperialist America." So far as countries such as Holland, Belgium, Luxemburg, Canada, and Norway are concerned, they are referred to in this way:

All these reactionary powers, together with the Kuomintang reactionary clique, are willing to act as the running dogs of imperialistic America. Among them, the Kuomintang reactionary clique has been ousted by the revolutionary force of the Chinese people. Although the reactionary power of the other nations is still capable of maintaining their sovereignty, yet their fate will not be better than that of imperialist countries such as the United States, Britain and France. There will not be much more time for them to serve the imperialistic countries."

"Socialism must be victorious all over the world," the text-book says, and even that, it declares, will be only a "step toward Communism."

The tremendous development of productive power in a socialistic society achieves what is necessary for society to step forth to the further stage, communism. In this higher, Communist stage, all production will be done by electric power. All industrial processes will be highly mechanized. Products will be infinitely abundant. Everybody will get whatever he wants.

An incalculable number of the young men who were taught this as their history and economics were thrown only a little later into North Korea to fight the American and other United Nation forces. Is it any wonder, then, that they tore against the GI's like little beasts, their eyes popping with fanaticism? With all schools teaching this same line, the Peiping regime understandably feels that, in the long run, it has no worry about replenishment of fanatic manpower.

The second half of the book takes up Soviet Russia in the same way, only with opposite conclusions. A significant section is entitled, "All Anti-Imperialistic Democratic Forces Must Unite With Soviet Russia."

"Let all the anti-imperialistic democratic forces of the world be united into one fighting line headed by Soviet Russia," it declares, thus telling the Chinese young men and women that they must look to Moscow for leadership. Gradually and painlessly these textbooks inculcate a father-son complex toward Soviet Russia, which is usually referred to as China's "Big Brother" and the "father of socialism."

The student is instructed that he can show his highest patriotism toward China best by defending its strong ally, Moscow. Slowly but thoroughly he is drawn into a philosophy that makes loyalty to Moscow the first requisite of Chinese patriotism. Even China's loss of Mongolia to Soviet Russia is presented as a matter for rejoicing. Ignoring Mongolia's historic and racial ties to China, the textbook interprets the forced transfer of sovereignty to Soviet Russia as securing Mongolia's "independence and prosperity."

A portentous summary of Red China's stand on world revolution is given in a concluding section entitled "The Victorious Chinese Revolution and Its Effect on the World Situation." Here it is:

After V-J Day, imperialist America took the place of imperialist Japan. Chiang Kai-shek took the place of Wong Ching-wei.* All this was in the hope of turning China into a colony of the United States.

The people all over the world can now see clearly that the Chinese people have not only defeated Chiang Kai-shek, but have also defeated imperialistic America. By deeds, the people of China have proven, before the people of the world, that imperialistic America is nothing but a paper tiger.

Without doubt, the Chinese people's revolutionary war has met with the sympathy and help of the revolutionary strength of the world. If it were not for the struggles made possible by the strength of the peoples of the world, headed by Soviet Russia, then imperialistic America and other imperialistic nations would have been able to crush China with all their might, and consequently the total victory would not have been possible for the people of China. The aid of the people all over the world has helped the Chinese revolution. On the other hand, the Chinese revolution and its success are also most helpful to the people's revolution in every corner of the world.

Here, as in all such propaganda intended only for their own eyes and ears, I came across a phrase that the Chinese Communists don't use abroad. Referring to insurrections elsewhere in the world, they use the term "racial-liberation movement." After World War II, the book says, the colonial peoples "started a racial-liberation movement." There is subtle logic in this line by the Chinese Communists. By stressing

* Wong Ching-wei, Japanese puppet in World War II. The Communists refer just to this part of his career, ignoring his 1927 refusal to break with Moscow when Chiang Kai-shek did.

the racial aspect of guerrilla warfare elsewhere in Asia, they can distract attention from the nationalistic aspects of it. After all, if countries such as Indochina, Malaya, and Burma developed a true nationalism, this might prove very much of an obstacle to the political expansionism that is inherent in Chinese Communism. There is much evidence to show that Communist Russia is offering what in effect is an exchange of territories it doesn't possess in Southeast Asia for Chinese soil, such as Sinkiang and Mongolia.

The textbook finishes with a section entitled "All Roads Lead to Communism," which refers to "all the people of the world who are still oppressed." I had only to go back to the earlier pages of this textbook to know specifically whom they meant by the "oppressed"—the inhabitants of the United States, Britain, France, and all other non-Communist countries.

INVESTIGATION

Investigation and Research seemed like a curious title for a high school book. Just what did it mean? I noticed that it was classified as a political reader, but this made it all the more perplexing. Not only was it unusual; it was unprecedented. Formerly, school children were taught civics; here was an entirely new subject to replace it.

The book appeared to be an entirely new approach to the problem of responsibility in society, and so it was. In the old civics courses, the emphasis was on the individual's role in society, the give and take of being a good citizen. Here the emphasis was on investigation in the police sense of the word. The research part of it was supposed to make it scholarly and academic, but like the psychiatry in the indoctrination course at the Revolutionary University, and like the evangelism in the learning and self-criticism meetings, this was quack undercover work, an attempt to habituate minds to the secret police mentality while they were still young and malleable.

Instructors in this new course started out with a striking advantage. The old civics books were dry, uninteresting, monotonous. From primary school through junior and senior high schools, students had had to study civics, which consisted in each class of a tiresome repetition of what had been taught before. Only language and style were changed to suit the age of the students. In civics, students were taught to "salute the national flag," to "pay respect to the Generalissimo," and to participate in the New Life Movement (the Kuomintang's youth corps)—weak, uninspiring demands compared to the ecstatic praise now being poured on Stalin and Mao Tse-tung in the schools. All these hesitant forms of half-hearted discipline had had little effect on the students. Youths of high school age are energetic, hotheaded, full of curiosity, and full of a real passion for all activities which can provide an outlet for their excess of energy and their suppressed idealisms. Civics, full of protocol and doctrine, were not at all appealing to youth under the Kuomintang. Again, a vast realm of the mind was abandoned by default, and the Communists were quick to fill it, dropping the puerile course in civics and providing something more exciting than even playing cops and robbers. The new subject, investigation and research, unconsciously wrapped a halo of mystery and fascination around such relentless, dogmatic terms as "class standpoint," "village economy," and "relationship to exploitation."

The book gave no specific rules of operation, but what it did teach was of such a nature that the students would automatically organize themselves into groups. Catering to the ardor of youth for work they can do by themselves, this book is the most appealing of all in the indoctrination field for this age level.

All teachers know that, when a high school student steps into a laboratory for the first time to work out some experiment, his enthusiasm is unbounded. The same is the case here. The book outlines actual experiments that the students can do themselves. This is field work (investigating a village) or it is homework (investigating a family). The students are too young to appreciate the meaning of such investigation and research. In the environment in which these children are raised, it would be astonishing if they did not find such a subject utterly fascinating. It is far more exciting than what American youngsters of their age can do—listening to some gangland program on the radio or seeing it on television.

The text is written in simple, modern Chinese that a highschool student can read and understand without the help of his teacher. Part deals with statistics (how to collect them, what the average and the index mean, how to fill out statistical forms) and this is not so interesting; but the mathematics used is of the simplest. As the students have to use numbers before they are able to obtain concrete results from some of their field work, this part is not too boring, either. Many practical examples are given, which render this textbook the most exciting of all in the political field.

The Communists have been astute in adding such a subject to the senior high school program. Knowledge that it is being studied in school gives investigatory work in general a higher tone. The book is well written and very appealing for those for whom it was intended. The book is purportedly scientific, intended to train children in making an investigation and drawing accurate conclusions in the field of political thought. This, it must be stressed, is not investigation in biology or chemistry, or in any of the usual laboratory subjects at school; neither is it investigation in the ordinary field of crime. Politics, and political thought, are the subject matter.

Besides studying the book, the students are expected to do some actual investigating on their own. Home is always an easy place to start, as is the firm where father works, or a factory operated by some relative.

This is so unprecedented a subject for school study that how it is built up and glamorized, as a sort of Chinese "cowboys and Indians" game, warrants particular attention. The book teaches on page 1 that "a scientific attitude is most essential to the task of revolution"; on page 2 that "investigation and research must be guided by revolutionary theories and policies"; and on page 3 it quotes Mao Tse-tung's saying: "Without investigation, one has no right to speak out." The book goes on to say that the basic rule in investigation and research is "to understand facts objectively," using Marxism as the point from which "to observe and study society by this method of class analysis." No slipshod measures are wanted; "dialectic methods" have to be used.

When we investigate some fact, we have to ask, first of all, When did it happen? Where did it happen? How did it happen? What relationship has it to other facts? . . . We must not be content with its present conditions. We must try to know its past. We must find out how it developed into its present state and what is the tendency of its future development. . . .

We must try to find out the existing conflict, to find out the actual problem, for only by finding this out can we discover the solution. . . . Through scientific analysis only can we total up the results of the research work we carry out, and thereby draw a scientific conclusion, and make a scientific judgment.

In the midst of this extremely dialectical thesis, we are suddenly given a spiritual note:

Good organization is essential for efficient teamwork, while spiritual preparations are also indispensable. We have to realize the importance of investigatory work, and be prepared to meet with many unexpected difficulties during the course of the specific task.

Helpful tips are given on "distinguishing true information from false statements," by determining the source. "Was this a personal experience of the informant? If not, other proofs are required to back up its authenticity." What is the point of view of the informant? Has he anything to do with the case? Perhaps he is exaggerating. "Try to gather information about the same fact from different angles or sources, and compare them."

This is actually what was done with the information provided in background reports, self-criticism statements, and thought-conclusion theses in the Revolutionary University and in the other indoctrination classes described to me by participants. There the data in one part of a report would be compared to statements made in other parts, and the whole compared to different reports. Contradictions would be noted and used as leads in ferreting out further information and secrets. That this was an examining technique of Soviet Russia's secret police was perhaps purely coincidental.

The Chinese people were being taught not only to propagandize themselves, but to be their own secret police against themselves. The book taught this new twist on investigations:

Bring the problem before the masses. See how the masses react. Gather the opinions of the masses and study the information obtained with the help of the opinions expressed by the masses.

This is exactly what is done in China in mass trials and in public purges. In Soviet Russia, purges and public trials are a matter for trained investigators and special prosecutors. In Red China, the public was being entrusted with this responsibility, along with self-propaganda and self-espionage. This was the new democracy.

The book teaches, too, what to do with information supplied by an outside informant. In such cases, the class standpoint of the informer has to be taken into consideration. He may even be connected with the Kuomintang! Information from such a source cannot be considered reliable.

Practical experiments are outlined. One such is "Studying a Family." The first data that has to be gathered is the class to which the family belongs. In order to determine this, these lines of investigation have to be followed:

1. Family members: age, sex, past experience, profession, labor conditions, relationships inside the family

2. Property: land, house, production materials, living materials, money

3. Role in exploitation: extent to which the family exploits others or is being exploited

4. Income and expenditure: source of income, amounts, various expenditures and their amounts

How many enthusiastic teen-agers must have come home bringing the exciting news that they have been assigned to a most interesting political experiment, and won't Daddy please help? I can imagine the struggle that must go on in the parent's mind. If he objects, what will the school authorities think? and report? If he doesn't object, what will these alert, prying kids find out? And how can he feel sure that what these lads write, in their inexperience, won't sound very incriminating indeed?

Instructions are given for field work in investigating a village, in connection with farm reform. Working conditions, class relationships, political views, social education, culture and recreation, marriage and other social problems, all have to be outlined, and, finally: "How is revolutionary work being carried out in the village?"

I can imagine, too, what lies hidden in the minds of a group of peasants when a team of city schoolboys descends on their village with a horde of such questions. How must they feel when these lads go about questioning peasant by peasant, checking up the answers made by one farmer against what another farmer says. I can imagine, too, the mutual suspicions planted and the worries that remain long after these boys return to school. These reports, of course, like all such papers, become part of official records.

What I can't, or perhaps don't want to, imagine is the type of mind being developed by this sort of investigatory work—a mind which will regard such activity as normal in society, a mind which has been indoctrinated to enjoy just this sort of inquisition.

HISTORY

The Communists take no chances with the teaching of history. A school is not allowed just to pick its history teachers simply because they know history, as if this were some comparatively inconsequential subject such as arithmetic or calligraphy. They first have to be examined by the Communist Education Bureau, which has the right to order school authorities to discharge teachers whom it deems unfit (which it frequently does).

The requirements for a teacher of history, or of politics (the two are usually considered together) are neither academic achievements nor experience. The decisive factor is whether the teacher's "mind has been straightened out." If an uneducated country bumpkin "has his mind straightened out," though he has never read a history book in his life, he is qualified to teach. If his mind is not "straightened out," no degree can help him.

This is what the principals of high schools in Shanghai were informed after "liberation." This is the deciding factor throughout Red China. In addition, the Board of Education had a large roster of specially trained, Party-approved history teachers whom it distributed among the faculties of various schools, irrespective of whether a qualified teacher, even a Communist, had to be dropped or not. This was Party patronage.

The Party authorities refused to approve any name on a list submitted, either of Party or non-Party men, until they had placed their own cadre of these specially trained history teachers in jobs. Persistent refusal to approve submitted names ultimately put the headmaster in the position of closing up his institution or (as always happened) "voluntarily" employing the new teacher offered.

Instructors in all other subjects are required to coordinate their lessons with the teaching of history and politics. They have to study those textbooks, so as to be able to use them as references on their own subjects, and then they have to explain how they do so in their regular weekly reports. This emphasis on history and politics, even in the lower schools, is further demonstrated by the unwritten rule that no student can be promoted or graduated who fails in either of those subjects.

The new textbooks were not ready immediately after liberation in Shanghai or many other cities, so the schools were instructed to tear out certain pages in the old books and to use the whittled-down portions without referring to the deleted matter. When the new history books appeared, practically everything in them was found to have been taken from one source—the publications of the Chinese History Research Association. This is one of the supreme academic bodies in the Red government, organized under the new Research Yuan (ministry). Its setup is similar in structure to the Kuomintang's Central Research Yuan and to the National History Editing Bureau. There the similarity ends. History has to serve the purposes of propaganda, and everything related has to have a purpose; nothing can be told just for information's sake.

The history books are by far the most impressive of all the textbooks that the new regime has put out. By comparison, other subjects, such as literature and science, have been carelessly treated. Because of the perhaps decisive role that the teaching of history occupies in the indoctrination of the new generation—the fighting generation—a rather extensive survey is warranted.

The way the old Kuomintang regime obtained textbooks was comparatively simple. Orders were placed with one of the main textbook publishers, such as the Commercial Press and the Chung Hwa Book Company. These firms, which are now putting out Communist textbooks, employed their own writers and editors. A representative of the Ministry of Education had to give his approval before any textbook could be used in the schools, but this control was exercised spottily and usually moderately. An effort to step on no toes succeeded only in irritating all circles. The Red regime makes no such blunder. Any of its officials who would approve a textbook containing the whisper of a bourgeois thought, either out of carelessness or for a bribe, surely would be purged. No corruption is allowed to interfere with Party policy. The old textbooks were dry and uninteresting, full of dates, with little descriptive matter and less opinion. The narration was dull and methodical. The writing was semiclassical or semimodern, another compromise that was annoying. The language was stilted, which further repelled students, who had the impression that history was being stuffed down their throats without opportunity for reasoning things out.

The Kuomintang histories were mainly a collection of historical writings gleaned from preceding books, actually an awkward selection from a colossal collection. Without opinions being given them, the young students were at a loss as to what was to be believed and what was legend. They were in no position to judge, and they were too young to understand the parts tolerance or political pressures might have played in such a strained objectivity. Kuomintang histories, for instance, simply ignored the Communist Party, never attempting a history of the relations between it and the Kuomintang. This was like writing the story of modern American history without referring to the interplay between the Democratic and Republican parties—only more so. These Kuomintang-Communist Party relations were a subject of current interest about which students were extremely curious. The Communists, once in power, quickly exploited this field, going into minute detail and at the same time giving their own coloration to all events. The students never had had anything of this sort before and, lacking any standard of comparison, were easily led to believe that the Reds were telling the truth when they said they had nothing to hide.

Chiang Kai-shek made another error. He felt that it would be immodest of him to allow his biography to appear in history books, and so it did not appear. The Communist histories give his biography, telling how he rose from a mere clerk in a Shanghai banking office to become ruler of the nation, but they tell it with vinegar and sulphuric acid. Nevertheless, once more the Communists win by default. In addition, they take advantage of the opportunity to glorify and virtually deify Stalin and Mao Tse-tung on every possible occasion.

Contrary to the even dullness of the Kuomintang textbooks, the Communists made history as thrilling as a novel. They weighed every word. When modern Chinese is used, it is vivid and forceful. When classical Chinese is occasionally employed, it is concise and exquisite. Anecdotes are frequently employed to press home a point. When some event which the Party regards as important is brought up, every device is used to make it clear and unforgettable. The main point is repeated again and again, with plenty of picturesque comparisons, so that it sinks deeply into a comrade's mind. Junior high school textbooks overlap in subject matter, which has added emphasis to summaries.

The Communists give a great deal of space to discussion of the evolution of social status and the development of society, which includes a great deal of research material. This, far from revealing a desire to press home a political slant, appears to the young students as evidence of the care taken to provide proof for everything said. Ideas and viewpoints skillfully planted in these immature minds thus take root. The students, when they become older, acquire their own way of looking at history—the Party way. Their brains are cleansed, so that whatever facts are presented to them are tested in this framework and they are able to think for themselves only within this narrow framework.

Drastically new ideas conflicting with popularly held versions of history are not presented too abruptly in the junior high histories. Political and economic conditions are described first, then the historical event or battle is mentioned. An effort is made to avoid giving the impression that these histories seek to revolutionize traditional concepts, although this actually is the basic objective. Only later is this bluntly done, after the mental framework has been molded.

Confucius, for example, is assailed only indirectly and with caution, because of the universal respect in which the sage is held in China. He is brushed aside.

Kung Chiu was a petty aristocrat of the Lu State. He was well versed in feudalism. Not being very lucky in politics, he turned to teaching. He upheld feudalism and emphasized the class system. He urged the people to be loyal to the emperor and was thus the mentor of conservatives and aristocrats. He had many disciples. Kung Chiu was adored by various feudalistic emperors who came later, was looked upon as a saint, and was addressed as Kung Fu-tse [Confucius].

Even this approach, without the usual vituperation, sounds very exciting and terribly daring to junior high students, for it completely breaks with a 3,000-year-old tradition of homage to the Great Sage. Such revolutionizing of traditional concepts is extremely stimulating to youth, for it makes them feel superior to the past.

Scholars have always been held in highest prestige in China, and so, instead of being attacked directly, they usually are presented in adverse and ridiculous situations. When they are finally criticized openly, it is done with generalizations.

The scholars sought a good life, and yet they despised laborers who lived by their own efforts. So the scholars went to work for the rich and the powerful, and in this way obtained fine clothes and luxuries for themselves, and were able to support all their families. Then, why should the rich and the powerful have favored the scholars? They did so because the scholars could draw up plans for their masters, proclaim their fame, and fortify their positions. If the masters did not treat their scholars well, they would have gone over to their enemies and have worked for them.

The young student, constantly coming across such belittling and degrading allusions, naturally comes to feel that there is nothing praiseworthy in becoming a government official, but that what is most worth striving for is to become a Party member. They will plunge headlong into work for the Party while still in school.

History is presented in simple narrative language, as if the author were reasoning things out with his readers, a manner of writing that sounds extremely convincing to the students and gives an impression of modesty on the part of the Reds. Much of the text has the flavor of a discussion meeting. This gives students a feeling of having participated in reaching the conclusions given them. They were never flattered this way by the Kuomintang.

Students do not ordinarily appreciate diagrams and maps; so, no matter how necessary they may be for a thorough knowledge of the subject, they are rarely, almost never, used. This is again completely opposite to the old history books. Occasionally the Communists provide a series of dates and figures to give the impression of authenticity and to back up some concept in which the Party is particularly interested. The students, grateful for no longer being required to memorize dates and place names, do not question what is told them in the new, easily absorbed manner.

Studying history under the new regime is just like reading a thrilling novel. Of course the youngsters like it. In all of these histories, every war of the past, anywhere in the world, is described as simply an ugly fight between capitalist nations over the division of ill-gained loot. All civil wars or internal disorders are called either glorious farmers' revolts or labor strikes.

There is only slight discussion of theory in the junior-high books, which present history as though it were mathematical equations—that is to say, permanently unalterable fact. Even the indoctrination portions are written as straight narrative. The new concepts are accompanied by anecdotes and references that purport to prove the point. The minds of the students are thus well prepared to receive, later on, what is called "higher Communist education."

World history is taught in junior high schools, along

with ancient and modern Chinese history. The juniors are given one textbook in addition, *The Modern World Revolutionary History*. The opportunities for political slanting in the ordinary histories apparently are not sufficient to guarantee that the minds of the students might not be changed later by the discovery of facts conflicting with what they were told in school. This supplementary history makes use of the same facts related in *World History*, except that the approach is directly from the standpoint of Communist dogma. Most of the book consists of Communist Party doctrine on world events.

In the senior high schools, the emphasis is virtually complete. The children are taught from books with these revealing titles: *Chinese Revolution Reader, History of the Chinese New Democracy Revolution*, and *The Chinese Modern Revolutionary Movement History*, and three other books on Chinese history with more conventional titles. Unlike the usual practice in schools, where education is presumed to be absorbed gradually, all these histories are used simultaneously in all the senior years. They are written so simply that no teacher is needed to explain them. True history receives little attention in some of these, which are outright Communist pamphleteering on Party dogma and pet hates.

The new textbooks speak of ancient Chinese history as a mixture of fact and legend, backing up their findings with many references and much discussion, which gives the impression of a scientific approach. The Kuomintang had lumped ancient history together as legend, at best unconfirmed, and let it go at that. The Communists lay great stress on a description of the oppression of the people by the ruling class, and they elaborately describe social systems which fit into their doctrines, and build up a class viewpoint. They back up their points with quotations carefully selected from the great mass of ancient Chinese literature, rewriting the paragraphs they like in modern Chinese. This strikes the students as original research; they have no way of knowing the way the material was selected.

The following passage from a first-grade textbook demonstrates the way in which Communist dogma is inserted into the middle of straight history.

If a struggle should long endure between two systems of the social order, such as capitalism and feudalism, the inevitable result is that the new system will defeat the old and take its place.

If this be social law, the student will naturally think that Communism, coming after capitalism, is sure to win out. The textbook doesn't have to say so in those words.

A snatch of dialectical materialism is inserted into the story of the way in which the primitive Chinese tribes formed China's first recognized dynasty, the Hsia, two thousand years before Christ. The student is informed that politics in that prehistoric era consisted mainly of "exploiting and oppressing slaves," and that the "slave labor boss" became the highest authority or ruler.

This research, a hodgepodge of legend and political fancy, is welcomed by the students, for whom it is an exciting new approach. The new histories also gratify a universal taste for sensation with such historical titbits as:

They [the ruling class during the late Shang Dynasty, about 1500 B.C.] lived extravagantly and licentiously, drinking day and night. They often went out hunting, gallivanting about. They neglected the soil, which became barren, and let deer and birds multiply on it. They invented all sorts of cruel tortures to squeeze wealth from the people.

What child, or grown-up, would not be excited over a vivid description of the different varieties of tortures used in the olden days? They were given, as part of the history for the youngsters, in this way:

He [the emperor] invented new methods of exploitation, called the redemption of punishment. These were cruel tortures, inflicted on the common people by the ruling class. They were of five kinds: the ink torture, in which the face was slashed and the wounds inked; the nose torture, in which the nose was cut; the foot torture, in which the feet were cut; the palace torture, in which the genital organs were cut off men [apparently to provide eunuchs] and women were confined in palaces as slaves; and the great chop torture, which was beheading.

Officials were corrupt at that time, receiving bribes openly. Emperor Mou wanted to turn all this to his own benefit, so he proclaimed the system of redemption of punishment. Ink torture could be avoided by paying 40 catties of copper; nose torture, 80 catties; foot torture, 160 catties; palace torture, 200 catties; and great chop torture, 400 catties. This was done wholly to squeeze wealth. Actual criminals were not allowed to redeem themselves this way; only suspects could be ransomed with money. Anyone could be suspected, therefore anyone could be punished. From this viewpoint, it can be seen how private properties were accumulated and the common people divided into the rich and the poor. The rich were punished and squeezed while the poor were tortured.

The old histories had merely mentioned that various tortures were inflicted on suspects, and that certain emperors were tyrannical and lost their thrones as a consequence.

Tantalizing details are given on the different kinds of torture during the early T'ang Dynasty. The names of various tortures can be sure to arouse the imagination of children. Among those listed are the "hundred pulse," the "cannot pant," the "lost-soul," and the "dead pig." Sometimes more elaborate details are given, as:

The victim is hung upside down with a stone attached to his head. Or hot vinegar is poured into his nose, or wooden wedges are driven into his head, or his nails are pierced with bamboo pins. Or he is prevented from sleeping, and his mouth is stuffed before he is beheaded.

In this manner, horror toward the past is built up.

Old wars among the Chinese are related in exciting story form so as to leave a political impression. The students find such accounts as the following quite refreshing:

Chieh was the last emperor of the Hsia Dynasty and was a tyrant. He and his officials exploited the people exceedingly, and employed all sorts of cruel methods of physical torture to force the people to work like slaves. The people of the Hsia Dynasty began a strike, and, uttered this curse against the emperor: "If only you would perish, we would be willing to die, too." Tang used this opportunity to overthrow Chieh, but Tang's courtiers did not approve. So Tang threatened his courtiers, saying: "If you disobey me, I will kill you and enslave your households. If you obey, I will reward you."

This, based on actual tales in the *Chinese Annals* and other classics, is put into story form in modern Chinese. Then something new is added—Communist dogma, which teaches that society originally was Communist in form and is passing through an inevitable spiral before it returns to Communism. Slave ownership is supposed to be the first step in the downfall of man from his original purity. So the history book gives this comment:

When the people of the Hsia Dynasty began their strike, they must have been struggling against their masters; it must have been slaves against slaveowners. If they had been self-supporting farmers, a strike, on the contrary, would only have starved them.

The Communist theory of inevitability—the bandwagon psychology by which they have won so many opportunistic converts—is frequently met with in these histories. Here is an example, from a discussion of new systems of rule created in the brief, Napoleonic Chin Dynasty, two centuries before Christ, when the family principle was established and when the emperor was regarded as the father of his people:

Emperor Chin Hsih-huang would never have succeeded in centralizing power by his own will or his capability alone. It was history that pushed him into this. Thus he was able speedily to realize his wish.

The Han Dynasty, which lasted a couple of hundred years on each side of the start of the Christian era, has always been regarded as the age when Chinese culture flourished in the arts, science, literature, and music, when emperors were just, and when the people were happy. The Communist histories accordingly give special attention to this era, of which the Chinese people have always been so proud. However, they do not praise it. With the same curious consistency with which the Communists strive to prove that every American deed in China has been motivated by bad will and evil purpose, they seem to be possessed by the fear that, unless they can prove that every individual or group ever in power in China's long history has been downright wicked, their own grip on power somehow will be drastically weakened. The new histories go to great length to disillusion the students concerning the Han period, which is particularly signifi-cant because the Chinese people have always described themselves as "sons of Han" and hence an essentially civilized people. The Red assault on this conception is indirectly a blow at Chinese nationalistic feelings. The Han period is presented as one of uninterrupted exploitation of the masses.

Whereas outlaws are consistently referred to as leaders of people's revolts—there surely must have been some actual bandits in China's past—once one had won power he is vilified as a virtual bandit. The first Han emperor, Kao-Chu, referred to only by his common name, Liu Pang, is described as "a village ruffian."

Earlier histories had referred to the "Hwang-chun bandits" and the "Huh-shan bandits" during the Han Dynasty, but the new histories, with their upside-down inflexibility, interpret the bandits' roles this way:

Armies formed by farmers, such as the Hwang-chun and the Huh-shan, rose up, but they killed only the officials, seizing their wealth. These people's soldiers never killed other people. Only the violent and ruthless ruling class, the war lords, massacred the people, causing the productive force to collapse, the population to decrease, and creating the deplorable spectacle recorded in [the classical Chinese poem] "coming out of the house, I see nothing but skeletons which cover the earth."

An ideological plug is inserted here for Communist dogma about the eternal interplay between productive power and productive relationships. This build-up becomes the basis for this generalization on conditions during the Han Dynasty:

How did the farmers live? They wore shabby coats. They ate corn husks, wild cabbage, and drank cold water. Tung Shung-shu, the great scholar of the West Han Dynasty, said that they were clothed like horses and cows and were fed like dogs and pigs. People of the north had nothing to wear in winter and hid themselves in the hay all day long, crawling out only when they were wanted by money-exacting officials. The poor people were able only to sell themselves and their children as slaves at very low prices.

Historians who have praised the Han Dynasty for its good rule are in reality only encouraging landlords to take away more of the land, leaving the poor farmers nothing on which to lean.

World history is taught in a manner intended to arouse racial and international hatreds. Indirect attacks are made at all non-Communist countries, whenever an excuse arises. Religion is discredited by this pseudo-historic approach:

Jesus, the illegitimate son of a carpenter's fiancée, reformed the Jewish religion. . . . Later the disciples of Jesus rewrote the dogma and changed it into something to uphold the teachings that the property of the rich should not be touched and that the poor should resign their fate to God so that they might enter Heaven. Thereupon, this religion was at once accepted by the Roman emperors.

Every effort has been made to arouse antipathy against foreigners and to play upon it. Such prejudices had been breaking down in the past, but they are now being reinforced by paragraphs such as this:

When the Allied army entered Peiping [during the Boxer Rebellion], its generals permitted it to pillage openly for three days. Later, under the pretext of looking for remnant Boxers, the soldiers continued to plunder and rape women. All the precious ancient books and antiques were partly destroyed and partly stolen by these bandits. These foreign bandits took this loot back to their own countries.

Atrocities by "foreign aggressors" are described in exciting, detailed, story-book form. Extra large characters are used over the section entitled "Invasion by the Imperialists."

The most fluent writing, and the most vitriolic, is expended on the United States, particularly in the *Chinese Revolution Reader*, a textbook on politics written against a background of history. A separate, hate-arousing chapter includes every anecdote and rumor that could be collected to prove the unlawful conduct of America and Americans in China. The section on economics avoids mentioning America entirely, in a way that makes it all the more forcible. It has frequent references to China's economy and numerous comparisons with Soviet Russian economy, which is casually accepted as the world's most prosperous and most industrious nation.

The *Chinese Modern Revolutionary Movement History* refers to America's role in ending World War I in this way:

At the conclusion of World War I, in 1918, during the Peace Conference, the American President Wilson presented all the other nations with the Fourteen Points. These were intended to cheat all the people of the world. Among these Fourteen Points was one "to help the weak peoples and nations." Such deceitful suggestions produced a sort of hallucination in the minds of all the oppressed people in the world. . . .

The *History of the Chinese New Democracy Revolution* ignores such a detail as America's opposition to Japanese aggression in China, which led directly to Pearl Harbor; and it describes America's relations with China as alternating between cooperation and competition with Japan in such aggression. A more brazen distortion of history cannot be found. Yet, the pupils who read this in their textbooks are too young to know what actually took place—they only know what they are told. Here is an example of what they are told:

During World War I, the American imperialists sold ammunition and made loans, thus becoming rich. Gradually America became the most powerful nation in the world economy. It became more and more ambitious. The Japanese imperialists also wished to grab more rights in China, so the United States and the Japanese imperialists became the two contending imperialistic nations in China. . . . In name, the United States acknowledged the integrity of China. In fact, it instigated England and Japan to aggression against China, so as to colonize China "legally."

The young minds of the junior-high-school students are indoctrinated, in *World History,* with descriptions of the United States as a land of poverty and depravity. The early history of the United States is presented with seeming objectivity; only gradually is the student carried over into vivid tales of a viciously capitalistic country permeated by vice. The hunger-and-misery theme is used again and again. This mood is carried over even into the study of geography in junior high school, a decisive time in schooling because most of the children don't advance beyond it, and because if they are to be fanaticized this is the best opportunity in the sacrosanct surroundings of the classroom. *World Geography* begins with a description of the Soviet Union and other Soviet bloc countries. When the textbook reaches other countries, its titles are illuminating. They are printed attractively in big characters. "European Countries Under the Control of the Anglo-American Imperialists" and "America Under the Control of the United States Imperialists" are two such captions.

Finally, to make sure that the point is not missed, a separate chapter is included on "the great division between the nations—the democratic countries headed by Soviet Russia and the reactionary countries headed by the Anglo-American imperialists." The One World concept is simply disregarded in these textbooks, except in the form of a Communist world that can be achieved only by struggle under Moscow's leadership.

Young men who have studied from such textbooks are sure to have been among those Chinese prisoners of war in North Korea who have been asked if they ever received any special indoctrination. Their obvious answer was no. And they hadn't. They had simply gone to school.

If these teachings had not been sufficient to make these young students anxious to go out to fight against the United States, there was still the literature course to fulfill its role of hate.

LITERATURE

There is a folk song in Shensi Province about a lovely girl named Blue Roses, who is married to an old man who cannot satisfy her. The song relates, in local dialect and with descriptive vulgarity, that she has plenty of lovers, that she is perfectly happy in the arms of these lovers, and has full right so to amuse herself.

This is the language of the singsong house and the brothel. There is no fine writing about it; it is just a ditty of the back room. The last place one might expect to find it would be in a schoolbook, surely not in a high-school literature text. But, like the editors of the yellow press that the Communists have so persistently condemned as antisocial, the editors of the Communist schoolbooks feel that their first job is to gain the sympathy of readers. And what simpler procedure than doing exactly what the yellow journalist does?

There is the excuse, of course, of their way of looking at life. This second-year, senior-high-school book is for young men and young women between seventeen and twenty-one, which is already the marriageable age. If the purpose were to help break down the family system by teaching that adultery is justifiable, the lesson couldn't have been put in a more appropriate context.

Children and grown-ups alike can be expected to be avid

readers of another literature book, in this instance for students sixteen to twenty years, which contains such juicy passages as:

Two magpies caw. Wen-kai's heart thumped. Magpies, too, go in pairs. Wen-kai could not even compare with them. Lying in his bed, he couldn't sleep. It was as if he lacked something. He had been a bachelor for thirty years. Turning about in his bed, he felt alone. Stretching his legs, they felt cold. King Yu had been widowed for one year already. She had no children. The more he thought, the more uneasy he felt. "King Yu, King Yu," went through his mind, like dawn.

The moon shone brightly. Wen-kai strolled down the street. To and fro, he never went beyond a few yards. King Yu's house still had its door open. He could see the light through the slit in the door. He coughed twice, and stamped his feet. King Yu came out.

"Now I found the woman who makes shoes; I have been walking to and fro," he said in a whisper, and smiled. Swiftly he entered her house, and sat down on the bed.

"Look at yourself; you are shivering. Go to bed at once."

"Oh, my heart is going to jump out of my mouth. Come and feel it with your hand . . ."

The language is as crude as the plot; there is nothing about it that can be properly regarded as literature, either modern or classical. This quotation is a typical example of what is usually called "people's literature" in China. In America it would be called the cheaper sort of pulp-magazine hack writing.

These literature books teach as much ethics—Communist ethics—as they do ideology, and they are almost wholly geared to politics. The so-called decadent civilization, which Communism is supposed to replace, teaches that "you never kick a man when he is down." The Chinese had an equivalent for this; they talked of "not beating a drowning dog." Now the contrary is being taught, as bluntly as that, in Communist literature.

Third-year senior-high students (in the seventeen-to-twenty-one-year age range) read a piece entitled "'Fair Play' Should be Postponed." In order to give the impression that fairness is an alien conception, the words "fair play" are not translated into Chinese but are given phonetically, in four characters which sound like "fe-er-pe-lay." The author, Lu Shuan, well known for his contempt of Chinese who adopt foreign styles or use foreign words, writes that "to beat a drowning dog" is not a cowardly act, for, drowning or not, a dog is always a dog. He says that if you pity a dog because it is drowning, and let it come ashore, it still will be a menace to you. This article refers to those who criticize others for having turned Communist. He draws a comparison with those who criticized the Chinese in 1911 for establishing a republic. "These pretentious, respectable gentlemen at once hid their pigtails in their hats and ran for their lives like dogs without a master," he writes. "The Revolutionary Party did not want to beat the drowning dogs. The dogs climbed ashore and later helped Yuan Shih-kai* to bite many revolutionists to death." If a justification of and a call for the "liquidation" of Chinese who express criticism of those who capitulated to the new government could be more effectively indoctrinated into young minds, this writer cannot imagine any better way than printing this essay at this time. The reference to present conditions will escape no reader. But the author has been dead fifteen years, and the essay is dated December 29, 1925!

Lu Hsun was hailed as China's greatest modern author. If he actually sympathized with the Reds twenty-five years ago, while the Kuomintang was in power, the lesson that this conveys to young students is that they should believe in the Party that much more today.

Beating the drowning dog has always been considered a cowardly act by the Chinese, equal to bullying the already defeated. Lu Hsun wrote that certain conflicts could never be

---

* Yuan Shih-kai, a Chinese general in the army of the Manchu rulers, was sent to suppress the republican insurgents. Instead, he made a deal with them, becoming president of the new republic. He later plotted to become emperor and to start a new dynasty, and died broken-hearted when this was frustrated.

resolved except by the destruction of one side or the other. This excerpt from his writings, reprinted now with elaboration and high praise for the author, is just one of innumerable evidences that the Chinese Communists themselves believe in the inevitability of war with the United States and other non-Communist countries, unless all the latter "peacefully" recognize the error of their ways and surrender wholly to a totalitarian philosophy. In this respect they are sincere when they talk of peace. They feel that it would be just too bad to have to force those other countries to become Communist, but that if these countries remain "stubborn" there can be no other way out. This sounds reasonable enough to a brain-cleansed ideologist and is the theory conveyed in the new primary and high-school textbooks.

The Communists know the revulsion of others to shooting at children (especially young girls) or old women, and so their literature supports the tactic of using these people as guerrillas. They glamorize the participation of children who cannot yet conceive of the difference between actually dying and playing dead. There is a sinister practicability to the inclusion of such teachings in primary and junior-high-school literature. Their readers are the right age to go out and do likewise. A primary schoolbook, for instance, relates this incident of the war with Japan:

A Japanese soldier pursued a boy of twelve, who was actually a communications officer of the 8th Route [Communist] Army. An old woman, seeing the boy, understood what was happening. She pretended to thrash the child, severely scolding him as if he were her grandson and had tried to run away. The boy saw his chance, and embraced the old woman. The Japanese soldier was deceived by this camouflage and the boy escaped free.

Siah Tih-tsui, the subject of another lesson, was older; he was fifteen and he ran secret missions for the Red troops. Once he disguised himself as a shepherd and entered a Japanese-held compound, where he made himself useful feeding the horses. He pretended that he was taking the horses out to graze, but instead he fled back to his troops. Another lesson tells how children captured a spy. Here is what they did:

> During the anti-Japanese war, the Children's Corps at Li Chia-chuang provided the best sentries. Two children acted as sentries in uniform, and two others were disguised as detectives. Once a stranger offered candies to the disguised sentries and asked them what regiment was in the village and how large it was. One boy lied and returned to the village to report to the people's soldiers, leaving the other talking with the stranger. The troops came and arrested the stranger, who was found, indeed, to be a secret agent.

The creation of a Children's Corps is the subject of many lessons. The youngsters are taught that many children joined it for its revolutionary activities. They "entered the army, supported it and its policy, arrested traitors and secret agents, participated in production, and became little teachers. They joined anti-American parades, consoled teachers in their fight against starvation, and helped distribute propaganda." And it concludes: "We must adhere to discipline and consider the welfare of the Children's Corps as our own welfare, decisively fulfilling what has been decided, and joining all sorts of activities."

Right from earliest school days, the children are taught the principles of partisan warfare, one of which is that any farmer is simultaneously a guerrilla soldier, so that an enemy cannot tell a peaceful civilian from a sniper who will shoot him in the back when he passes. Here is how it is taught in the literature course for early teen-agers:

> Ding-ding-dong! Ding-ding-dong! First beat the iron, then the steel. Make the scythe like a crescent, make the gun that gleams light. With the scythe we cut the crops, with the gun we fight the enemies. Strive for production behind the lines, win victory at the frontier.

The high-school literature consists mainly of selections of Chinese writings and a large number of translations from the

Russian. They are practically all of an indoctrinating nature. Primary school literature consists mainly of original writing along the same lines.

Ai Tze-chi, whom we first met as the lecturer and the sole professor at the North China People's Revolutionary University, is represented in the textbooks by his description of the learning procedure. He explains a typical three-month course, which consists of "a comparatively detailed study of the history of social development [historical materialism] in the hope that the student will systematically understand three basic concepts: (1) labor created the world; (2) class warfare; and (3) Marxist doctrine on the meaning of nation."

"Using Marxist-Leninist concepts to contradict our own non-Marxist-Leninist ideas, and thus straightening out our own minds, is a preliminary method of learning Marxism-Leninism," he says. This is one of the most remarkable statements in a most remarkable article; its logic offers an excellent key to what the Communists call a "scientific approach." Yet, ridiculous as the logic may be, its influence on young minds should not be underestimated. This simple and expressive style of writing wins sympathy from the start. It gives students impressive subjects to discuss in the numerous meetings which are often the most interesting part of the school day. For then it is play, as the pressures that are imposed on older minds are not generally needed in schools for the young.

What particularly arouses the enthusiasm of the youngsters is the sense of superiority given them by Ai Tze-chi's approach. Earlier scholars were not supposed to be interested in politics. An old Chinese proverb says, "All professions are lowly; only scholars are noble." Scholars were supposed to study only for the sake of knowledge itself, not for any practical purpose. Youngsters always find it fun to smash traditions. They therefore agree with Ai Tze-chi's essay, a large portion of which is devoted to emphasizing the importance of associating theoretical learning with practical realism.

The children are taught how to write letters, and an example is given them which teaches much more than the art of correspondence. The sample salutation to one's own father, in contrast to the tradition of China as far back as letters have been written, is as blunt as to a stranger. It begins with "Father," and ends with the factual "Your son." Just that, no more. The pitting of the prestige of the schoolroom against the parent is further evidenced by the contents of the letter, as most of its subtleties, of course, escape the child, who also absorbs only its spirit.

Father:

This term, the teacher says that I have shown willingness to learn, and that I know how to use what I have learned. I was first in the learning contest, and won a *Liberation Songs* album as a prize. I am very happy. Elder Brother is also good. He loves labor and was third in the production contest. He was given a Red Star badge as his prize. Younger Sister is tidy and also got a prize. Guess what? A towel and a toothbrush.

Papa, are you glad to hear that? I hope you will soon come to see our prizes.

Your son,
Siao-ping (July 2)

"Papa, are you glad to hear that?" Is there an overtone in this of, "I dare you to say no?"

American writers are represented in these literature textbooks, too, but only by the example of a letter "to his son" by one of the convicted American Communist Party leaders, Gilbert Green. The indisputable authenticity of the American nationality of its author makes what it says against the United States, and in favor of the Soviet Union, a particularly effective weapon for propaganda.

Further on in the same textbook is an analysis of Gorky's bitter diatribe against the United States—seventeen full pages of this, forcibly written. Here again, the Communists have shown effective wile in picking a foreigner with such prestige value. This lesson is replete with livid descriptions of the United States as a literal hell on earth, a "yellow devil's empire," and the United States is compared to a melting pot where people are melted down into the yellow metal, gold.

Almost every high-school student in China used to dream of going abroad to finish his studies, particularly to America. Those who had to support their families after graduation, and so couldn't go, envied those schoolmates whose families were able to send them to the United States to continue their studies. After "liberation," it was evident that sons even of well-to-do families would not be able to travel to the United States. A natural consequence was that they began to comfort themselves by imagining that the United States wasn't such a good place after all and that they were probably lucky not to be able to go. Such a vitriolic essay as that by Gorky appeals to these young people, for in this respect they find relief in it.

The more eager a student once was to go to America, now that his hopes seemed smashed forever, the more anxious he becomes to indulge himself in imagining how woeful it must be in America. The Communists here have only followed their usual pattern of determining the frustrations of the people they wish to indoctrinate and then feeding them what they want to hear. This is the most effective way of building up hates, for it provides a common meeting ground between the propagandist and his subject.

Another bit of literature attributed to a Russian indicated that the Chinese, even under the various pressures put upon them to work harder and harder for less and less pay, weren't producing fast enough to satisfy Moscow. Perhaps there had been murmurings for the better life that the Communists promised. Anyway, a purported Soviet Russian engineer, in an article in a Manchurian newspaper, related his alleged experiences in the United States twenty years earlier, a period when he had been sent by Moscow to study American industrial methods at one of the Ford plants. The account he gives is supposed to spur Chinese workers on to even greater competition in production, to be paid for by their sweat. In this newspaper article, reprinted for high-school seniors, the Russian says that after a few days of apprenticeship he felt fully prepared to stage a production contest with the other work-men. He selected the American next to him, and "by lunch, there was a heap of manufactured products on my workbench, and he also had a heap, but his was much lower than mine. It was evident my production had surpassed his."

After lunch an American worker reproached him, accord-ing to this tale, calling him a traitor to his fellow craftsmen, as the new rate of production would now be made the norm and there would be mass firings.

"In my nation," the Russian said he told the American, "every worker wants to compete with every other this way, and nobody worries about losing his job." The American is quoted as having replied that this was because there were no such men as the Fords in the Soviet Union, for "it is your country."

Such writings fit well into the pattern of allegiance to Mos-cow as it has been adroitly built up in the new Red textbooks. "The imperialists will certainly attack Soviet Russia," is the warning in one lesson. The quicker these "imperialists and their running dogs start a war, the sooner will they perish," it adds, warning the students against believing rumors con-trary to Moscow's interests. The article continues, for the benefit of the fifteen-to-eighteen-year-old students:

The devil wants to strike. . . . Between the imperialists and us, except for their running dogs, every interest of ours is a dis-interest of theirs. Our paralysis is their joy. Then their enemy must be our friend. They themselves are crumbling, unable to support themselves. So they hate Soviet Russia. Seeing that this is without effect, they can only prepare for war, and will only sleep well with Soviet Russia destroyed. But what will we do? Are we to be cheated any more?

If the running dogs of the imperialists want to fight, let them. Ours, the people's, interests, are the opposite of theirs. We are against attack on the Soviet Union. This is our way of life.

This, too, is classified as literature.

One of the essays of Ilya Ehrenberg, entitled *The Great*

Feeling, offers another lesson. In it, the foremost Soviet Russian propagandist tells about the "love" that the peoples of all countries have for Stalin, that he is "adored" by them, and that he ascribes an "international" quality to Stalin. This implies that Chinese students would only be doing right in paying more homage to this "universal savior" than to any Chinese leader. The beat of war drums is hardly muffled in this example from a lesson entitled "Be Ready at Any Moment."

We must love the People's Army. . . . We must love our faithful friend, the fortress of peace and democracy in the world, Soviet Russia. We must be ready at any moment. We must be ready to offer our energy to protect our nation and world peace, and to fight for the fundamental liberation of the people of the world. . . . We must love the Chinese Communist Party, which led the people of China toward victory, and we must love the teacher of revolution in China and its leader, Mao Tse-tung. . . . We must love to be obedient to discipline and organization, to be ready at any moment to struggle for the heroic career of the revolution, and stay firm before our enemies.

Are you ready, children of New China?

This call, with the usual Chinese sense of timing, was printed in a junior-high-school reader, as the culminating lesson of the textbook.

Yet the compilers of these textbooks have not been able completely to conceal their neurotic fear that, just as they won power through their calculated manipulation of people's minds, they will lose power through losing control over these same people's minds. Hence their pains to eliminate the traditional role of the jester in the peasants' *yang ko* dance. "The role of the jester is now abolished," says an essay on the *yang ko.* The jester had been needed during past regimes, for, through his privileged mouth, "the existing order was criticized and wrongs were righted." But with the Communists in power these students are taught that "the satirical parts of plays are no longer necessary." Criticism that is not controlled by the group technique cannot be trusted. The new *yang ko*, the lesson goes on to say, is called the "struggle *yang ko*," for it "teaches the people to struggle, to fight." The jester, if he had been allowed to remain, might have been able to express the people's true ideas on those whom they are being sent to fight.

The principles of journalism are taught, too, in these literature courses, with the inference that accuracy is secondary. An article on writing for the press, translated from the Russian, says: "Your articles must be like artistic paintings, and not be mere photographs." The budding journalists are taught to pour their "own emotions" into their writings. They are warned that they are the eyes and ears of the public and are powerful, so that "none of their faults can be forgiven." The effect is to justify control of the press and the imposition of a ban on foreign newspapers.

A lesson is included on how to write editorials, also written by a Russian. Before writing an editorial, it says, "you first must ask yourself whether or not what you are going to write is useful and good for the public." That this guide on what is "useful and good" is in strict accordance with Party line is taken for granted.

Even Robinson Crusoe's story is regarded as a danger to Communism's grip on China, for it teaches children to depend on their own wits. The form which the attack on Defoe's classic took is a supposed discussion meeting at which the book is criticized. Someone remarked that, so long as an individual can use his head and hands, he can get on all right. But the meeting decides this is not so; it resolves that the story does not have much truth or meaning in it, because "man is a social being, and all that Robinson achieved were gifts of the community in which he had previously lived." He had learned from this society, so the book did not represent "mankind's actual struggle" and therefore was to be condemned as a bad influence on youth.

The same lesson indirectly teaches the procedure by which writings which the Communists do not favor can be criticized and condemned without being read. In this discussion group, the secretary read a summary of the book to the meeting. The questioning took place on the basis of this summary. Whether the secretary read the book through or was given his version of it by a safe, brain-washed source, was not told in the lesson.

SCIENCE

Science, which embraces all the social studies, is a junior primary-school subject in China. In the senior primary-school classes, it is broken up into geography, history, natural science, and political science. (The primary school classifies its first two years as junior, the remaining four as senior.)

Whatever indoctrination material cannot be conveniently fitted into the other courses is lumped together in these. The child is taught learning in his first few days in school, and there is no beating around the bush regarding the new political interpretation given it. The child, from almost his first days in class, is taught the organization and methods of discussion meetings. The young are given their first formalized teachings in patriotism, and it is interpreted for them as a matter of loves and hates, the former for the Soviet bloc and Stalin and Mao, and the latter for the United States and other "imperialists."

The first science lessons given the new pupils, presented in big characters and illustrations, are: "I love teacher, teacher loves me"; "Raise your hand when you want to talk"; "Chairman Mao loves us, we love him"; and "Farmers plow, workers work, children learn." The next term they progress to such teachings as, "Clothes are made by workers, houses are made by workers, utensils are made by workers"; "Landlords don't till the soil, they live on what the farmers grow"; "Landlords don't work; they eat well and clothe themselves well, nevertheless"; and "Farmers feed the landlords, while they themselves starve and lack clothing."

The second year of schooling takes the children a jump forward; there are more words and fewer pictures in their science books. Terminology is used in a particularly Communist Party manner, and the children are given their first lessons on holding a meeting. Now seven or eight years old, they are given a description of other children of their age organizing a learning meeting and holding an election for a Children's Corps leader. They are taught about wild life, too, about rabbits that steal peas, and wolves that kidnap sheep. "They are called beasts; they are harmful; we must kill them." The ass, cow, and mule are domestic animals, "we have to protect them."

They are taught about the Children's Corps (which ultimately contributes many recruits to the Red Army) in this simple way:

Many school heroes unite. They want to do well in their "learning" work. They want to be accomplished. What is this organization? It is the Children's Corps.

The lessons they received in their first year of schooling are now amplified. For instance, here is what they are told about "Why Landlords Live Well":

Landlords don't work; then why do they live well? They lease land to farmers. They collect heavy taxes. They lend out money at high interest. Their good livelihood is stolen from the farmers.

Then "Why Do Farmers Live Poorly?" The next lesson gives this answer:

Farmers grow the crops. They have to rent their land from the landlords; they have to pay heavy taxes; and, if they owe anything, they have to pay heavy interest and have to work for the landlord, and make him gifts. The farmers are robbed by the landlords.

The textbook adds:

In the old liberated zone, after farm reform, farmers could own what they grew, and starved no more.

Between indoctrinations, the children are given helpful household hints on such matters as sanitation and are taught not to believe in superstitions. Word guessing (which means any analysis of Chinese writing, palmistry, physiognomy, and fortunetelling) "is all fraud." This lesson is not without political significance, for fortunetellers were used by the Communists in psychological warfare and espionage, and they know that now that they are in power these can be used against them just as easily.

Simple physics, zoology, and botany are begun in the last half of the second grade. Lessons are worded in such a way as to assume that all classes already have been divided into groups in the democratic-discussion manner and that each has selected its own leader. One lesson describes an enthusiastic learning group. Helpful hints continue on the care of the eyes and ears, and such terms as "friction" are defined. There is this start on the facts of life:

How do animals produce their young? Mammals produce the same way as man. Birds produce eggs first and then hatch the eggs. Some insects hatch from eggs worms which turn into larvae and the larvae become grown-up worms.

The Party gets down to ideological brass tacks in lessons entitled "We Chinese":

Our China has a history of 5,000 years. The Chinese people have been traditionally cheated, insulted, taken advantage of, and tricked by three kinds of ruffians. These are the imperialists, the feudalistic landlords, and the Kuomintang reactionaries. Now these bad eggs are being broken, and the people are liberated.

There are lessons, too, about the happiness that comes to a peasant family after it has "turned over." They "no longer have any worry about food and clothing," and the little boy can go to school. The children are taught that China comprises a number of different "races"—"living together as one big family." These races are enumerated as the Manchus, the Mongolians, the Moslems, the Tibetans, and the Miaos, as well as the Chinese.

Armies and war make their appearance in third-year science. The children are instructed to "love the People's Army," to "imitate their good example," to send the soldiers "consolation" (the tactful word for gifts and contributions), and to be enthusiasts in learning. Lessons on the composition of the human skin, on how plants propagate by scattering seed, and how air circulates in a room are included.

The science class is now considered advanced enough to be taught history. In accordance with the technique of constant repetition from all possible directions, the textbooks return again and again to the important points—always of an ideological nature. The same subjects are repeated in textbooks on supposedly different subjects, the only difference being one of emphasis.

Early history is described in Party terminology to leave the impression that ancient happenings were similar to present-day events. Solutions always are fitted into the Communist pattern of inevitability in dialectical materialism. For instance, about all that was told in the ancient records about the latter days of the Chin Dynasty was that there had been some sort of uprising. The following is what third-year science has made out of this:

At the end of the Chin Dynasty, able men were drawn from everywhere to build gardens for the emperor and to construct the Great Wall. People lived miserably. Sheng Shun was an employed farmer. He once went with his comrade, Wu Kwong, and with a few hundred other forced laborers, to a construction job. They were caught in the rain on the way and were late. According to Chin Dynasty law, people-laborers [this means forced labor] were executed if they came to the job late. The men held a discussion. "It's death anyway, so let's strike," they decided. They used wooden staves as weapons and bamboo poles to carry a banner, and started a revolution. People everywhere killed Chin's officials and followed them. In two months their troops increased to 100,000. The aristocrats who were against Chin's reign took this opportunity to rise up, too. Although they were annihilated by the Chins after half a year of revolution, yet the tyrannical rule of the Chin Dynasty was soon overthrown.

The second half of third-year science gets down to cases on foreign affairs. In the Opium War, the people themselves are said to have risen and their successes to have terrified both China's ruling class and the British, who collaborated to suppress them. The inference is that the Chinese people were only prevented from winning the war by their own rulers. "Since then, the Chinese people have always been under the oppression of the imperialists," the lesson concludes.

The textbook then describes the building of railways and the construction of churches as part of a program of aggression. "The people wouldn't believe what the missionaries said," so the only converts they could get were "ruffians and other local rowdies," the lesson says.

These ruffians, with the foreign missions at their back, perpetrated all sorts of evil, increasing the hatred of the Chinese for the imperialists. The people of Shantung and Hopei provinces got together, organized an association called the Boxers, and took as their slogan "Annihilate the Foreigners." They planned to drive out the imperialists and burn all their properties. The Ching [Manchu] Dynasty, seeking to make use of them [Boxers] to protect their own interests, bade them come to Peiping. Thus followed the incident of the siege of the foreign ambassadors' residences, when the German ambassador and the secretary in the Japanese ambassador's residences were killed. England, France, Germany, Italy, America, Russia, Austria, and Japan—the eight imperialistic nations that had long been desirous of perpetrating a great robbery in China—took this opportunity to form an allied army, which captured Peiping. The Ching Dynasty made peace with these countries and signed the Sing-chiu [Boxer] Treaty. Since then, China has remained independent only nominally. In reality, all the imperialists were able to rule China.

This history skillfully shifts all the discredit to the imperial family. The old textbooks described the Boxers as local gangs and bandit groups claiming to possess supernatural powers and inflicting great hardships on the people.

The next lesson tells of the formation of the Chinese republic and the abdication of the emperor:

The Ching emperor was overthrown and a republic was born. The revolution did not suppress the war lords, officials, and landlords. The emperor was gone, but in his stead came many warlords, and imperialism still clung to its privileges. Thus the revolution did not save the people from oppression, and there was nothing real in the republic but its name.

The textbook ends on a happy note:

Thanks to the Chinese Communists and their leadership, the imperialists have been driven out and the reactionaries suppressed. The Chinese people turned over. . . . Since then, the people have their own Central People's Government to lead them in annihilation of their enemies and in the construction of a happy nation.

These junior primary-school science books then go into detail about the growth and activities of the Communist Party of China. The anti-Japanese war is presented as a wholly Communist enterprise. "In 1945, Soviet Russia attacked Japan, and Japan surrendered." The next lesson is entitled "The New National Disgrace":

After the conclusion of World War II, the American imperialists wanted to rule the world and turn China into its colony. The Kuomintang wished to oppress the people, and to annihilate the people's strength. But their own power was not enough, and they needed the help of the American imperialists. The latter wished China to become their colony, and this appeal was exactly what they were waiting for. Thus the Kuomintang betrayed its own country in order to get help, and the American imperialists were glad to assist the Kuomintang in fighting the civil war.

On November 4, 1946, the Kuomintang reactionaries signed the pact that betrayed their own country—the Sino-American Commercial Treaty. According to this pact, the American imperialists were allowed to build naval bases in China at will, to travel and investigate in China without any restriction, to dump its products into China, to fly its planes in the Chinese sky, and to send its armies to whatever port it chose in China. . . . No other treaty has ever been so utterly treasonable. The Communist Party announced that it would never recognize such a treaty, and all the people and the democratic parties in China were against it. November 4 was named the New National Disgrace-Shameful Day, and the Party called for the cooperation of all people to wipe away this disgrace.

The children who read this cannot know what a succession of distortions and untruths have been fitted into this lesson, how the gift of powdered milk for babies (under the United Nations Reconstruction Relief Association program) has been interpreted as "dumping," and how the simple right of commercial ships of any country to call at the ports of other countries is made to appear as an extraordinary abandonment of sovereignty. The subordination of fact to fancy through double-talk has forced the use of some very awkward logic and phraseology, as in the sentence that says the Kuomintang wished "to annihilate the people's strength." Here, "people's strength" is used as a synonym for Red Army. Unless a reader understands such manipulation of language, he may think he understands what he reads, but it will not at all be what the able Party member who wrote it had in his mind. This, too, is psychological warfare—making people fool themselves.

This type of teaching leads naturally to the lesson that reads, "we must bring about the downfall of Chiang Kai-shek and drive out the American imperialists." This is repeated a few sentences further on, in slightly different form to lend emphasis:

The Chinese People's Liberation Army is the army of the people. Under the leadership of the Chinese Communist Party, it will annihilate the Chiang Kai-shek gang and drive out the American imperialists.

Each succeeding lesson builds up the same theme. In one, the United States is presented as abetting the defeated Japanese to attack China once again. In another, the pan-Asiatic aims of the Party are outlined. A lesson entitled "Our Neighboring Countries" reads:

There are about ten countries neighboring ours. Some are our good friends, some are colonies oppressed by the imperialists, others are our enemies, the imperialists. The Mongolian People's Republic is next to us in the north. Soviet Russia is to the north of the Mongolian People's Republic, and adjoins us only in the northeast and northwest. Across the Yellow Sea from Shantung, on a peninsula directly connected to our territory in the northeast, is the Korean People's Democratic Republic. These three neighboring countries are our good neighbors and good friends.

In the southeast are India, Burma, Indochina, and Nepal. They are all colonies of the imperialists and are all struggling for independence. In Indochina and Burma, the people have already organized their own armies and have started the liberation war. They are very happy over the success of our efforts in realizing a New China.

Only the neighbor to our east, the Japanese imperialists, is our worst neighbor and the aggressor of our territory. Although they have been defeated by us, yet the American imperialists are now helping the recovery of Japanese imperialism, which plans to attack us again. But the people of Japan are our friends, and they are now fighting for democracy under the leadership of the Japanese Communist Party.

This incidentally points up the fact, as do Communist Chinese statements generally, that no country is recognized as having gained its freedom unless it simultaneously becomes part of the Soviet bloc and subject to Moscow. The India of Gandhi and Nehru, which had attained its independence before this textbook came out, is classified along with any other colony.

Along with this go lessons in self-criticism and discussion meetings. The children are taught to ask themselves:

Do I always obey the decisions of meetings and conform to discipline? Do I have attitudes of personal freedom? We must be impartial; we must obey discipline and work for the masses.

The casual manner in which personal freedom is alluded to as a bad personal characteristic cannot help but impress itself on children's minds.

The textbook ends with a lesson on Soviet Russia, which it describes as "the most happy and fortunate people in the world." An ideological basis is now given, in a sweeping generalization, for the Russia-First line, and this is that Soviet Russia already is "preparing to enter Communism," which is described in this sweeping language:

In a Communist society, the people's political consciousness is the highest. They are all capable. The production rate is therefore higher than in a socialist society. The community is richer, and the following is realized: "Each does his best and gets what he needs." This is the happiest new society for all of mankind.

The Chinese child is thus instructed, in his early school years, that it is to Soviet Russia that he must look for the achievement of the world's greatest civilization. The foundation is laid for that curious twist in ideology by which the Chinese people are supposed to believe that the most effective form in which they can express their own national patriotism is by supporting Soviet Russia in all things.

THE PAY-OFF

KOREA

A CHINESE NEWSPAPERMAN, DRESSED AS A COOLIE, WAN-dered about the countryside outside his home in Central China to get the feel of the land. He wandered into a parade grounds where a high-ranking officer was addressing his troops. This was autumn in 1950.

"They were the best—the warmest-dressed—Chinese soldiers I ever saw," this reporter told me shortly afterwards, when he had managed to leave Red China. "I stood among some villagers and listened to what the soldiers were being told. Imagine my surprise when I heard the speaker exclaim, 'When we were in need, before our liberation, our Big Brother came to our assistance. Now our Big Brother needs our help. We are going to Soviet Russia, therefore, to give our Big Brother the assistance he asks of us.'" (Big Brother is the well-understood label commonly used by Chinese Communists when referring to Soviet Russia. Korean Communists use the same expression when referring to either the Chinese or the Russians.)

"Of course I knew, and the speaker evidently knew, that his troops weren't going into Russia—they were going to Manchuria and Korea," the Chinese reporter said to me. "But his men didn't know it. North Korea, North Manchuria, or Siberia, it was all the same to them."

The Red officer's statement just didn't seem to make sense. At first hearing it sounded as if this political officer had simply lied to his men. This wasn't necessarily so. Outsiders would evaluate his words in the framework of their own normal lives, and put their own sense of values on them. Then, of course, what he said sounded like a lot of nonsense. The Chinese troops were not crossing the Soviet frontier, and Moscow was not yet engaging in an overt war with anyone. But this wasn't what the Chinese officer meant when he made his statement. He was thinking in terms of the North China People's Revolutionary University, in the language of discussion meetings and "The Questions of Thought," and in the mental framework of guerrilla camps in Indochina, Malaya, and Korea. Then, what he said made sense, a great deal of sense.

This was because we were thinking in narrow channels, while the Communists were not. The Americans always referred to the "Korea war," the Britishers to the "Malaya war," and the French to the "Indochina war." But I never heard either the Chinese Communists nor any other Communists in Asia use that terminology. This applies to their writings and propaganda for external consumption as well as for one another, to the diaries which they write for themselves, and to their so-called discussion meetings.

No matter whether it was in Korea, China, Indochina, Malaya, the Philippines, or even Japan, they always spoke in some such manner as the "All-Asia War," or the "Korea-China-Indochina-Philippines front," or the "Anti-Imperialist War." What was more, the Reds were not merely thinking of the fighting in those broad terms, they were planning their operations and implementing them on that basis. While non-Communist authorities outside the Communist sphere were thinking and acting locally, the Communists were operating globally. While each of us was considering some one area as a complete problem in itself, focusing our interests and energies on it, the Communists of Asia were planning and acting on the basis of all Asia's being one front. Japan, Korea, the Philippines, Indochina, Malaya, Indonesia, Thailand, Burma, all the lands of Asia were only sectors, along with China, on that one front, to be dealt with as opportunity provided. This factor alone was worth many army divisions to the Communists. Handling Asia as one big front meant that the Communist High Command could keep the pressure going indefinitely, allowing a lull in one sector when tactics required it, and putting on the heat somewhere else. They were able to keep the United Nations sitting idly by in all other sectors, while one or another of their flanks was being mercilessly pounded.

Let me give an insight into what this strategy means on the battlefield. This will require an excursion back into Malaya, when I was traveling with a British detachment in the north, near the Thai border. I was with part of the Malayan forces that were battling what the British officials said was a hard core of only 3,000 to 5,000 guerrillas. Officially, the British weren't even admitting that these guerrillas were Communists, using instead the euphemism "bandits" that fooled none of the native population, only made it shy from stepping into fields where even the authorities seemed afraid to tread. Before I visited the sector, I wondered whether the British weren't minimizing the number of guerrillas. Now, after having been there, I wondered whether they weren't exaggerating.

The sort of jungle that exists in Malaya is so dense that a handful of men can keep a regiment running mad circles. The British were losing only a few men each week in the Malaya fighting. They talked to me confidently of the day when they would finally kill off the 3,000 to 5,000 guerrillas and restore peace in Malaya.

But I found that each Englishman killed wasn't just another fighting chap who could be replaced overnight by another Englishman from the homeland. He frequently was a long-experienced jungle fighter, a man who knew the jungle and its ways as one can only after hard training and experience over a long period. He couldn't be replaced in less than a few years, and even so, a man had to have a special kind of temperament to be any good in that environment.

As for the 3,000 to 5,000 guerrillas, I found that the Communists were deliberately keeping the number that low—confident that if the British killed a dozen or so in a day, or in a skirmish, these easily could be replaced. What was more, this kept the news value low, too, for newspapers abroad had no space for such small, seemingly petty skirmishes. This allowed the Communists to proceed without arousing the alarm of the West.

Guerrilla losses were particularly easy to replace, for the Malayan guerrillas were virtually all Chinese. Many were born in China. Some of their key leaders came from China— from Yenan, for instance—during World War II. These Chinese could be replaced, if not from Malaya itself, from Thailand, Indochina or China. The bleeding of the British could be kept up indefinitely this way, with the fantastic monetary expense that it entailed. (This was what the Communists meant by "economic warfare.")

A couple of Chinese interpreters with the British troops explained it to me. "The guerrilla detachments don't recognize borders," they said. "They stay comfortably in Thailand, across the frontier, resting up and training in the big rubber plantations over there.

"They are given a mission inside Malaya, perhaps to roll a hand grenade down a theater aisle, or ambush a British jeep, or assassinate a Chinese merchant who isn't paying the subsidy demanded. They go across the Thai border into Malaya to do the job, then return. The British make believe this border exists for the guerrillas as much as for themselves."

This make-believe went to fantastic lengths. The British at that time were distributing millions of leaflets to Chinese villagers, telling them that they needn't supply information and food to the guerrillas any more, that they needn't be afraid to refuse to do so, for the fight against the guerrillas was to the finish. The Chinese interpreters in the British Army told me how it worked out.

"The Chinese love to go to their little inns, or to sit in tea houses. At least one Chinese-language newspaper comes to every village, and at least one person in every village is able to read the news to the others.

"Well, yesterday the big headline in the Chinese press was on a talk given by a British Cabinet Minister. He denied that there was to be any change in British policy toward Peiping, and said that the Peiping regime was in de facto control of the mainland, inferring that it was here to stay, and said we should be realistic about it. Well, this is what the Chinese Communists are telling the villagers. They are telling the Chinese population that they had better bet on the right horse—the Communists—that they should be realistic. Whom are the plain people to believe? The British in Malaya, or in London? If the British in faraway London are willing to deal with the Reds because it is opportunistic, what do they expect of the poor villagers on the spot, whose lives and properties are wide open to guerrilla incursions?"

This sort of global reasoning was what gave point to the thinking of that Red officer whom my newspaper friend had overheard talking to his troops in Central China. What he said made sense, too, when considered within the context of the history, literature, and the science books of Red China's schools. He was brushing aside all trivialities and make-believe. After the ideological defeat that Stalinism had suffered in Yugoslavia, world Communism simply could not allow a territorial defeat in Korea. It was as simple as that.

Of course, if the North Koreans could handle it themselves, this would have satisfied Communism most. When they got into a really tight spot, then naturally the Chinese Communists had no alternative; they had to send help to that stricken sector. And if the Chinese Communists got into a really tight spot, then it was up to the Russian Communists. This was the mental framework for this officer's remarks.

He had been taught—or he wouldn't have been allowed to address these troops—that the highest patriotism a Chinese could show his country is to support Soviet Russia. He was accepting the fact that all the area in which the fighting was taking place in Korea was in the Soviet Russian sphere. Maps might say differently, but maps are just matters of convenience and control in the totalitarian way of thinking.

Another factor in this Red officer's mind was that any younger brother feels mighty good when Big Brother asks for his help. This gave the Chinese troops a morale lift and made them feel, for the moment, the equals of the Soviet Russians. This is psychological warfare, too.

About that time, eyewitness reports were coming from China proper telling of Communist divisions being dispatched to Manchuria for service in Korea. I had an interview with Maj. Gen. Claire Chennault on July 4, 1950. His "Flying Tigers" had been enabled to achieve phenomenal results in China through a strategy in which a large role was occupied by the unprecedented intelligence network he had set up, which gave rise to the phrase that has now become a part of the language, "the bamboo wireless." This was an adaptation by Americans of age-old methods in China of passing along information by utilizing every primitive and modern means to complement each other, from word of mouth to radio.

In developing this network, the tanned schoolmaster-flier-technician had recourse to the same practical ingenuity that was responsible for his World War II strategy of strangling Japanese war industry by depriving it of some basic supply en route, a strategy that was credited by America's Japan Bombing Survey with being the most effective, beyond even the exploits of high-flying B-29s.

Five years after V-J Day, when I interviewed "the old man," remarkable remnants of this World War II network were still keeping him in touch with what was happening on the Chinese mainland. His "bamboo wireless" was penetrating the bamboo curtain. Gen. Chennault told me that he had just learned that 200,000 Communist troops, fully armed, had been moved from China proper through Manchuria to the border of Korea, under orders to enter the fighting as soon as the need arose. "And I hear that more are being sent all the time," he told me.

The Free World didn't want to believe this. We preferred wishful thinking. I was with the ill-fated Thanksgiving Day push of United Nations forces in Korea that, according to the headline across the top of the English-language Seoul *Daily News* on November 26, 1950, was the "Drive to End War by Christmas." I was witnessing—had been witnessing for some time—as extraordinary an effort at self-deception as I had ever seen in my more than a quarter century of journalism around the world.

America's—and the Free World's—worst enemy was not the Communist troops. As I sat in a command post tent a couple of nights before, listening to the shells swoosh overhead, the generals of the 25th Division explained their offensive to a small corps of newspaper correspondents. The UN advance had not yet begun. The shells were for what the military called triangulation. Airplanes overhead supervised the firing. Figures were being calculated which would be used, once the drive started, as the points from which the air spotters would keep the artillery advised on where to aim.

There was a complete blackout that night; even smoking was forbidden, for the faint tobacco glow would have betrayed our presence in this amphitheater of mountains. We felt our way over the frozen sod, from the press tent to the headquarters tent. Inside was an improvised map room, where a steady stream of officers came to report and receive final instructions. One batch of officers after the other would congregate in front of the big map that covered one wall, while a general or his chief of staff would explain some position, using his finger or a pointer. The weather outside was way below zero; inside the tent it was comfortably warm from the heat of the oil stove and many bodies.

The chief of staff stood up, and in schoolmaster style gave

us a briefing. Then the three generals, seated in a row in front, answered our questions. They patiently explained the offensive, which would start at the break of dawn. If any secrets were held back from the world press, they were technical details in which we had no interest. By the time they could leak, the army should be at least within spitting distance of the border. The important details were all being told to us, and the offensive, as it was being described, sounded thorough and ship-shape, supporting the belief in all ranks everywhere at the front and behind it that this, indeed, was the final campaign of the Korean fighting.

Earlier that afternoon, I had eaten my second Thanksgiving Day dinner in two days, with all the trimmin's—there had been so much at the front that in some battalions there was enough left for a second day, as well as a second helping each time. At our Thanksgiving feast I had heard the troops discussing Gen. MacArthur's visit to Sinanju, at the western end of the front. Everyone was telling everyone else that MacArthur had said "the boys are going to eat their Christmas dinner at home." There seemed no reason to doubt this. Gen. MacArthur's bold Inchon landings had taken place ten weeks before, and the captured territory had now become a springboard for the final leap forward. The North Korean army had crumbled, and the advance to the Manchurian border was to be mainly a mopping-up operation. Some Chinese Communist troops were known to have entered Korea, but there was general agreement that Peiping did not intend to join the fighting in any decisive manner. This was to be a token operation, a face-saving device.

Previous UN setbacks in Korea had been caused by the overwhelming superiority that the Communists had in manpower and equipment. The numerically inferior UN troops had been obliged to shove forward in only one sector at a time, leaving their flanks unprotected against guerrilla forces that might linger and filter behind. This time the enemy was not to be given any opportunity for such a maneuver. Although the distance to the frontier was only 50 miles, several days were to be taken in traversing this. Along the width of northern Korea, in the valleys and across the mountains, we were shown on the map how the UN armies were going to proceed slowly and cautiously, like a comb, making sure that no enemy soldiers remained behind to snipe at and harass our forces as before.

We didn't have appreciably more troops than formerly, so in order to extend our front all along this line we had to thin out our forces considerably. But so what? The North Koreans had been cut up and thinned out far more. Nobody saw any danger in this strategy.

I remember the Ranger vanguard that I had met that afternoon, in a jeep trip that threaded a winding, hilly way beyond the walled, natural mountain fortress city of Yongbyon to within sight of Communist-occupied villages. The small Ranger detachment was to accompany tank squadrons and was under the command of a lanky lieutenant who was grimly sure of himself. "We're fighting to kill this time," he said. "I've seen a couple of hundred of my classmates at West Point killed out here so far." Thus he expressed his sense of unity that made him feel that he had been present at each of these deaths. For my part, I wondered how far we could endure such loss of highly trained young officers, while the European power that had incited this bleeding wasn't losing a man.

As I listened to the briefing I could not know, of course, that this young West Point graduate was not going to die— he was only going to lose both his legs—and that the bulk of his small force of less than 100 Rangers was to be destroyed.

As the briefing proceeded in its methodical manner, I began to feel more and more restless. I was well acquainted with the situation. A question was forming itself in the back of my mind that was out of harmony with the general feeling. I would try to hold the question back, but it would press itself more and more into my mind, and finally, although I felt it was almost tactless to let it out, I would have to do so, for I would know that this was the hub of the matter, which it would be so nice and so polite not to mention, and yet I would have to do so. How often have I found that people build up their whole case with everyone tacitly not mentioning some one awkward detail on which everything else hinged. This is human nature, and to go along with it is natural, but it is not good reporting.

In this briefing other memories were protruding into the professional atmosphere of a headquarters tent. These were memories that I had brought with me to Korea: of the Chinese newspaperman who had listened to the Communist officer addressing his troops in Central China, of Gen. Chennault's bamboo wireless information, and what the Chinese Communists themselves were ceaselessly saying.

Ever since the fighting started in Korea, the Chinese Communist government had been proclaiming, in every medium of communication that it possessed, from its multilingual radio programs that reached all of Asia to its regimented newspapers and its controlled discussion meetings, that the Korea fighting was part of its own "All-Asia Defense War."

Chinese Communist Army units, months before, at carefully manipulated political meetings everywhere from the capital at Peiping down to Kunming, had begun passing resolutions expressing determination "to defend the Chinese People's Republic" against a so-called American aggression, blithely ignoring the fact that a neutral UN committee headed by an Indian had found it the other way round.

A flow of eye-witness reports came at the same time from China proper of Chinese Communist divisions being dispatched to Manchuria for service there and in Korea.

Yes, America's—and the Free World's—worst enemy that night, as I stood in that command-post tent, was wishful thinking. Wishful thinking about the scope of the warfare and about the duration of the war. Wishful thinking that had the enemy fold up after the masterful Inchon landings, instead of its being only the North Korean element in the Communist armies. Wishful thinking about whether we could terminate the warfare at the 38th parallel; wishful thinking about whether the 38th parallel meant anything more to the enemy than did the 37th or the 39th. Wishful thinking over whether the Chinese Communists even were in the fighting.

This last phenomenon—wishful thinking over the presence of the Chinese Communist troops in force—was responsible for a self-deception that permeated all circles and made a make-believe of everything else. As a consequence, there was a "dirty word," a hush-hush word, at press conferences in Tokyo, and behind the front in Korea, and at the front. Nice people just didn't speculate over the possibility of the Chinese Communists' coming into the Korean war in a big way. Too many reputations were at stake. When the subject was brought up, a pained silence would fall over the assembly, the same heavy sense of disapproval that silences a boor who utters a filthy word. Outside of this theater of war, in places such as Hong Kong, and here, too, a state of mind had been created that made you seem a very backward individual, indeed, if you fell for such sensationalism as the reports that the Chinese Reds were moving into the war in force. "Did you hear the latest Formosa rumor?" was the tone required in mentioning such a subject if you didn't want to lose face. People can make believe around a conference table, but on a battlefield, if you make believe that a rifle isn't there, you get shot.

The push that early morning turned into reverse fast, as history records. After the retreat, everyone blamed somebody else for the strange psychology that made us fool ourselves. This again was an unrealistic approach. Every sort of person was taken in by this, from my fellow colleagues in the press corps to the diplomats, the military, and the businessmen. With a few notable exceptions, they were all using their own frame of reasoning in judging what the Chinese Communists were going to do, instead of the point of view expressed in "The Modern World Revolution History" and the "Chinese Modern Revolutionary Movement History."

This was literally make-believe as well as wishful thinking that the Free World still was indulging in—a combination which, if persisted in, would be enough to destroy any civilization.

The reasoning that seemed mainly responsible for our belief that the Chinese Communists would not join the Korean fighting in force was an argument I always heard when I did succeed in bringing up the subject. It was a clincher, and it made sense to all "practical people." This was that if the Chinese Communists had intended to come into the Korean warfare, they would have done so in the beginning, when they could easily have flung the few Americans and unprepared Koreans into the sea and occupied all of the country.

But if they had done this, they would not have been Communists. They would have been us, and there would have been no war in the first place. The entire Soviet strategy in Asia, the strategy which it is confident will win, has been, since V-J Day, a delaying tactic, a bleeding operation. Anything that interfered with this slow draining of the physical and economic blood of the Free World, principally its huskiest member, the United States, interfered with this fundamental Communist program and so had to be avoided. There was nothing racial about this attrition program, except in the callous revival and exploitation by the Communists of race hatreds that the twentieth century had believed it finally was well on the road to eliminating. Asian and non-Asian blood and treasure were being spilled indiscriminately, so long as it would keep the pot boiling.

Indeed, incalculably more Asian blood and treasure had been lost to this Communist strategy, not only in Korea, but ever since the post-World War I Bolsheviks had sent their agents into Asia to capture the revolutions that President Wilson's 14 Points had activated. Either an all-out victory or an all-out defeat for the Communists in Korea would have been an interference with this delaying, bleeding strategy. The former would have brought the entire world conflict to a head, the last thing Moscow wanted at this time; and the latter would have been too costly a setback in morale. Either

of these would have ended the Free World's bleeding on
that sector of the Asia front.

The make-believe and wishful thinking had assumed all the
characteristics of the "as if" mentality on the eve of our supposedly final drive in Korea. "As if" the Chinese Communists
weren't going to participate; "as if" so much that existed
didn't exist. How often this dogmatic way of thinking has
destroyed all that individuals and nations had built up
through years, sometimes centuries, of painstaking effort!

So my restlessness increased as I listened to the briefing
and to the questions and answers. I thought of the night before in the press tent, just before we turned out our kerosene
lamp, and we had nestled snugly into our sleeping bags and
pulled up the zippers, and the press relations chief was still sitting at the edge of one cot before leaving for his own bed in
another tent. We were chewing the fat. Everyone was taking
for granted the finality of the coming drive, and when I
asked what would happen if the Chinese Communists entered in strength, I heard once again that they just wouldn't;
if they had wanted to, they would have done so months
earlier.

I could hold back no longer as I listened to the briefing
and cut in. "There's one point that still puzzles me," I said.
"Everything seems to have been anticipated and prepared for.
There seems no possibility of not keeping going all the way
to the Yalu, once we get started. But what if we don't find
just a token force of Chinese Communists fighting us; what
if we find a really big force of Chi . . ."

I never finished the word. The same feeling came over me
that any man must have in polite, mixed company if he happens to let out a nasty word—a four-letter word, perhaps—and
senses the silence of heavy disapproval around him, a silence
that is almost vocal. My question never was completed. Someone else had spoken up, and the general was replying in the
same polite manner by which another couple might relieve
the tension in a drawing room when some boor had made a
tactless remark.

When we were stepping out into the darkness a few minutes later, the briefing over, I found myself next to the correspondent for one of the world's most important publications.

"What in the world did you have to bring that up for?" he said. He didn't repeat my nasty expression. He was being tactful, too.

"But, man," I exclaimed, "I've just come from the rest of Asia, and I've talked to too many people who know that the Chinese Communists are up here, and I know the psychological build-up in Red China that has been on such a tremendous scale as to make it virtually impossible for Peiping not to intervene."

"They can't!" he retorted. Then he said something that sounded ridiculous only later, under different circumstances, but which didn't sound at all ridiculous at the time, in that environment. "They can't be going to intervene; we're going to be home for Christmas," he said.

Now, with the knowledge provided by judgment after the event, we can laugh at this naive remark. But then it had all the finality of faith. Once you took it for granted that the troops would be home for Christmas, well, obviously they couldn't be home if the Chinese Communists entered the war, and so that ruled out their entry. And the belief that everyone would be eating his Christmas turkey at home had settled into all minds, like a rumor that everyone hears everybody repeating.

The United Nations was being given "the China treatment." The manual on warfare written years ago by Mao Tse-tung, Red China's military bible, was being thrown at us, page by page. Take the American prisoners of war who were released in no-man's land just ahead of the 25th Division. I encountered the first ones, where they had trudged into our cautiously advancing lines. These freed POWs talked exuberantly, as was natural with men who had been in captivity for weeks, who had been anticipating the sort of atrocities perpetrated against other American POWs, but who instead had been treated with kindness and care and unexpectedly told, "Go home; you are free."

"We were treated swell," they kept saying to me with youthful exaggeration. They told me wonderingly about the kind of questioning they had constantly undergone—man-to-man talks, sometimes so paternal, always so cordial, by Chinese Communists who spoke English well. Yes, they said, these Chinese carefully took down their names, serial numbers, and home-town addresses. I didn't have the heart to tell these men, still under the warming realization of their release, that the Communist radios were quoting their sentences out of context and broadcasting them around the world to show that the Americans were criminally naive and to persuade the other peoples of Asia to consider Americans as they would a man-eating tiger—a beautiful animal, perhaps, but one that had to be slaughtered at sight. I didn't have the heart to tell them that this had been the Moscow-Peiping-Bucharest theme ever since the fighting started; that the U.S. was warring against the peoples of Asia.

Yet we should have been familiar with and prepared for this maneuver. It was one of the oldest tricks of the Chinese Communists. They had used it against the Japanese armies, when the Red capital was in Yenan.

The military tactic that the Chinese Communist always had exploited the most—the guerrilla maneuver of melting in front and infiltrating behind, only hitting at such enemy groups as could be split off and outnumbered—was also certain to be utilized against the United Nations. And so it was. This was one of the ways Chiang Kai-shek's armies had been whittled away and his "annihilation campaigns" against the Communists frustrated.

A few days after the collapse of the Thanksgiving Day drive I was back in Pyongyang on the curving banks of a wide river where the Communists had their North Korean capital. While I was there a Chinese was caught distributing leaflets to the populace. These leaflets, in Korean, told the people that the Communists would be back and that those who cooperated with them now would be remembered—and woe be to those who gave any aid to the Americans. The Chinese agent was actually recruiting guerrillas. He had been in town for some days. The identical Communist techniques that I had found elsewhere in Asia were being utilized here, too, so far as opportunity provided.

NORTHERN
KOREA

SOME REPORTERS ARE LUCKY. DESTINY SETS THEM DOWN IN
places where big events are about to happen, where they have
to be present just then—not before or after—in order "to get
the story," at a time when there is no way of telling that anything spectacular is going to happen there short of what
appears to be just crystal gazing, or good luck. Luck is a big
element in anything as unpredictable as news, which when
reduced to its least common denominator is the story of what
is happening among one's neighbors, particularly as it may affect oneself or reflect one's own experiences and aspirations.
This is what most interests all people.

The improvement in the channels and mechanisms of communications, which first created the penny press and then
immeasurably increased its scope and form, has brought
about two parallel phenomena, of a contrasting nature; it
has made our world larger, insofar as it has brought more and
more people into our vision as neighbors, and it has made the
world smaller, because it has shortened time, as calculated in
the distance between places. No place is farther than the time
it takes to go to it, or to talk to it. The Chinese peasant who
told me years ago that it was less li to go down a hill than up

it was correct; his thinking was realistically and scientifically up-to-date. Only an old-fashioned, narrow-minded man nowadays would calculate distance only in miles.

Similarly, no neighborhood is smaller than the number of people whose daily lives we can mutually influence. Like most things in life, this approach is a combination of philosophy and materialism, and out of it has come our modern "One World" thesis.

This is why the typical American in, say, St. Louis, and later the typical Thai in Chingmai, and the Australian in Adelaide, and the Turk in Alexandretta, found themselves in Korea. They had answered the call of a neighbor for help. As neighbors, they were all equally concerned in preserving their individual liberties.

So, as neighbor too, I found myself in North Korea. I had no way of knowing, while I was patiently and methodically making a news-gathering survey of this area, that the Communists would shortly take over again and that the curtain would descend once more for an indefinite period. My presence there exactly then was the part of it that was my "lucky break." This is what enabled me to do what had been impossible hitherto in any Communist-dominated territory, to go anywhere I wanted, without any eavesdropping escort, to ask any questions I wanted, so I could tell others what I had seen, and heard, and learned, without anybody's having the power or the authority to shut me up. This right is inseparable from freedom.

Nowhere else in the world had anybody yet been able to conduct such reportage in any area that had been governed by the Communists, especially one from which they had been expelled abruptly, unexpectedly, before they had had time to repare the setting for onlookers. Because of the unitary system of world communism, under which what it does in one area is done in all other areas it controls, what I saw in North Korea opened the window into what I would have seen, in larger or smaller measure, on a similar tour, free from all restraint, in Red China or Romania.

This similarity of procedures and objectives has enabled those who view communism as a world mechanism to predict almost eerily what was going to happen in such places as Red China, while those who insisted on making believe that the Communist hierarchy in China was not under Moscow's stern dictatorship were constantly falling into erroneous analyses, in spite of intimate knowledge of the country. Events kept catching up with them, disproving their persuasive findings.

Thus, when Mao Tse-tung and his foreign publicists were speaking so beautifully about the peasantry and their improved lot in the "New China," it was certain that as soon as the opportunity provided, the interests of these same peasants, whose blood had fertilized the revolution, would be nonchalantly cast aside, under the theory that it was the workers who must constitute the vanguard of the revolution and who must receive all prior consideration. And it was equally certain, at a time when so much was being made of Red China's tolerance toward those officials and businessmen who had not been Communists before, that this was a temporary expedient, soon to be replaced by the inevitable purge, with the reinstitution of the death penalty on a scale wider by far than that exercised by any medieval tyrant such as Genghis Khan. Thus, it is predictable, too, that the Chinese Communists will consume themselves, "improving" on the purge trials of Soviet Russia, and this has begun with the so-called "three anti" and "five anti" movements that constituted the so-called anticorruption campaign of early 1952.

So what I was able to see for myself in North Korea had unavoidable implications for Red China, as well. This was an unrivaled opportunity to find out on the spot how internationally acclaimed policies such as farm reform were actually working out. Questions about farm reform were among those I asked in every village, town or city I visited. Peasants who had been given land for the first time in their lives, farmers who had always owned their land, workers, merchants and officials, everyone, so long as he had lived in the locality during the Communist occupation, was grist for my journalistic hopper.

What first impressed me was the similarity of the replies that I was receiving everywhere. If only the merchants, or the officials, had answered me this way, I would have suspected a bias, perhaps centrally directed. But when the simple peasants in localities far from one another, whom I met by chance, answered the same way, there could be no doubt as to the veracity of what I was hearing.

My conversation with an erstwhile farm worker usually went along these simple lines:

"Did you own the land you tilled while the Japanese were here?"

"No, I worked on somebody else's land."

"Do you own any land now?"

"Yes."

"Who gave it to you?"

"When the Communists came in, they divided up certain lands and gave me a piece."

"You're a real landowner now. You don't have to work on anybody else's land any more. You must be better off now, aren't you?"

The peasant would seem puzzled how to answer, so I would ask, "Weren't you better off? Didn't you make more money under the Communists?"

There was no hesitancy now. "No, I wasn't better off. The taxes were too high."

"What do you mean?" I'd ask. "Before, you used to be a tenant farmer or a farm worker, and you didn't own a grain of the crops you grew. Now you have land of your own, and the harvest belongs to you."

Obviously this was how it should have been only it wasn't. "There were too many taxes," the farmer would repeat.

He had been given a plot of land, yes. Continued questioning would bring out that this didn't mean at all what it sounded like. The words had their usual different meaning. Farmers were landowners on sufferance. There was no un-

questioned inheritance by one's sons. This whole inheritance matter was hedged about by so many interpretations
that if ownership meant possession of something that can
be left to one's descendants, this simply wasn't the case. Few
farmers had the deeds to the farms they were supposed to
own.

The farmer had been allotted a plot of land, rather than
given it. At the same time, the government figured out exactly
what each such piece of soil should produce and set a comparatively fair tax upon it; fair, that is, if it was the whole tax.
That is to say, perhaps 35 per cent of the crop. Even so, the
rest had to be sold through government granaries, at a set
price. This price, usually lower than the farmer could have
obtained in a free market with protective controls, was in effect an indirect tax. In addition, there were a host of other
obligatory levies, the usual Communist array of contributions, donations, dues and fees that couldn't be avoided under the same penalties that would have met refusal to pay the
original tax.

By the time all these levies were added up, they left the
grower less than he had earned while working another man's
land.

The Communist Party everywhere makes a big point of
being incorruptible, and this also was interpreted in a party
manner. This meant that no matter what misfortune befell
the farmer—a death in the family, drought or flood—the tax
collector would say very sorry, but the people's government
had set a production figure for a farm of this size, and
would the peasant please show his gratitude to the people
for making him a farm owner by paying what he owed? Corruption was interpreted as meaning any consideration given
to personal circumstances, to what elsewhere are called "acts
of God." Such consideration could only be given to the party.

"What if you hadn't enough to eat?" I'd ask.

"You had to sell something to buy food."

"What did you have that you could sell?"

"Maybe a table or a coat."

"Would you have to sell them if the rice you grew wasn't sufficient to cover your taxes?"

"Of course."

The Communists had given a new emphasis to the old adage that taxes, like death, were inescapable.

What the Communists called land reform was thus shown to be merely the revival, under a new terminology, of the old serfdom that even the czars had discarded in 1861. The Korean peasant was given his piece of land, but he was attached to it like a prisoner, and he had to farm it for the benefit of the state. He was more shackled than the serf; he was a slave, handcuffed to his galley, and he had to row or die.

Even this division of the land had a time limit to it. This was the honeymoon period, when the Reds were placating the peasants, and the succeeding phase was already under way in neighboring Manchuria. This was when the agricultural population, divided into family groups too small to present any organized opposition, would be called upon to contribute their lands for collective farming. The peasant, temporarily a landowner, became a factory worker in effect. This was how it had been in eastern Europe and Soviet Russia. Collective farming had not yet come to North Korea, where farm reform had not "progressed" beyond the frustrating taxation stage.

There was something else I wanted to know. "So you earned less at the end of the growing season than you did when you tilled somebody else's land," I would begin. "This means, doesn't it, that you would prefer working on somebody else's farm, and making more money. Would you like to go back to the old system before the Communists came?"

The peasant's invariable response left no doubt as to his feelings. "Oh, no," he would say, with the farmer's stubbornness in his voice. He didn't want to give up his land. He didn't want to give up the idea that he owned it, even if the title deeds were kept from him. He liked the feeling of being a landowner. "Only I would like to keep some of the crop I grow; enough to live on," he would say.

The Communists had been able to achieve a psychological victory by making the peasants believe that they would be given a fair portion of the earth's soil and the goodness that grows thereon. Here, I felt, was the Free World's great opportunity: to take the Red slogan and to give it substance. To actually give the farmer his land and most of what he grew on it with his own toil and sweat.

The population of North Korea was estimated at 12,000,-000 on V-J Day, and South Korea's at 18,000,000. By mid-1949 at least 2,000,000 refugees had hazardously crossed the 38th parallel from the north. These, excepting some thousands of Communist agents, were entirely people fleeing from the harshness of the totalitarian state.

Had the situation been reversed and had it been South Koreans fleeing north in such large numbers, the Communists would have made this the subject of a worldwide propaganda drive, and everybody in Korea would have had it dinned repeatedly into their ears. As it was, they made a big to-do over the handful of southerners who did go north, broadcasting the fact around the earth, and emphasizing it again and again by every conceivable propaganda means. The attention they did succeed in gaining this way was another example of how we had been softened into a double standard of appraisal of what was happening.

The effect that the 2,000,000 northern refugees could have had on the attitudes of the farmers and workers of southern Korea, if representative refugees had been sent from village to village to relate the true story of Communist oppression, might well have made it impossible in any coordinated program for the North Korean Communists to get away with their infiltration and guerrilla tactics in the south.

Another set of questions that I asked wherever I went dealt with the administration of the areas freed from Communist domination. I hadn't expected to pay any special attention to this problem when I came to Korea. The questions developed out of what I discovered when I visited the mayors and other officials that had just taken over. I was dismayed by their meager capacities. They certainly were not qualified for their jobs.

I promptly went over to the Civil Assistance officials attached to the UN forces. Theirs was the responsibility, on entering a new locality, to see to the restoration of normal government. "Are these the sort of people you think should rule these places?" I asked. The replies I got were disheartening, and I often would be met with some such challenge as "Why don't you recommend some better ones?"

The Communists had been making a great deal of propaganda over their claim that all the Korean intellectuals had fled when the Americans showed up. Were the Communists telling the truth? Surely these officials I was meeting could not be the best brains of the country. Where were the Koreans of initiative and education?

I added this question to my collection, and everywhere I went I would ask, "Where are your intellectuals? Where are your men of leadership ability? Have they all gone with the Communists?"

My replies did not come out of official reports by "prejudiced" sources. They came from the lips of plain men and women. Nobody, anywhere, denied the story that was told me. Before leaving any community, the Communists rounded up two kinds of people, in addition to those who were suspected of having conspired against them. One were the intellectuals who weren't Communists and didn't have an unblemished record of fellow-traveling. The other were persons with leadership qualities. Christians in particular—Korea has the largest Christian communities on the Asian mainland —were taken into custody. All of these were "potentially dangerous" to the so-called people's republic.

Except for the comparatively few who could be used as hostages, most of the rest were simply done away with, physically. Possible enemies in the present conflict and individuals who could be obstacles to the long-range program were thus disposed of at once. This was "preventive killing."

These people were rounded up without fanfare and were led to the outskirts of town and then put to death as if this were the most normal procedure in the world, nothing to make any fuss about. There were no foreign correspondents present, nor newspaper photographers. So although these were calculated killings, part of a pattern centrally directed, of thousands of Korea's most capable men and women, they got nothing like the columns of atrocity stories sent out from South Korea and published throughout the Free World. For the latter there was Tom Driberg to get up in the British House of Commons to solemnly protest; there was the United Nations Commission for the Unification and Rehabilitation of Korea to put the Korean Foreign Minister on the carpet. For the former—silence.

This was symptomatic of the dual standard in judgment that has been so useful to the Communists. The motivation and psychology of it is a separate subject; here we are discussing how it worked.

I was invited to a press conference for European and American correspondents at Seoul, following the widespread publication of eyewitness stories of atrocities by South Koreans. Dr. Chough Pyung Ok, Home Minister, who was responsible for the police administration, gave the interview. "What puzzles me," he said, "is why the same publicity wasn't given to the substantiated accounts of the slaughter of thousands of Koreans at a time by the North Korean Communists, of whole villages being wiped out. I don't remember seeing stories about this in the foreign press."

He distributed a written statement on a piece of flimsy paper; it is published here for the first time:

"It is not within my power to refute articles that have appeared in various publications concerning alleged abuses of prisoners and citizens by the National Police of the Republic of Korea; however, in fairness and justice to the police, one must realize that during the onslaught of the Communist Armies through the Republic of

Korea their acts of barbarism, torture and other brutalities were directed with particular savagery and viciousness towards the police and their families.

"When the tide of battle turned in favor of the UN forces, it was anticipated by my office that reprisals of some nature might be taken against captured prisoners, Communist sympathizers, or collaborators—therefore, I took definite and positive action to prevent any such reprisals by issuing both written and verbal directions to the Provincial Governors and Provincial Police Chiefs that acts of brutality on the part of the police would not be tolerated.

"There might have been some isolated instances of inhuman behavior for which some particular policeman might be held responsible. But it is not fair and just for some correspondents to make a sweeping condemnation of the Korean National Police."

That the Home Minister had a case appeared indisputable, although this was no reason to whitewash excesses on the part of his government. A story on the first page of an important English-language newspaper in the Far East some weeks later showed what he was complaining about. A two-column headline read "56 Prisoners Shot by South Korean Police Without Trial." The long account ran over into an inside page. This was an unquestioned atrocity and should have been exposed, as it was. But what was an obvious lack of balance was the short, two-paragraph item that I found tacked onto the end of this long story. Most newspapers that ran the former never ran the latter. Here it is:

"Thousands of South Koreans have been summarily shot by vindictive North Korean guerrillas when they captured Chorwon in the guerrilla-infested area 50 miles northwest of Seoul, according to refugees. In Chorwon, just north of the 38th parallel, the Communists rounded up every male in sight when they retreated and killed them without questioning, said these refugees. When the Communist guerrillas left town after six days of occupation, they looted practically every house of rice and clothing.

"Residents of Chorwon who miraculously survived the

Red reign of terror said over 60 per cent of the town's male population were killed by the Communists. The biggest casualties were suffered by the newly recruited police who were sent there after the liberation in October."

The important point in my mind, as my on-the-spot tour of northern Korea confirmed, was that these excesses by the North Koreans were part of a far-seeing political program and were thus of incalculably greater significance than any outbursts of violence by individuals or groups operating contrary to the policy of their own government. There can never be any accurate knowledge of the number of Koreans with leadership qualities who were deliberately sought out and slaughtered by the Communists. This was genocide on a new and harrowing scale. Genocide in World War II had been imposed by one people against another, or against a racial minority. Here was a new, "improved" form of genocide, in which a so-called political party selects an entire class of people among its own blood relatives, and liquidates them.

In the coming generation what history might well judge to have been Communism's most heinous crime in Korea will be the massacre of this element of the population. How many generations of Koreans will have to pay for this crime? How many generations will it take for Korea to replace these leaders? The effects were already evident in the poor quality of administrators. The world had already witnessed the casualness with which totalitarians destroyed the economic resources of their own country for political advantage; now it was witnessing the destruction of the mental resources of one's own people. Only a fanaticism that has turned to madness can put such a strategy into effect. That it was being implemented in Red China, too, was evident from the increasing recourse to public trials for grown-ups, along with the intensification of "brain-washing." Only, in China the process was being more slowly dragged out in an effort to avoid dangerously alarming the populace.

The Koreans who filled the public posts in spite of their lack of adequate qualifications, who were appointed because of their availability rather than their ability, had to possess more than average heroism. They were subject to constant threats and violence. One of the main tasks of UN divisions supposedly behind our own lines, while I was in Korea, was to answer calls from village leaders for help. The guerrillas were just as ruthless against Korean civilians as against regular troops. Indeed, under the Red strategy the law-abiding civilian, without any firearms, who was seeking to restore normal community existence, was a greater menace to the Communists than a soldier carrying a tommygun. He was the special target of guerrilla attack.

Shortly after the Korean fighting started, when I was on a news assignment in Taipei, capital of Formosa, I met a much confused man who sat deep in the reassuring upholstery on the sofa in the Friends of China Club, where most foreign correspondents congregated. The war map of Korea was at his left. The war news came over the radio, and as I was looking on the map for the towns mentioned, he got up to help me. He knew every village. He began talking fast, letting out his suppressed feelings.

"I just can't understand it," he said again and again. He was one of the Americans who had been engaged for several years in the rehabilitation of Korea. "Everything seemed so well arranged," he went on. "We had built bridges and repaired railways, we had rehabilitated villages and farms. We had raised the standard of living."

"How did the North Koreans manage to press ahead so fast?" a foreign correspondent asked.

"You are riding in a jeep outside a village," the visitor mused. "Several farmers are working peacefully ahead of you. Just as you approach, one of them reaches in his jeans, pulls a tommygun, and lets you have it. They weren't farmers, you see. They were soldiers from the North, who had infiltrated behind the lines."

"Didn't we explain to the farmers what we were doing in Korea?" the first correspondent asked.

"Of course," the traveler said. "We sent mobile units into the farm districts with films and posters."

"What did the films and posters show?"

"Oh, they showed how to use fertilizer, and how to get the most out of the new plows."

"What were the Communists saying all this time?"

"They were exploiting every grievance, promising the farmers that they would become prosperous and free, and have farm reform. They were blaming every difficulty on the Americans."

"And so we met this challenge with movies about fertilizer," remarked an American pilot for CAT (the airline started by Chennault). "We expected to arouse their fighting spirit with a lecture on sheep manure."

The visitor from Korea smiled. "Yes," he nodded, "I suppose we missed the boat there."

Guerrilla warfare, as developed by the Communists, was no longer a hit-and-miss affair. Actually, it is impossible nowadays to draw the line where orthodox warfare ends and guerrilla warfare begins. The same overall direction is given to both. Here is an example of its role. In a command post tent one day above Kunmori, close to where the Turkish Brigade later made its glorious but costly stand, an American officer turned to me and said: "There's something that's been puzzling me for a long time.

"Our convoys and certainly our tanks can advance no farther than their gasoline supplies. How did the Communist vehicles and tanks keep coming down our roads—I saw them do so—without gasoline supplies being brought down behind them?"

I learned the answer from American advisors with the ROKs—the South Korean Army. They had been fighting in the mountainous and wild backbone that runs through Korea. They had found underground stores containing supplies of every kind, including gasoline dumps, all the way up the center of Korea, from Pusan to the 38th parallel. One such sub-soil storehouse contained tons of equipment, neatly packed. It included tanks.

"We noticed a bit of bayonet poking out of the ground one day," I was told by Capt. James Jordan, of Des Moines, Iowa. "When we dug it out, we found a complete rifle, and heaps more. A little spadework discovered more and larger pieces of equipment—tons and tons of it." He stopped talking a moment, then mused, "How many more such underground dumps exist that we haven't found?"

That more existed I knew, for others had told me similar experiences. These stores could not have been cached after the start of the war. Such extensive preparations for guerrilla warfare must have taken years. The Reds undoubtedly had sufficient underground supplies still buried to keep guerrilla warfare going for years more, if they could get to them.

One old ordnance man, Capt. Francis T. Smith, of Vallejo, California, one day detected a strange coloration on the boring of a rifle that had been removed from such a cache. He took out his cleaning rod, attached a bit of cloth, and thrust it through the long bore. He sat down for a job that would take, at a minimum, five minutes.

When he pulled the cleaning rod out for the first time, he was amazed to find that most of the dirt and rust had already vanished. He pulled the cleaning rod through just once more, and held the boring up to his eye. The boring looked as if it had been taken new from the rack. He could peer clean through!

Close examination showed two shades of metal—obviously some new alloy had been cast inside the old metal. He could see the two concentric circles at the end of the bore. He took out his steel knife and jabbed at both metals. A metal that cleaned so easily probably was soft and wouldn't last like the old. Again he was amazed. He easily scratched the outer rim, but pound as he did, he could not leave the slightest impression on the new alloy.

Here was the ideal metal for guerrilla weapons, particularly in farming areas such as Asia, where guerrillas pose as farmers by day and bury their guns in the damp earth. Regular Communist troops, when used as a vanguard, or as a reconnaissance force, or behind the lines, regularly use this disguise, wearing native civilian clothes. Partisan fighting, as developed by the Chinese Communists, had long since done away with "bourgeois" conceptions of there being any difference between "regular" and "irregular" fighting.

Along with such advanced guerrilla tools of war, produced in Soviet Russia, were crude weapons such as I was shown in the office of Brig. Frank S. Bowen, Jr., who commanded the Sunchon airborne operation in which, for the first time, everything from ¾-ton trucks to 105-mm. howitzers were floated to earth by parachute. When I saw him at Pyongyang, he picked up a sawed-off shotgun to show me. The stock was crudely sawed off, and so was the metal bore, leaving a ragged edge that made any long-distance aiming impossible.

The gun wasn't intended for long-distance aiming; it was intended for surprise, close-range attack, perhaps on a sentry, or on the recalcitrant mayor of a UN-liberated village. The Korean fighting had confirmed, if such proof any longer were needed, that under totalitarian thinking there is no difference between a soldier and a civilian—if he is on the opposite side he is an enemy, to be dealt with summarily, unless he is a Communist guerrilla or underground worker. No other classification is recognized.

This explained why Maj. Gen. Keane, of the 25th Division, riding to the front one day in an open jeep, anxiously watched as one of his soldiers searched the pack of a passing Korean peasant woman. "Remember that other young mother?" he asked his driver. "Oh boy," the youth exclaimed. "She had a baby at her breast, and looked so innocent, you felt like a heel searching her. But when we glanced into the bundle on her back, we found a high-class radio transmitting set. Oh boy! What an act! She even looked pregnant."

The Reds even exploited their own policy of killing off intellectuals and potential community leaders. They left agents behind to apply for key jobs, including that of police chief.

Their task was twofold: to fulfill orders recklessly and harmfully, and to keep the Reds fully informed.

The popular conception of guerrilla warfare as unorganized is true only in its initial phase, when a situation becomes so fluid that control cannot be wielded. Then individuals are supposed to indulge in whatever activity fits into the pattern they have been taught, and to do so on their own initiative. This is part of the long-range planning.

Only a few weeks after the stunning defeat dealt the North Korean Communist armies as a result of the Inchon landings, evidence began to reach the UN forces of the central organization of guerrilla troops. Proof was obtained by the 25th Division. When I first came upon it, in the interval when it was stationed on both sides of the 38th parallel, its mission was to fight guerrillas far back of the front.

The core of the guerrilla movement was not composed of civilian elements, as the Communists say, but army people cut off from their own forces by the Inchon maneuver. They had been taught not to surrender under such circumstances, but to go underground. They were joined by Communist agents among the civilian population of South Korea, who had taken posts under the Reds when the North Koreans first invaded and who now had to flee to save their skins. These elements reorganized army units under the direction of Communist agents left behind for this purpose. Lieut. Richard Wozmak, of Buffalo, New York, while shaving in his tent that afternoon when I toured the vanguard area, before the start of the Thanksgiving Day push, told me of an order found on a guerrilla leader at the beginning of September, 1950. It was a formal document, signed by the guerrilla commander in the area.

What did all this add up to? A new form of warfare, absorbing the old into it, but not discarding it. What can we call it? Guerrilla warfare? Partisan warfare? Irregular warfare? No, none of these terms fully covers it. Total warfare gives an idea of its extent. But the term that best fits this twentieth-century warfare, perhaps, is "psychological war-fare." It embraces all of these things.

The Communists work on the assumption that whatever contributes to achieving the neutralization or the defeat of the enemy is a weapon. This weapon can be a bullet, a leaflet, a broadcast, a speech—or the publication of the works of a frustrated writer. Meanwhile, the Free World was still mainly in the stage of considering war a conflict with purely lethal instruments.

During my stay in Korea I asked another stock question. This one had far wider significance than for just Korea. The question was, "How would you feel about having Japanese troops come to help fight the Communists?" I asked it in the towns which the Communists had never occupied, and I asked it in North Korea, which had been under long Communist domination.

In the south, except where the Communist armies had extended, the reply was in the negative, and usually strongly so. The memory of the unhappy years of Japanese conquest was too close. Even President Syngman Rhee has too vivid a memory of the half century before to enable him to reach judgment about the Japanese without emotion. He sees his hands in front of him, and he involuntarily lifts them to his face and blows at his fingers. These are the fingertips that were mashed between wooden blocks when he was young and an ardent independence worker in Korea.

In the north, and in those localities below the 38th parallel where the Communist troops had gone, the attitude was different. The people there had a closer memory than of the Japanese; what was in the forefront of their minds was the recollection of the marauding Russian Communist troops that had rolled into the country in the "five-day war" and of the Korean Communist government that was set up as a consequence. These northern Koreans weren't interested primarily in whether it would be Japanese who were coming, but in whether they could help rid their country of the Communist forces. They asked, "Will they be part of a temporary world army, along with the Americans?" If the answer would be yes, they said, "Let them come; let everybody come, just so long as they will expel the Reds."

This has become the attitude everywhere where people have experienced Communist rule. When I asked people who had come from Red China what the attitude was toward the Nationalists, they would tell me that the big issue was no longer who they were, but what they could do. Everyone's help was needed. Meanwhile in the council chambers of diplomats, in newspaper editorial offices, in clubs with after-dinner speakers, in backrooms of bars and in incalculable parlors, people outside the satellite countries were still discussing those lands in terms that had already become outdated.

This stint of mine as a roving correspondent in Asia taught me that many of our difficulties arose from our refusal to face the facts of life in China proper. First, we underrated Chinese Communism's chances of winning a military victory on the mainland; we said that the Chinese were too individualistic to allow it to happen. This was over-optimism. Then, stunned by seeing it happen, we went to the other extreme and over-estimated the strength of the Communist hold on the Chinese people. We began to talk as if the Chinese people were supporting the Peiping regime, which wasn't true. This was over-pessimism. The one error can have consequences just as disastrous for the free peoples of the world as the other. Both created the blind spot that made China a hush-hush subject in press conferences and permitted diplomats to solemnly pontificate—safely "off the record"—that the Chinese Communists weren't going to enter the war in Korea in force. The diplomats then were still talking as if Mao Tse-tung were the agrarian democrat that his publicists so skillfully made him out to be. "As if" once more.

As I write this, the fact that is outstanding among all others is that the governing authorities of a country with a population of 450,000,000 are methodically engaged in a "brain operation"—"cleansing" and "washing" and filling the minds of its people with the sort of hate and warmongering that I have recorded in this book. This is aggression, and aggression of the worst sort, because it is not a short-range tactic but long-range strategy. If we and the other free nations permit this to go on, and if the same is being done in the other countries of the Soviet bloc, the price our children will have to pay makes the heart sick. There can be no greater mission for any man than to prevent this.

The unique and terrible thing about this mass indoctrination is that it is planned and directed by central governing authorities. This is psychological warfare on a scale incalculably more immense than any militarist of the past has ever envisaged. This is what has to be stopped and counteracted, and the mentally maimed must be cured, if we are to be safe ourselves from "brain-washing" and "brain-changing"—and "liquidation" and "evaporation."

APPENDIX A

A SON DENOUNCES HIS FATHER

A TYPICAL EXAMPLE OF THE SELF-CRITICISM AND THOUGHT conclusion that are required in brain-washing is the paper written by Hu Shih-tu, the son of Dr. Hu Shih, one of the great liberal scholars and philosophers of this age. Dr. Hu Shih began the use of the vernacular in Chinese writing, for the first time bringing the written language to the people, and is regarded as the "father of the Chinese Renaissance," known in China as the "May 4 Movement."

The thesis, in which the son denounces his highly-respected father as "a public enemy of the people, and an enemy of myself," was exploited by the Chinese Communist Party in publications throughout China. It was reprinted on September 22, 1950, in *Ta Kung Pao,* a pro-Communist Chinese-language newspaper in Hong Kong, and a translation appeared on September 24 in the *Hong Kong Standard,* a Chinese-owned, English-language newspaper.

There is perhaps no better example of the pathetic corrosion that the democratic group discussion technique perpetrates on young minds than this document.

In the old society, I considered my father as an "aloof" and "clean" good man. Even after the liberation I felt deeply insulted whenever my father was being criticized. Within my heart I strongly objected to Premier Chou En-lai's calling my father a man who never understood what imperialism means. After I had read the *History of Social Development, State and Revolution, History of Chinese Revolution* and many other books written by Communists, my concept of my father began to change. Now I shall analyze his effect on historical development.

My father came from a fallen family of bureaucrats. He was a student from 1904 to 1910. When he went to the United States at the age of 20, the American material and spiritual civilization dazzled him and swiftly conquered him. His educational environment changed him as a man from a semi-feudal, semi-colonial country to a bourgeois. His article on "The Improvement of Chinese Literature" won him popularity in China because it was anti-feudalistic. He was considered as a progressive.

When he returned in 1917, China was under the despotic rule of Yuan Shih-kai and Twan Chih-jui. He made up his mind "not to talk politics in 20 years" and buried himself in books. But during the period of "May 4" he could no longer escape from politics. So he published his *Problem and Doctrine,* to attack the growing socialistic ideas with evolutionism. He believed that China could have progress without making fundamental changes. His opinion represented the entire class of bourgeois intellectuals when confronted with the "May 4," and "June 3" movements. What he objected to was a revolution that would demolish the war lords, bureaucrats, landlords, and state machine.

The Wrong Way

After 1919 he drifted farther down the wrong way. He praised Ibsenism and battled materialism with experimentalism. He himself was wandering among the rulers of those days, hoping his "evolutionism" would be adopted by them. At the ebb of revolution he hoped to establish a good school. He thought through education a society might become good. He organized the China Public school. But under the threat of the Nanking government his dream was shattered and he was forced to leave the public school. The weak capitalist intellectuals never dared resist the "government." He, like all other members of his class, bowed his head

to the reactionary government, and turned to Chiang Kai-shek
to practice his doctrine of reforms.

In the year when he was forced to leave the public school he
voluntarily became the dean of Arts School of the Peking University. It was in that job that he laid down his foundation of a
political and cultural ruler. He became one of the pillars of the
Rockefeller Foundation and the Sino-American Cultural Fund
Society. He turned to be the docile tool of the imperialists.

Greater Power

When the reactionary government was campaigning against
the Communists, he praised it as a "good men's government."
Wong Wen-ho and T. F. Tsiang under his "inspiration" all joined
the reactionary government. The people who had long suffered
under the oppression of the reactionaries thought that the government might change for the better after such "liberal" professors had joined it. The reason why my father refused to become the Minister of Education under Chiang at that time was
because he thought that by remaining "aloof" he would enjoy
greater power.

In 1937, when the Japanese invading hordes began to storm
into East and South China and the rich compradors of the Anglo-
American imperialists were forced to take up their cudgel against
the aggressors, the interests of his class were gravely threatened.
In 1938, he finally became Chiang's ambassador to the United
States. In his post as the ambassador to the American imperialists,
he signed all kinds of trade agreements and was greatly instru-
mental in obtaining loans from the American government to fight
the Communists.

Booming Tide

In 1946, when the booming tide of the people's revolution was
threatening the ruling class, he considered it as a sacred duty to
serve for his class. He returned to his country and worked faithfully for the Chiang government. At that time he was carrying

out the orders of the reactionary government as the president of the Peking University on the one hand and was deceiving the people by writing middle-of-the-road articles on the other. He more or less had given the people an impression of a "worldly man."

But his loyalty to the reactionary government had not saved the common enemy of the people from the fate of extinction. At a time when final victory was about to descend to the people, he left Peiping and China to become a "White Chinese" living a life of exile.

Today, after my education in the Party, I begin to recognize his true qualities. I have come to know that he is a loyal element of the reactionary class and an enemy of the people. Politically, he has never been progressive. After his publication of the *Problem and Doctrine,* in 1919, he wandered on the road of indecision. For 11 years, he groped in the labyrinth of darkness. In 1930, he began to participate actively in the work of strengthening of the reactionary government.

This time he went to the United States in an endeavour to form a third party and took care of the U.S. $4,000,000 relief fund for Chinese students in the United States on behalf of the American State Department. He was willing to serve for the United States and for those reactionary individualistic students.

Enslavement Education

In the past, I was subjected to a long period of enslavement education of the reactionaries, and I was ignorant about the policies of the people. A friend of mine who came to Peiping from Hong Kong on business asked me what attitude I would adopt toward my father. I replied that perhaps he could never learn about "group doctrine" and would probably stay in the United States.

Today I realize the lenient policy of the People's government. It gives a chance to all those who have acted against the interests of the people to live down their past and start life anew, only if they can come to realize their past misdeeds.

Until my father returns to the people's arms, he will always remain a public enemy of the people, and an enemy of myself. Today, in my determination to rebel against my own class, I feel it important to draw a line of demarcation between my father and myself. Except that I should be vigilant enough not to let sentiments gain the upper hand, I must establish close relations with the working and farming class.

APPENDIX B

THE MINISTRY OF CULTURE

THE CENTRAL DRAMA SCHOOL IS UNDER THE JURISDIC-tion of the Ministry of Culture. Its titular head is Dr. Mei Lan-fang, the great Chinese actor-singer. The Central Drama Institute is also known as the Chinese Opera Experimental School. There is also an Institute for Research in Chinese Opera. The Chinese Communists have exerted great efforts to "reform" the traditional Chinese arts, in accordance with the instructions laid down in Mao Tse-tung's "On Literature and Art," at a meeting on this subject in Yenan between May 2 and 23, 1942. He said then:

"Literary or artistic criticism is a major weapon in the struggle of writers and artists, and it must be perfected. . . . We demand that politics should be united with art, that content should be united with form, that revolutionary political content should be united with the highest possible level of artistic style. . . . All the dark forces which endanger the masses should be condemned, and all the revolutionary struggle of the masses should be praised. This is the fundamental task of revolutionary writers and artists."

All others were cast outside the pale of writers and artists by his edict on literature and art.

The Ministry of Culture is part of a complicated but thorough official propaganda network. The State Department of the People's Central Government at Peiping has jurisdiction over various governing committees, including the Culture and Education Committee. This committee directs work in the following departments: the Ministry of Culture, the Ministry of Education, the Ministry of Hygiene, the Science Academy, the Ministry of Journalism, and the Ministry of Publications. The Central Institute of Fine Arts is under the jurisdiction of the Ministry of Culture. Kuo Mo-jo, the "leaned over" intellectual ("leaned over" refers to those who joined the Communist bandwagon after "liberation," or the occupation of the Chinese mainland by the Communists) is chairman of the Culture and Education Committee, is in charge of the Central Institute of Fine Arts, and is also one of the Vice Premiers or Vice Chairmen of the Peiping government.

The Culture and Education Committee has six ministries under it. The Communist Party has its own propaganda and education committees, its own cadre schools and administrative organs. The two parallel propaganda and indoctrination setups are linked and the government groups are made subordinate to the Party by putting Party people in key posts in all of the former.

Each of these government committees has subcommittees. These include all such nationwide organizations as the Anti-U.S. and Aid Korea committees, which are actually such subcommittees. Although given the form of popular organizations, formed spontaneously by the public, these are all just as much government bureaus as the Library of Congress at Washington. They are invariably organized at the initiative of the Party representative in any such government ministry or other official body. The *Propaganda Cartoon Reference Book* thus is not merely similar to a government directive; it is a government directive.

APPENDIX C

THE MEANS OF MIND REFORM
by Ai Tze-chi

THE MIND REFORM OF THE VARIOUS CLASSES OF PEOPLE IS entirely different from the struggle against enemy minds. Since the nature and the policies of such reform are fundamentally different from those of a mind struggle, the means with which it is to be achieved are bound to be different.

The spread of the destructive ideas typical of the evidently reactionary faction must be sternly suppressed, defeated, and uncovered by means of dictatorship. Every one of the people, being one of the masters of the nation, is charged with the responsibility of suppressing, defeating, and uncovering the reactionary ideas. Everyone should spontaneously participate in the struggle whenever needed.

The wrong ideas among the people, or those contaminated with the influences of reactionary ideas, should be overcome by democratic means—in the form of criticism, self criticism, and patient persuasion. The reform of the people's minds is a complicated, painstaking, and long task. We cannot hope to eliminate all the backward, passive elements in the minds of various classes of people within a few days or a few weeks. Even against the influences of the ideas typical of the reactionary faction among the people, we have to keep struggling for a long time instead of hoping to accomplish the job within a few days or a few weeks. As Chairman Mao said, "The influence of the reactionary ideas is still quite great and will continue to exist. It cannot be eliminated very quickly." (*On the People's Democratic Dictatorship*).

A hurried, harsh, and imperative attitude, which does not emphasize the stimulation of the learners' apprehension and willingness, would be not only wrong but also fruitless. This principle, fundamentally, is applicable both to regular universities and the Party schools or the learning campaigns conducted in the Party for better discipline. But, we should not allow the principle to interfere with our schedule of achieving certain aims within certain periods of time. (The length of time is to be determined by the circumstances.) Neither should it be allowed to prevent us from solving certain problems, which is possible, nor from overcoming certain shortcomings in their minds, which is both possible and necessary.

In the campaign of opposing the United States and aiding Korea, for example, the people learned very fast to hate, despise, and look down upon the United States, having overcome the ideas of associating with, worshiping, and fearing America. If our plans were made in coordination with the actual circumstances, we would be perfectly justified to expect certain achievement within a certain short period of time. It can be done, and it has been repeatedly proved with our experiences.

If we bluntly considered the mind reform as a long task, which would take a lot of patient persuasion irrespective of any time limit, we would be drifting off from the right course and making a serious mistake. Of course, under different circumstances of learning, where the demands for learning, the experiences of the leaders, and the foundation of the mass vary, the prescription for the task and the length of time required would be different. It would be wrong to simply apply the requirements of Party schools or campaigns for better discipline within the Party to non-Party schools. It would also be wrong to apply the requirements of short courses of political training to the political studies at regular universities. All of this will have to be handled properly by the leaders in coordination with the actual circumstances.

APPENDIX D

"LEANING TO ONE SIDE"

FEW PERSONS, EVEN THOSE PRIDING THEMSELVES ON THEIR knowledge of Chinese contemporary history, know that Mao Tse-tung did not begin his "leaning to one side" policy after World War II, but before it, while his publicists were saying that he was not a Communist of the standard ideological type. Translators completely altered the text and sense of what he wrote in "New Democracy." These distortions are of historical importance because they provided source material for writers, lecturers and officials, particularly in the U.S. and England. People couldn't conceive that what was palmed off as a translation was actually a rewrite. How people who had long contacts at Yenan could have failed to know this is incomprehensible.

Here are some expurgated paragraphs from "New Democracy":

"You may say, 'There is a difference between eastern and western imperialists. This person allies himself with the eastern imperialists, but I will do the opposite. I will ally myself with the ——, the western imperialists.' That sounds indeed brave! Unfortunately, the western imperialists will be anti-Soviet and anti-Communist. Then good-by to your revolution."

The word left out in the above is the filthiest expression in Chinese invective, meaning incest with one's mother. This

340

alone, if the translators had not concealed its inclusion, would have made Mao's position clear.

"The whole world is going to be embroiled in the war of the two camps. In the world thereafter, 'neutrality' will be merely a term to deceive people."

That this policy was part of a Stalinist world program was made clear when Mao wrote that the peoples "of the colonies have to stand on the imperialist front and play a role in the world counter-revolution, or on the anti-imperialist front and play a role in the world revolution. They must choose either one of the two. There is not a third role."

For those who were guided by Dr. Sun Yat-sen's "Three People's Principles" (San Min Chu I), Mao said that they have to consider it a movement "allying itself with the Soviet Union, and can never be one that allies itself with the imperialists to oppose the Soviet Union." Thus he interpreted in double-talk fashion any statements made that he was supporting Dr. Sun, telling his party people that yes, indeed, he was supporting Dr. Sun, but with an interpretation that Dr. Sun's words meant what the Communist line desired.

POSTSCRIPT

THE INTERVENING YEARS HAVE SHOWN THAT A NEW ERA entered human history with the introduction of that strange and sinister word, "brainwashing." Now our thoughts and energies are focused on dual realms: the finite space of the brain, and the infinite space beyond the brain. Cybernetics, computers, subliminal advertising, the exploding of the atom, nuclear fission, and a walk on the moon are all manifestations of these realms. All demonstrate the eternal search by man for answers to what may seem unanswerable.

During the past few decades on the Chinese mainland, much that is bizarre has been happening within the area of brainwashing. The human brain—the mind—is, of course, the most important subject in the world, and the most important issue of all time is the susceptibility of the human mind to attitude-changing devices and pressures.

Therein lies the significance of this book. The locale is China, for two reasons. First, the psychological attack upon the mind is being most exhaustively practiced in Red China, more nakedly so than even in the Soviet Union. Second, this writer was able to discern the brainwashing pattern in a great mass of detail because he fortunately had spent a large portion of his adult life in China, and in work involving the Chinese. He watched mind warfare develop at close range, as a newspaper editor and foreign correspondent, and also as an analyst

343

of propaganda pressures and as an activist in the wartime manipulation of attitudes.

Communist China's primary significance, when the history of this second half of the twentieth century is written, is likely to be its development as a brainwashing laboratory, in which the relevant processes in the war for the mind were being worked out at a forced pace, without subtleties. The Chinese people are being experimented with frantically in a race with time by a desperate chemist who is using them as ingredients for his ideological test tubes.

The chemist is Mao Tse-tung, whose closing years have given him the same sense of insecurity he has imposed on his people, as a control tactic. His rationale has been dialectical materialism, allowing for no faith except in the present—no yesterdays and no tomorrows, only the present. His frenzied changes in direction during the past, fast decade have shown his deep sense of desperation—actually, the product of frustration. He has been portrayed during his lifetime as a veritable god; during his last years a pocket-sized, red-covered book, entitled *Quotations From Chairman Mao Tse-tung*, has been distributed in quantities comparable to, and recited in the manner of, the Bible. This volume has been sold throughout the world, and has been used by terrorist-type political groups as their unquestioned guide and conversion medium. Mao has fiercely tried to fill the role of master chemist, determined to outmaneuver death. If he could do so, he would bring death up on charges of counterrevolutionary activities.

But at this writing Mao is still alive, reacting as if approaching death were in alliance with those still living to undo his life's work. He obviously fears that life is in some sort of collusion with death, just waiting for him to die in order to destroy his main handiwork, his effort to change man's human nature, to create "the new communist man."

No wonder, with his present so irrevocably short, given to an ideology that eliminates trust in one's fellow man, Mao has become so demonstrably desperate. No wonder that the supremely confident, artful fighter of the Long March has become the mad chemist as he approaches the terminus of the most personal march of all—the march to the grave. His collective ideology can be of neither comfort nor guidance to him during these last, most lonely moments of all.

Nobody ever imagined Mao apart from the Communist Party of China; everyone was sure he was inseparable from it. None could foresee that his purges of people and institutions ultimately would include the Communist Party of China itself. But the time came when everything was being sacrificed to an all-embracing intensification of brainwashing. Finally, the military had to be called upon to assume control. A return had to be made to the oldest, most reactionary formula of all.

The conflict of conflicts in which Mao was engaged, that spread out from mainland China and was as wide as the world, is between control of the mind and freedom of the mind. All other issues of our time will derive their ultimate importance in the scheme of lasting things from their impact upon this fundamental issue of all time. It is the ultimate struggle. The Communists have based their ideology on this basic reality, and their destiny on the outcome of this struggle. We are yet to recognize this, although Peking considers us its irreconcilable enemy because it knows that we are the primary protector on earth of the free mind.

Desperation put the Chinese military in control of the brainwashing program, along with practical domination over everything else, from colleges and communes to factories. Only time will tell whether this will turn out to be just another throwback to China's war-lord past, as well it can be. Mao Tse-tung has brought it on himself. So long as he remains alive, the titular power is his by right of his successful past. But what then? This is the gnawing problem.

If Red China could have been cut off from the outside world to the extent it sometimes has been in the distant past—or as Japan was closed off during the early Tokugawas—Mao would have had a greater chance to achieve more lasting results from brainwashing. They would not have been healthy results; quite the contrary. But in this age of jet planes and electronics, a conditioned environment cannot be maintained effectively over a vast stretch of territory, as even the Soviet Union has learned.

As the reader has seen, brainwashing is a clinical, rather than a political, technique. It consists of two parallel processes —softening-up and indoctrination. The former need not even pertain to the latter. Each of these two processes for the destruction of a mind consists of a number of elements, used as a doctor may use medicines in a treatment. These elements are: hunger, fatigue, tenseness, threats, violence, and, on occasion, drugs and hypnotism. They are chosen—one or more—and prescribed as needed, selected for effectiveness, over whatever period of time is required to destroy a mind, and then to re-form it—not reform it, but to form it over again, fundamentally changed. The treatment is an unnatural one, because by applying it normal minds are made abnormal, instead of the process being the other way round.

Protection against this kind of mind attack, a cure for it, similarly requires the application of one or more elements in whatever arrangement proves effective. The formula for the preservation of a mind is, of course, far more important than any formula for its conditioning and control. The elements for its protection and a cure are: faith, conviction, clarity of mind, purpose, keeping one's mind busy, confidence, adaptability, crusading spirit, group feeling, being yourself—and high jinks, deceit, and a closed mind.

The last three need a brief clarification. High jinks refers to any morale-building tomfoolery that safely makes game of one's inquisitors. Deceit—undesirable under normal circumstances—must be understood within the framework, say, of intrusion into one's home by an armed madman. Any artifice that would humor and render such an assailant harmless would be perfectly proper. A closed mind ordinarily is contrary to our fundamental beliefs, but is the only recourse for a person caught within a conditioned environment, fed only data scientifically selected to deceive, and put under pressures systematically devised to change attitudes.

The conditioned environment needed to brainwash an individual cannot be relaxed after a treatment is completed without danger of the brainwashing weakening or even disappearing. Control tends to fade once the brainwashed individual leaves his conditioned environment. Brainwashing is costly and intricate enough without its being temporary, and needs the constant application of psychological booster shots.

In January of 1956, a conference was held in Red China to discuss the sticky problem of intellectuals, because of the lack of progress that persisted in science and technology. The intellectuals were urged by Chou En-lai, as prime minister and foreign-affairs chief, to catch up with the West in these strategic fields. The intellectuals were complaining that stringent indoctrination pressures prevented them from putting forward their creative efforts. A few months later, in May of 1956, Mao himself tackled the problem by announcing a "blooming-contending" policy at a specially convened session of the supreme state conference. Its full title was, "Let a hundred flowers bloom and hundreds of schools of thought contend."

The "flowers" were to be ideas, and the "schools of thought" different approaches in science and technology. Mao added the categories of literature and the arts, for they were required as channels for all those wonderful thoughts that were expected to "bloom" and "contend."

The time was overdue for relief from the relentless process of bloodbath after bloodbath that had been going on at short intervals ever since the Red regime was set up in Peiping—renamed Peking—on September 21, 1949. The "three-antis," the "five-antis," and every sort of mind-repressive movement have marked the whole course of the Communist regime.

The initial response was negligible: Everyone was waiting for someone else to make the first move, and nobody dared. How right they were, but how tragically late they found this out!

On February 27, 1957, Mao gave a conciliatory talk at the eleventh session of the supreme state conference, entitled: "On the correct handling of contradictions among the people." Mao asked for the "rectification" of "three evils," which he listed as bureaucratism, sectarianism, and subjectivism. The "blossoming-contending" slogan was alluringly reiterated. The intent was to spread the word that Mao was "sincere" about this and could be "trusted" by the intellectuals.

Even so, the response lacked enthusiasm until reinforced a few days later, on May 1, by official action of the central committee of the party. A directive was issued for a "rectification campaign" inside the Communist Party itself. "Rectifications" hitherto had been launched against the middle class and other segments of the public, leaving the Party immune to any serious criticism. Now, intellectuals and non-Party people were appealed to by the Party for help in improving itself and life generally.

These cumulative pledges of good faith by the topmost Communist leaders unloosed at long last the repressed feelings of intellectuals. They forgot that such words as "sincerity" and "trust" have a different meaning in the dictionary of dialectical materialism than in regular dictionaries, as is the case with words such as "truth" and "good." The sole standard by which words are defined under Communism is the utterly pragmatic. What is to Communist advantage is correct, truthful, and good; what is to its disadvantage is wrong, a lie, and bad. This is dogma. The same approach motivates Red jurisprudence, determining legality and illegality. Indeed, this standard covers and conditions all use of language, whether casual conversation, solemn negotiations, a promise, or a treaty.

The intellectuals knew that past promises had been broken at will, but convinced themselves now, through their own desires, that they could believe the Communists this time, rationalizing that it was to the Reds' own interest. They wanted to believe, and so they did. They began to speak out frankly. Soon they were reacting as if they had left their conditioned environments. They began speaking out more and more boldly; their inhibitions disappeared.

This recalls an incident at Ivan P. Pavlov's laboratories outside Leningrad. His kennels took fire. Something extraordinary followed, of hopeful significance to all mankind. The dogs that escaped reacted as if they had left their conditioned reflexes behind, in the conditioned environment in which they had been indoctrinated, which now had burned down. They no longer reacted to the signals and symbols that had been scientifically inculcated into their brains and bodies.

The "blooming-contending" period had much the same impact as removal from a conditioned environment. The writers, scholars, artists, journalists, scientists, students, and even Communist Party cadres issued declarations, wrote articles, and gave lectures that denied the achievements claimed by the regime. They opposed one-party rule, denounced proletarian dictatorship, repudiated socialist reform, and rejected collectivization. They particularly asked that an end be put to thought control and to all forms of brainwashing, and for the restoration of personal freedoms.

Once the "flowers" began to "bloom," the growth became too luxuriant for the Red hierarchy to handle. What Mao called "bourgeois thinking" was too ingrained in human nature, and just as immune to elimination as it was in Soviet Russia. Labels could be changed at will, but not the actualities. This was not what Mao had meant, or maybe he was repeating his old guerrilla-warfare tactics, when he lured the enemy to where ambushes would be most effective.

Within the short space of five weeks the flood waters of pent-up feelings that began pouring forth on May 1, 1957, were violently dammed up again. They flowed only until June 8. But possibly no more important demonstration ever had taken place in the history of man's thought. An anti-rightist campaign was then launched—"rightist" being the usual catch-all label used against intellectuals as a class—and was vigorously carried on for four months. Those who had believed the Communist promises, and the pledged word of Mao himself, had succeeded only in disclosing themselves. They were rounded up as anti-Party, anti-people, and anti-socialist. Tens and tens of thousands were arrested, imprisoned, or executed; the complete figures may never be known. Whether Mao contrived this "blooming-contending" drive as a trap from the start, or because he hoped against hope that his brainwashing program had successfully created the "new Communist man," can be argued indefinitely. Probably it was some of both.

"Rectification and reformation"—renewed brainwashing—was proclaimed. An even more intense pressure drive was called "deeper rectification and reformation." Part of this was a "heart-surrender" movement, aimed at inducing intellectuals who were affiliated in some manner with any Communist enterprise to engage in "self-reformation," and to give themselves up wholly to "mind reform" and "re-education."

The punished totaled millions, according to the delayed, eighth Communist Party convention, held in Peking in early May, 1958.

After the convention a personnel change of the utmost significance took place at a meeting of the central committee. Lin Piao was named a vice-chairman and standing member of the all-powerful Politburo. Lin Piao was important enough as a general, and was likely to become more important, but was not considered a rival for Moscow-trained Liu Shao-chi. Only Mao could dislodge Liu, and this seemed inconceivable.

But brainwashing was not working for Mao sufficiently or in time. The terms used were many, such as rectification, mind reform, and re-education; in the United States there is a wide range of labels ranging from mind engineering to sensitivity training, all dealing with some phase of processed reactions or attitude-changing. All may be called a behavorial approach that has its origin in the simple, old-fashioned concept of teamwork. One need only read the detailed description of brainwashing procedures in this book to realize the influence it has had in some phases, at least, of sensitivity training. The use of identical terminology, such as "self-criticism," and the stress given such factors as "confession," are no mere coincidences. The reader will be sure to notice the similarity between the "small groups" described in these pages, and the "workshops" into which "new left" political meetings divide nowadays in the United States. Maoism has had its impact abroad!

Mao himself was not satisfied, but it should not be ignored that these psychological pressures have had a deep impact on the minds of the people on the Chinese mainland. After all, the Chinese public, and not outsiders such as American prisoners of war, are the primary target of this conditioning technique.

Mao had made China an ear-splitting, mind-deadening laboratory for propaganda pressures that were kept at a constant hysterical pitch. But even this was not enough. So he took a draconian step. He established a communes system for all of China. On December 10, 1958, he put a prosaically written resolution of historical importance through a plenary meeting of the Chinese Communist Party. It reads:

"Within a few months starting in the summer of 1958, all of more than 740,000 agricultural producers' cooperatives in the country, in response to the enthusiastic demand of the mass of peasants, reorganized themselves into over 26,000 people's communes. Over 120,000,000 households, or more than 90 per cent of all China's peasant households of various nationalities, have joined the people's communes."

Thus the communes system was imposed upon the vastnesses of mainland China. The first the peasants heard of it was when their families were split up and herded into separate huts or barracks, and they were informed that this was in response to their "enthusiastic demand." The communes were organized as a short cut to the creation of the collective mind, by exterminating family life and obliging everyone—in all matters and for all things—to belong only to, and to look only toward, the state.

The commune inescapably became a conditioned environment. Mao was confident that now, at long last, he had hit upon the unbeatable formula. But along with natural docility, the Chinese have developed a limitless capacity for quiet, stubborn sabotage that became almost an instinct during the millennia of their history's despots. The Chinese people went through the motions of life within a commune, but the more things changed, the less there seemed to be a change! The comm;unes did not work out as intended. The ancient *hsien* or county system had been abolished, but in its place, frequently within the same borders, much of what had been before was reinstated. Only it bore the new name: commune.

Within a few months the more hallucinatory aspects of the communes program had to be abandoned. The Central Committee of the Party, on December 10, 1958, formally dropped the effort to absorb the cities into the communes, and called off the demands that the peasantry be totally deprived of the slightest personal possession, even of a teapot. Even the graduates of the "revolutionary universities," where only Red dogma was taught, could not be completely brainwashed.

This ideological retreat was typically camouflaged as Communist liberality. What it represented was the Pavlovian tactic that first deprives a dog—or a human—of practically everything needed for survival, then restores a wee bit of it, earning a sort of animal gratitude. The resolution passed at the meeting declared, in Communist language:

"The people's commune is the basic unit of the socialist social structure of our country, which combines industry, agriculture, trade, education and military affairs; it is, at the same time, the basic unit of organization of socialist power. . . .

"The principle of combining education with productive labor must be carried out thoroughly in all schools, without exception. Children above the age of nine may take part in some labor to an appropriate extent. . . .

"What we describe as getting organized along military lines means getting organized on the pattern of a factory. It means that organization of labor in the people's commune should be as organized and disciplined as in a factory or in the army. . . . Militia organizations should be set up at corresponding levels of the production organizations in the people's commune. . . ."

A few communes operated as planned, and these became the showplaces of Communist China. They were more or less Potemkin villages, serving to divert attention from the others. The idea of the commune was too unreal, too much of a throwback to some tribal past. Yet the commune system drags on in China, a superficial refurbishing of the sociological household.

Mao showed by his actions that he realized this artificiality. He is an intellectual. His ultraextremism, surpassing Trotsky's, make him an impractical intellectual. He is a cunning politician and an astute guerrilla leader, but as an intellectual, the son of precisely the sort of small landlord his regime terrorized and wiped out, he has been a failure. His lashing out at intellectuals was by implication a self-criticism and a confession. He found it easy to condemn and distrust intellectuals as a class, knowing himself. Similarly, he lashed out at small landlords, perhaps identifying them with his father.

Security could not be achieved without the creation of the "new socialist man," or the "new Communist man." He would have to be a man whose innate nature had been changed fundamentally, so there could be no danger of a bourgeois throwback. Mao was constantly harping about people relapsing to past thoughts, which he called "burdens." One of the primary tasks of brainwashing was to remove such "burdens" from the minds of men.

This "new man" would react only to collective thoughts, wholly divorced from individualistic traits. He would be "reliable," in its Communist meaning. He might be thousands of miles away from his crowd, but he still would react as part of the mob, as if he were immersed in its conditioned environment. This phenomenon was recognized by the French writer, Gustave Le Bon, three-quarters of a century ago, when he explained in his imperishable book, *The Crowd . . . A Study of the Popular Mind:*

"For individuals to succumb to contagion their simultaneous presence on the same spot is not indispensable. The action of contagion may be felt from a distance under the influence of events that give all minds an individual trend and the characteristics peculiar to crowds. This is especially the case when men's minds have been prepared to undergo the influence in question. . . ."

Mao envisaged such controls wielded by the Communist Party.

But this wasn't happening, or happened to too few to be relied upon. Simultaneously, a division began to be perceptible on the Chinese mainland, particularly inside the Communist Party. The crack was becoming noticeable. Mao saw it being created by those who did not share his point of view that security had to be complete and worldwide—total—or never really be secure. These others were satisfied with less than the whole. Liu Shao-chi was one of these, and he was identified in pragmatic minds with the Kremlin's point of view.

Liu Shao-chi, indoctrinated in Russia for many years, was Mao's heir-designate. The Kremlin, especially under Khrushchev, had become somewhat critical of Mao. Moscow had been quick to point out that the communes system had been abandoned at a very early period by Soviet Russia. Liu represented Moscow's views, which did not differ from Peking's on ultimate objectives, including the defeat of the United States as the paramount, ideological need. But Moscow and Peking differed nastily on tactics—on how most effectively to achieve these ends—and both had contrasting interpretations of some of the Red dogma.

Liu Shao-chi was just too objective in his appraisals for Mao Tse-tung's subjective haste. What must Mao have thought of observations by Liu, as at the party congress of May, 1958, that anti-Communist sentiments would persist in China for the next "ten thousand years," and that "the present class character" of the opposition could not be eliminated until the "distant future"? This was a confession of failure by the vice-chairman in the campaign to let "a hundred flowers bloom and hundreds of schools of thought contend." Much more, though, was implied, including the unending existence of a police state—totalitarian dictatorship—with no cessation to internal turmoil, uninterrupted brainwashing, and incalculable, international strife.

Diverse attitudes regarding Communist policies and objectives began to develop inside the Red Chinese hierarchy, now

freed from the necessity of concentrating solely upon capturing power. Mao was more the purist than his Russian counterparts, at least more so than those who remained after the
Stalinist purges. Those now in control seemed opportunistic,
more willing to let the future unfold while concentrating on
the present. But didn't only the present exist? Wherever one
turned, a Marxist came up against contradictions. Mao was
not tortured by doubts regarding these contradictions. In
others, the contradictions simply were errors, heresies, devi-
ations, and outright betrayals. While opportunistic and patient
regarding military tactics, Mao was impatient and inflexible
concerning political objectives. He wanted them implemented
as speedily as possible—right here and now. He did not have
the time to wait. Too many did not think as he did, so he had
no alternative but to subordinate all else to his program for the
conquest of the mind. Until this was assured, the state could
not wither away, as was the promise of Communism—the
ideological will-'o-the-wisp that made Communism bearable.
Meanwhile, socialism would have to remain, with full police
state controls. Authoritative articles in the Peking press organs
made this plain.

Chu Teh was already twenty-one when Lin Piao was born.
Mao was fifteen and Chou En-lai was ten. Liu Shao-chi was
closer to Lin Piao's age bracket. In practically all else the ca-
reers of these two differed fundamentally. Lin remained in
China and was a soldier. His focus was on Mao, whom he
consistently supported ideologically. He commanded the Chinese army divisions, made up of make-believe "volunteers,"
that fought the Americans in Korea. He is the Chinese commander with most experience fighting the Americans.

All Mao's life, he pitted himself against the United States
as the decisive enemy of the Communists. First, he had to employ his keenest talents in psychological warfare to divert and
exploit the power potential of the United States, so as to
achieve military victory on the Chinese mainland. Second, he
is building up his own power potential, including nuclear
weaponry, based upon his reiterated, unalterable assumption

that victory ultimately has to be achieved through the mouth of a gun. He makes no secret that he considers the United States the real obstacle to creation of the Communist world that alone signifies security to him. Herein lies his major difference with the Kremlin, which believes the United States can be softened up far more and far longer than Mao thinks, perhaps even obviating the need for a nuclear showdown. This holds no attraction for Mao, for it would deprive him of his consummate piece of "psywar," the hate-creating impact of American attack upon the Chinese masses and the cutting down to size of the impossibly large Chinese population.

Mao has feared that Moscow is not as eager to take on the Americans as he would like. After all, Soviet Russia still was vulnerable militarily, in spite of phenomenal construction programs in every military area, and obviously had not been able to win over the sincere cooperation of its own allies. How could it even be sure of the people within its own borders, not merely the Russians themselves, but all those others, Cossacks to Uzbeks? Much less could it trust those whose comradeship it claimed outside its borders, the Poles, Czechs, Germans, Romanians, and many other nationalities. Could Moscow, therefore, really be considered reliable?

Nothing could serve Mao's economic and military needs more than a reduction of a couple of hundred million or so in China's population, which has been estimated to be as great as 700,000,000. A mere million would be hardly a drop in that bucket. Indeed, if the estimates are wrong by a hundred million or two, it still remains an impossibly unwieldy figure. If the Americans could be induced to eliminate his unwanted hundred million or more while he regained control of the propaganda channels, this would well suit the "rational" Mao. The Americans could be presented as history's most ruthless murderers, their brutality beyond anything ever committed by the Khans.

He branded the atom bomb as a "paper tiger" when America alone possessed it. He believes that the nuclear bomb in American hands can be turned into a real tiger, whose actions at all times would be determined by Red "psywar" operatives. Its use was prevented during the Korean War. Now its use would be manipulated to the strategic disadvantage of its American possessors. Mao could solve his own impossible economic burden by liquidating these untold millions of excess Chinese population, if he could manipulate others into doing so and thus turn Chinese hatred against them. He could have his cake and eat it too. He was confident that certainly the naive Americans would be incapable of mastering the psychological warfare problems involved. Their government never has shown any talent this way. The nearest the United States ever came to it was under Woodrow Wilson, with his Fourteen Points.

An increasing number of Chinese Communist officials, many of high rank, supported Liu Shao-chi's Moscow-like position. Mao's intelligence reports kept telling him so. Mao suspected that Liu was only waiting for him to die in order to abandon the program of immediacy and adopt the more patient line followed by the Kremlin. Not only were the communes a disappointment, but Mao's fiercest efforts to capture minds were not having the anticipated impact. Something obviously had to be done, and drastically, while he was still here to do it. But where to turn? Whom to trust?

He turned to the children of China. He contrived a janissaries army of teen-agers and children sometimes younger in as sordid a maneuver as history has ever seen. He called on Lin Piao for military protection while he perpetrated his maneuver. Mao knew that China's intellectuals were not serving him with sincerity. Many were serving Liu Shao-chi instead, or simply had not shed the bourgeois burdens that had persisted in lingering on since the old Kuomintang Party of Chiang Kai-shek. Well, he would teach them all a lesson that none would forget. Everyone was considering Liu his sure successor. He would remove Liu, putting Lin Piao in his place. Lin always had been cooperative. The young people would accomplish this for him, in the garb of Red Guards. He remembered how useful the little ones had been as couriers and intelligence sources during the Revolution, and how oblivious to dangers they had been as "little devils," the popular term for children kidnaped by the Red Army. Now they would serve him again.

One of the first acts of the Communists upon capturing the mainland had been to seize the educational institutions. A secret police office was installed in each, where dossiers could be studied not only of students and faculty members, but of the townsfolk, the parents. Yes, indeed, the children always had been a great help to him.

Marxism was made the essential ingredient of every course. Marxism was becoming Maoism. Almost as soon as his conquest of the mainland had been completed, short-term "people's revolutionary universities" were set up where only ideology was taught. These were exclusively brainwashing establishments, operated directly by the Communist Party of China. What took place in one of these, related by a student who went through the course, is told in detail in this book.

A drastic overhaul was made of the curriculum in each educational establishment. Colleges and universities were merged and moved about. The Soviet model was adopted as completely as possible, and a great number of Soviet educators and administrators were brought in as advisors. They remained until about 1960, when Moscow withdrew all its technicians because of an ideological huff with Mao. The Sino-Soviet controversy was underway. Mao never could accept the crude debasement of Stalin by the nonintellectual, the boor Khrushchev. Stalin had studied to be a priest and engaged in Party polemics even while robbing banks. Neither he nor Mao ever engaged in manual labor.

All along, Mao has been impatient to institute an educational system to his own pattern of thinking, that put politics in the saddle in all things, down to the last detail. The inquisitiveness nurtured by any educational process, the inherently skeptical while outwardly docile minds indoctrinated into the Chinese through countless generations of survival under all too frequent despotisms, ran counter to Mao's needs. He wanted "reliable" minds—the "new men of socialism"—so

precisely alike in motivations and reactions that individual
initiative would be unthinkable, because their individual
brains might have been one, gigantesque, collective mind. His
inverted ideal was cogently expressed by Tao Chu, first secretary of the Communist Party branch in Kwangtung Province.
A dispatch from Canton dated January 12, 1959, published in
the Communist organ at Hong Kong, the *Wen-hui Pao,* read
as follows:

"The opening of kindergartens and nurseries has also solved
the problem of child education. Leading a collective life, the
child will as a matter of course receive social and collective
molding and education. They form from infancy a good collective and socialist habit, and will, when grown up, become
the new men of socialism."

These were the teen-agers whom Mao summoned in 1966
for the "Great Proletarian Cultural Revolution." What they
were revolting against was not the Kuomintang; it no longer
could serve on the mainland even as a whipping boy. They
were being called on for an internal insurrection, within the
Communist Party of China, an inside fight against it. Exactly
as the Stalinist regime had turned against the Old Bolsheviks
of Soviet Russia, under somewhat similar pressures, the Maoist
regime was turning against the Party. Too many had taken
refuge in it who did not equate the Revolution with Mao so
completely that one need only obey him and the Revolution
would take care of itself. This personalized approach was inherent in Stalinism too.

Mao's approach was the more intellectual; Stalin's, the more
pathological. Mao's purges, while ruthlessly widespread, did
not extend so high as Stalin's. Old comrades of the Long
March, who always had looked to Mao to interpret the Revolution, were not purged, but were expected to collaborate in
the purging, which they did. Mao's position always had been
that of a personality cult. Mao's mind—the universal expression was "Mao's thoughts"—represented the collective mind;
the job of other minds was to be so completely geared to it as
to express its will spontaneously. In Orwellian logic, "man"

became an abstract; only "class man" existed. This was the collective mind! In reality, of course, there being no single brain that existed separately from a great number of individual brains, the concept of a "collective mind" could work out only as leadership by one mind, faithfully or fearfully obeyed by the others. The adherents of Marxism always have had to live a myth, while professing an ideology that denied the existence of myths.

The young battalions of Red Guards, in their teens or younger, constituted the last trustworthy element among the civilians. They were trustworthy insofar as they had been raised to react without doubts, and to look to Mao as the master symbol. The little book, *Quotations from Mao,* was their Bible. They reacted to Mao in the Pavlov format. Here was a test of the Pavlovian-based, brainwashing technique. These children knew nothing about the outside world, or what a free mind meant; they knew only what had been obsessively dinned into them by spoken and printed word, carefully chosen for Red objectives. They were the "vanguards of the cultural revolution," the "revolutionary successors" to those now in charge. They were the Red Guards, and what they set about doing at once was to tear the Communist Party and Chinese society apart by sheer terrorist tactics. Before they were through, they had spread havoc wherever they went, whether on farms or in factories.

Minds can be twisted and deformed, and set off by stress and deprivation to go in discordant directions; knacks, traits, and capacities can be encouraged or held back. All this can be done, but none of it constitutes a change in the nature of the mind, and all of it together does not create a new human nature. A national neurosis can be created, and it was beginning to happen. But this was not the brainwashing intent.

All that the uninterrupted indoctrination of these younger intellectuals had achieved was to produce battalions of "sick" minds that Mao had set loose on a cowed and helpless society. The understandable consequence was chaos—civil strife rather than civil war. Fortunately for the Maoists, the loose, worldwide, Red propaganda apparatus composed of Marxists, sympathizers, and opportunists kept Red China's greatly weakened condition hushed up and even denied. Meanwhile, in the depths of continental China, as if in another world, highly skilled work continued apace for a nuclear arsenal.

Peking was unable to reliably brainwash "socialist discipline" and "socialist reliability" into the minds of plain folk and intellectuals alike, but it was developing a nuclear potential, and if all else failed, this conceivably could . . . could what?

What would it achieve? An extension of China's anarchic situation to all the world? World destruction? World conquest? Time would have to answer, if the question were allowed to reach that point. Nevertheless, failure to exploit the vulnerability that Communist China displayed during the chaotic period of the "Red Guard" disorders may prove to have been one of the decisive events—or non-events—of all history.

The Chinese Communist hierarchy provided all along for an elite of senior-scientists whose educational progress was scrupulously nurtured, comfortably screened off from the turmoil and tension outside. These brains were accorded privileges and favors quite commensurate with the distinctions in any capitalistic society. The Red hierarchy well knew that these senior-scientists could, in turn, be tossed off their soft perches once Peking achieved its worldwide goals, a prospect that some of the privileged characters might themselves have been keen enough to see coming.

Mao, in desperation, called on the army to put a stop to the ravishments of the Red Guards. The military took effective control little more than a decade since the communes system was begun. The military was back in the saddle, as it had been in war-lord days. How far would the similarity go? History's parallels usually are not true similarities.

The Chinese mainland presently is divided into what might be considered 2,200 or so counties, set up or confirmed under communism. Of these, only a couple of dozen have been reorganized under strict Party control. The best information, tenuous at best, is that 40 per cent are strictly run by the military. The control over about 30 per cent is vague, although more or less in opposition to Peking, while the remaining 30 per cent are fence-sitting, cautiously waiting to decide on which side it would be less dangerous to jump.

The military actually are in a position of domination over these commune-*hsien*-county areas. Where the army does not dominate completely, its influence is nonetheless potent. What was called a commune was frequently just a local administrative bureau. What noun best applies was a matter of accommodation and prudence.

The Chinese have learned the hard way how to outfox their oppressors. One might find every sort of local administration in China's communities, from dogmatic adherence to Maoist thought to an anarchy of sorts, from abandonment of controls to cautious, self-contained initiative. The normal, personal use of initiative is called corruption by the Communists, but actually is a brave, private-type effort, as yet on a very small scale, to retain one's sanity and to remain healthy in an atmosphere of mental upset.

Lin Piao, now picked as Mao's successor, was accorded the customary buildup that Communism gives to anyone in an important post who is being elevated to a topmost niche. Communist history constantly has to be revised or rewritten to give the latest perspective to past events. Some events have to be erased—thrust into the limbo of non-events—while others have to be emphasized or reorganized, so that the resultant historical pattern conforms to the new image. The emphasis in creating a Red image is not, as in America, on the individual's personality, but on fitting him into an ideological pattern. A Communist official does not have to overly concern himself about attracting votes; he must be completely satisfactory to his power-jealous peers, be able to balance them to his advantage; or he must have the favor of whoever is wielding power.

So, in Lin Piao's case, the Red theoreticians went back to

1929, to a Communist meeting at Kutien, about one hundred miles northwest of Foochow, when a decisive resolution was passed opposing the traditional peasant-worker military strategy that Chu Teh was following, and supporting the strategy of Mao Tse-tung that concentrated on the peasantry. The military focus was switched from city to countryside. Lin Piao had voted in favor of the Maoist strategy.

Somewhat the same kind of choice came up in 1960, at an enlarged session of the military commision of the Party's Central Committee. Liu Shao-chi's "polycentrism," which reflected Moscow's views regarding China, was represented in the military by Marshal Peng Te-huai as defense minister. Mao regarded it as a cover for his hated "bourgeois center." Lin again proclaimed his support of Mao's position, replacing the disgraced Peng as defense minister. Lin even wrote a foreword to the little red-covered handbook of Mao's quotations. The Red Guards were set barking at the heels of Peng, as well as at all others identified with Liu, who was condemned as China's Khrushchev.

This maneuver had tremendous ramifications. Political commissars had always been attached to the Chinese Red Army in the Soviet Russian manner. They made sure that troops and officers were properly indoctrinated and could be relied on to fight for Red objectives. Now, under Lin Piao, a change was made in emphasis. The military became primarily an ideological instrument, absorbing the traditional Communist Party role. The army was purged of Liu adherents and began to exercise the Party's control functions.

The official New China News Agency on August 3, 1970, sent out a long dispatch regarding the two resolutions—those of 1929 and 1960—declaring "all units of the People's Liberation Army have started activities to make a penetrating study of the two resolutions and to implement them. They have run various Mao Tse-tung thought study classes and organized teams to propagate the resolutions."

An equivocal situation developed. The Communist Party of China technically retained its old status, and in some areas, army men held both Party and military posts. In other regions, the military held exclusive sway. Every sort of combination existed. The military overwhelmingly has the advantage at this writing, while some effort is being made by Mao to rebuild the Party. But it would be a military party. The Party functionaries in an area may be allowed to mouth their prerogatives as long as they do not attempt to exercise them. What appears to be developing is a blend of Communist Party and Red Army, through ultimate control residing in the same individuals. The police state is becoming also a military state.

The draft of a new constitution was drawn up by the Chinese Communist hierarchy and put into the Party mechanism for formal approval late in 1970. Mao Tse-tung was named in it as "the great leader . . . head of state of the dictatorship . . . and the supreme commander," and Lin Piao was designated "successor, and the deputy supreme commander." This was unprecedented. Never before had a written constitution, supposed to endure beyond the lives of its creators, been employed as a vehicle to pinpoint the ephemeral positions of its contemporaries.

Even Mao cannot anticipate a prolonged survival; he is nearly eighty years old. What he obviously wanted to assure was the survival of "the thoughts of Mao Tse-tung," already in his lifetime memorized and repeated endlessly in the manner of Buddhist sutras. Never before in history have the admonitions and writings of any political leader so completely dominated a society as Mao's in Communist China. The most irrelevant or trivial enterprise, whether it be setting a broken leg or digging for oil, had to be credited—if successful—to one or another of Mao's sayings. Only in religion, in reverence to a Supreme Being, can we find anything comparable.

Whatever else the intent of the draft constitution at the time, it also served Lin Piao by etching his name and position indelibly at the top. His background, significantly, was basically military, not civilian.

The most important repercussions of these complex developments are in Sino-Soviet relations. Was Mao dealing primarily with ideological content, to mold China to his political thoughts, or, in effect, was he not looking ahead militarily? His vision always has been of a Communist world. Contradictions are taken in stride by Red theoreticians. Mao wrote a treatise, "On Contradiction," in 1937. Mao's dialectical skill has always enabled him to surmount any ideological or philosophical embarrassment. As he wrote in this treatise, contradiction is "the law of the unity of opposites"—a "basic law of nature and society, and, therefore, also the basic law of thought." In other words, he never allowed theory to interfere with practice where his objective was concerned.

The bulk of the violently dogmatic, terrorist groups of a revolutionary nature operating worldwide call themselves Maoist. That this is more than rhetoric is shown by their writings and teachings, confirmed by their deeds. The United States has not been immune.

Indeed, the 1970 annual report of the Federal Bureau of Investigation referred to a "rapid escalation in New Left extremism which presented a distinct danger to our national security." This was an extraordinary warning from so knowledgeable a body. The FBI has been calling attention for years to revolutionaries in our midst, and outlined their all-out objectives. But what the FBI now was stating was that these elements now constituted a clear and present danger to "national security." This was reinforced by FBI testimony in appropriations hearings in the Congress. The shift in emphasis was from a recital of subversive and treasonable ambitions to an acknowledgement of impact.

The organizations named had direct or indirect links with Peking. One such was the Black Panther Party (BPP), its official paper named the *Black Panther*. Its contents were unrestrictedly revolutionary. A dissembling name for the Black Panthers was National Committees to Combat Fascism. "Support groups" were established abroad and an "international staff" set up in Algiers. Both Moscow and Peking penetrated the Black Panthers in depth, in collaboration, and in rivalry.

The Black Panthers were in working relations with various

Arab guerrilla groups that operated under similar influences.

Another named in the FBI's annual report was the Students for a Democratic Society, out of which came an all-out terrorist group called the Weathermen. These were New Left, but the Old Left remained active. The report referred to "three main Old Left groups" in the United States, as the Moscow-oriented Communist Party, the Trotskyist Socialist Workers Party, "and the pro-Red Chinese Progressive Labor Party," the PLP.

Maoism helped link the Old Left and the New Left. The FBI report declared that PLP "leaders have been in contact with pro-Chinese communist groups abroad and its publications slavishly follow the line of the Chinese Communist Party." Simultaneously, the PLP was found to have "deeply penetrated" the New Left, particularly through the Students for a Democratic Society (SDS).

Much that this author is witnessing in the United States gives him the feeling, "This is where I came in," reminding him of the Maoist tactics he watched in China. Much of what he relates in this book reads as if written to describe such propagandist and terrorist occurrences in the United States.

Such similarities no longer are limited to atrocious crimes that are given a twisted rationale as political terrorism, or to Marxist "learning" courses and brainwashing parallels. They have spread to an entire category of publications, aimed at youth and the more impressionable, volatile elements in American society, including an activist segment in our academic communities. The "cartoon propaganda reference books," as summarized in this book, which teach revolutionary propaganda for popular use, have their counterpart in what is called our "underground press." In late 1970, a change in our so-called "comic books"—the nearest approach we have to the "talk books" of the Chinese Communists—was being widely publicized. Certain superheroes were being transferred into revolutionary types.

Pragmatic analysts—pragmatism so often being an extension of the practical to a conclusion that runs counter to the human nature it seeks to exploit—could not imagine the im-

poverished Red Chinese hierarchy exerting itself overseas. Soviet Russia, yes, but not Red China. These observers underrated the highly skilled use made by the Communist Chinese
all along of collaborative foreign sympathies and assistance. Indeed, this was the essence of the new "psychological warfare."
A great reservoir of experience and contacts thus was built up.

Ideological differences and rivalries inevitably arose, and
personality and territorial differences developed between the
two neighboring giants. The Communist Chinese outlook always has been international, not only from an ideological
standpoint, but for very practical considerations. During the
years of their uninterrupted drive for victory domestically, irrespective of agreements or world conflict, the Red Chinese
publicized their slightest foreign contacts in order to build up
morale at home. The most inconsequential delegate from some
paper organization in another country, no matter how small
and unimportant, received a booming welcome. Let a Chinese
Communist delegate, no matter how minor, be given a courtesy
dinner in some minuscule country, and it was sure to be published and broadcast by the Chinese Reds as if it were a
weighty meeting of state.

Now they are continuing this approach, adapted to the
changed power status of Peking and the resources at its command. The creation of Chinese Communist bases of revolutionary and ideological impact abroad strengthens Communist
China's position vis-à-vis the Kremlin. Communist Parties
everywhere are influenced in a manner that Moscow cannot
brush off.

The Palestine guerrilla movement, with incontestable,
strong Moscow links, nonetheless contained more dramatically
ruthless elements within it that were visibly Peking-guided.
The telltale Che Guevara poster-portraits and heroic pictures
of Mao are part of the office furnishings for a number of these
guerrilla factions. They intermittently collaborate and compete
with each other in a manner that reflects the Sino-Soviet relations of the day.

The Popular Front for the Liberation of Palestine (PFLF),

the terrorist band that captured and blew up four international passenger planes in early September, 1970, made no secret of its Red Chinese leanings. A hijacked Boeing 747 was diverted to Cairo, where it was blown up. The three other airliners were landed at a so-called "revolution airfield" in the Jordanian desert in a dramatically executed coup, where they were similarly destroyed. In each case, the passengers were allowed to escape only at the last harrowing moments. The world's attention was focused on this spot for a week while the guerrillas negotiated with the Western powers virtually on a basis of equality.

The Jordanian government declared, without contradiction, that it possessed "ample proof" that Peking masterminded the bloody warfare that broke out at this time between guerrillas in Amman and the north, supported ingloriously by Syrian tanks and King Hussein's forces. Israeli forces were ready to intervene, and U.S. troops to the north and the American Sixth Fleet in the Mediterranean were alerted. Syria obviously was fronting for Russia. If Hussein had crumbled, the confrontation could have skyrocketed.

The largest guerrilla organization was Al Fatah, its name composed of initials—reading right to left in the manner of Arabian writing—that stood for the Front for the Liberation of Palestine, usually called just The Front, or Palestine Liberation Organization. Its leader was Yassir Arafat, a burning nationalist, frequently described as non-ideological. Palestine-born, educated as a civil engineer at Cairo University, he held top posts in the Palestine Students' Union.

George Habash, PFLF chief, was in Peking at the time of the hijackings. He was a Christian medical doctor, graduate of the University of Beirut.

The clocklike precision of the coup testified to the professionalism of the guerrilla operators. They "played it cool," but, unlike movie and television gangsters, spoke familiarly of college and university life, and even of their degrees. Moslem nationalism, semi-religious in nature, was the usual motivation, but a Socialist-Communist-Maoist ideology colored it. Their conversation, as related to this writer by a keen observer with an extensive China background, was interlaced with a seemingly objective scholarship and a certainly subjective Marxism and Maoism.

They seemed a throwback to the old socialist revolutionaries who threw bombs at the Russian Tsar's ministers. These fire-brands of our day were equally desperate, and hence equally willing to accept help from all sources. But their intellectual-ism had a pathological—"sick"—tone to it, perhaps soured by greater expectations that higher education would be an "open sesame" to all gates. This frustration made them easy prey for "psywar" planners and manipulators.

Al Fatah gained early notice in America when Black Pan-thers were given training. The Middle East, particularly Egypt, has always been a crossroads for international agents, particularly Communist ones. Press and media correspondents covering the hijacked planes met trainees in terror tactics in Maoist-type, guerrilla groups. Some of these individuals claimed to be Americans, of both Christian and Jewish back-grounds. After all, Trotskyite and Maoist factions in the United States include every kind of revolutionary activists.

Cuba has been a busy agitational and training base for these types from throughout North and South America, along with those under Moscow's discipline who went there routinely. This has been going on at a steady pace ever since a program for precisely this kind of indoctrination and training was laid down at the First Afro-Asian-Latin American Peoples' Soli-darity Conference, or First Tricontinental Conference, in Jan-uary, 1966, in Cuba.

Chinese Communist indoctrination—brainwashing courses —and guerrilla or terrorist training have been given American citizens, white and black, in a number of newly independent African countries, as well as in Castro's Cuba. Indeed, Maoist training and planning confronted the United States, from Cuba to the southeast to Canada in the north. The same ex-ploitation as was being made of the American Negro was being focused upon the French Canadians. The French separatist

movement in Canada became a pushover for Red revolutionaries. The head of a Congressional committee gave this writer
details some years ago of the channeling of Communist money
into the United States through Canadian banks.

The Chinese Communists always have exploited race, taking advantage of their Asian race to interpret so-called "liberation wars" as racial as well as ideological. This blended neatly
into their reference to their own as "China's national racial
revolution." They now have adapted this into a war of all non-
whites against the whites, meaning specifically the United
States, at least for the present. They have even included the
American Indians as a target. Maoist propaganda papers and
booklets similar to those described in this book, disseminated
around the world, have been adapted to the American Indians, to persuade them to join hands with Latin America's
Indians, exactly as Americans of black skin were being indoctrinated in aligning themselves with African black revolutionaries.

Red China made its claim to leadership of the non-white
world in revolutionary warfare obvious in the Afro-Asian Conference at Bandung, Indonesia, April 18–24, 1955. Its role was
considered complementary to that of the USSR, itself partly
Asian. The Sino-Soviet alliance then barred even the thought
of this not developing in the most complete harmony between
Peking and Moscow. Every word had to be concentrated upon
an Afro-Asian crusade against "colonialism," in the revised
sense of the term that made it inapplicable to Communist
countries.

When Cuba slipped into the Red bloc, this was extended
into an Afro-Asian-South American "crusade." The Chinese
community in Cuba always has been large, so Peking had no
difficulty in placing Red agents there in the guise of newspapermen and merchants. Their numbers were greatly increased when Castro took over. They no longer needed a cover,
and were reinforced by oversized diplomatic staffs. They
gave tangible aid in the development of Red Cuba as a base.
The United States at all times was made the primary target of

this new Red base, for every variety of terrorist warfare, from assassination to street fighting and the destruction of military and government structures. Propaganda, preaching, and teaching such tactics was broadcast and sent as mail into the United States from Cuba and Peking. "The Crusader," an inflammatory periodical that gave lessons in sabotage and arson, was sent first from Havana and then from Peking, in the name of an American Negro, Robert Williams.

Communist China's intensive role in Africa is related to this interlocking program, and is facilitated by Peking's particular advantage in making a racist appeal, combined with a willingness to pay high for the opportunity. Time after time, Peking undercut Soviet Russian bids for commercial and industrial enterprises in Africa that had tactical and strategic potentials. The phenomenal financial costs had to come out of the hide of the Chinese peasantry, but Peking was more ruthless on such matters, or considered itself in a stronger position as regards the masses, than even Moscow.

The interest-free loan given by Red China for the Tanzania-Zambia railway is only one example. Similarly, Peking was helping Zambia build three broadcasting stations and a major highway. Tanzania was being helped to build a naval base. In October of 1970, Peking boasted that Equatorial Guinea had become the fourteenth African country with which it exchanged ambassadors. Thus, overt channels were being developed along with the usual clandestine ones. Politics—the "thoughts of Mao Tse-tung"—were inseparable from these deals. The announcement, for instance, of the addition of Equatorial Guinea—the former Spanish Guinea—to the list of recognized states, was presented in the Chinese Communist press, as in the *Ta Kung Pao* of Hong Kong, as evidence of the "development by the people of Africa of their struggle against imperialism headed by the United States."

All the non-white races are taught that they are in a war to the death against the white man. Eastern and Western Communism actually are one in this conspiracy.

Peking, at this point, was setting itself up as the capital of a regional, anti-American, united front, composed at the start of North Viet Nam, the Viet Cong, the Pathet Lao, and Prince Sihanouk's Cambodians.

A neatly printed English-language booklet of the Foreign Languages Press at Peking, dated 1967, entitled *The Chinese People Firmly Support the Arab People's Struggle Against Aggression,* is preceded, as is obligatory nowadays, by *Quotations From Chairman Mao Tse-tung.* The first of two declarations in this pamphlet of nearly sixty pages, taken from a "Statement supporting the people of the Congo against U.S. aggression," reads: "People of the world, unite and defeat the U.S. aggressors and all their running dogs! People of the world, be courageous, dare to fight, defy difficulties and advance wave upon wave. Then the whole world will belong to the people. Monsters of all kinds shall be destroyed." The other, similar in tone, came from a "Statement supporting the Panamanian people's just patriotic struggle against U.S. imperialism."

This booklet, published in Red China in numerous languages, its appearance and contents alike to those described in this book, when the Kuomintang was Mao's major target, was available, with countless others of the same, vile character, in bookshops in college and university communities throughout the United States.

The disgrace and humiliation of the Kremlin's favorite, Liu Shao-chi, who was put under house arrest, naturally inclined observers to believe that Lin Piao, Mao's choice, was oriented away from Red Russia, and that the prospect of a new, Moscow-Peking entente was most unlikely, if not made impossible by Lin's elevation. If the two Communist powers would keep sniping at each other, the United States might have its worries and defense needs comfortably cut. But this lulling interpretation could be as wrong as were interpretations of the "blooming-contending" policy.

Lin Piao was only a secondary military figure in China

until after Moscow's week-long war in 1945 against Japan. He was a name, one of the numerous generals under Chu Teh, the unquestioned military chieftain. But there is a generally unrealized side to Lin Piao. This writer recalls American military intelligence of the period when Soviet Russian troops were in occupation of the erstwhile Japanese puppet state of Manchukuo. The national forces of Chiang Kai-shek were barred by Russian troops from these "Three Eastern Provinces" of China, otherwise known as Manchuria. Even American ships—military or commercial—were effectively discouraged from docking in Manchurian ports.

Vast stores of excellent new Japanese military equipment had been taken over by the Soviet forces. But the West was lulled by Chiang's capture of Yenan, Mao's longtime headquarters city deep inside China, in the loess soil of Inner Mongolia. The Communist forces, impoverished and unequipped, had fled into Manchuria. A sigh of relief went up. Had not Stalin signed a treaty "of friendship and alliance" with the national government of China on August 14, 1945? Although it gave great advantages to the USSR, including virtual sovereignty over Outer Mongolia, this was considered a fair price for the Kremlin's solemn pledge.

This writer recalls items in U.S. intelligence, never released to the public, that told about conferences being held in Manchuria between the Soviet military commander and Lin Piao. These were no ordinary conferences, for they lasted several days. The American intelligence disclosed that details for military collaboration were being arranged. A secret entente was set up between the Kremlin and the Chinese Communists, behind the screen of alliance between the Kremlin and the national government of China. Diplomatically, Moscow was insisting that Chiang rely upon peaceful negotiations with Mao while, behind the scenes, Lin Piao's 200,000 men were rested, re-trained, and re-equipped with the captured Japanese military equipment. Soviet Russian officers helped man the bigger guns when Lin Piao's forces were sufficiently prepared to start their drive back into the Chinese mainland, striking against troops whose equipment required repairs or lacked ammunition.

Lin Piao obviously cooperates well with the Soviet Russians and is trusted by them. He had to be in similarly close working arrangements with the USSR when he commanded the so-called Chinese "volunteer armies" that struck at General MacArthur's troops in Korea that fateful Thanksgiving-Christmas season of 1950. Details of this historic episode are provided in this book, based on the author's eye-witness experiences.

As Mao's successor, Lin Piao would be in an excellent position to resume his past operational cooperation with the Soviet Union. He would be less suspect than Liu Shao-chi of favoring the USSR against the interests of his own country. Certainly, with Mao's departure from the earthly scene, Moscow would have a convincing excuse to reappraise its China policy and to re-orient it in accordance with changed conditions between the two countries and in the world.

But Lin Piao is China-oriented. The outcome could be determined in the clandestine world where nations seek to fulfill national policies nowadays, that sometimes seems to be the real world of the present.

Lin Piao's emphasis on indoctrination of the military, his assumption of control over the brainwashing program generally and over Red China's nuclear potential has limitless possibilities.

One can never tell ahead about a military regime, for soldiers are pragmatists, if not always practical. The best guides are power potentials. Rather than look into a blurred crystal ball, it might be better to await some future preface to some later reprinting of *Brain-Washing in Red China* to assess the post-1970 developments.